DATE DUE

GAYLORD			PRINTED IN U.S.A.

The Arts and Crafts of Syria

The Arts and Crafts of Syria

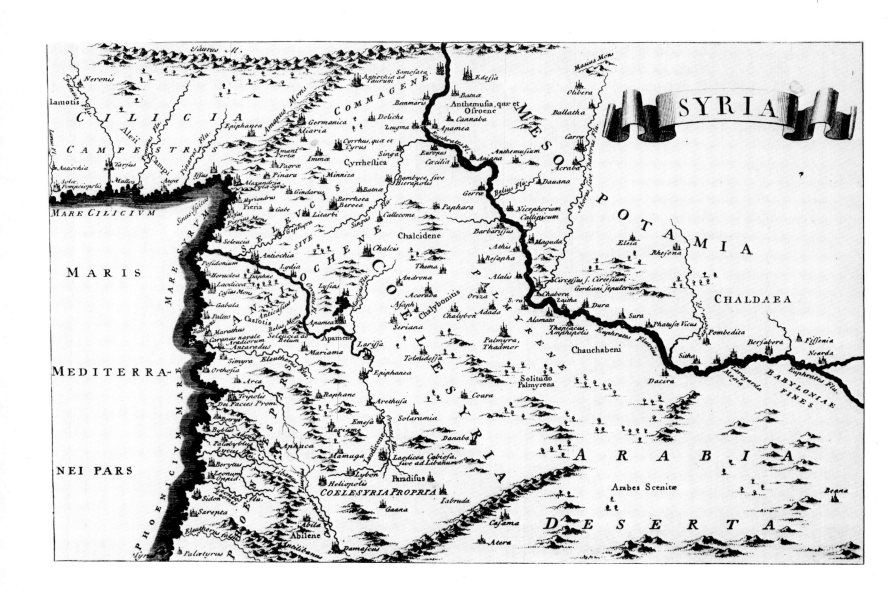

1 Historical map of Syria, mid-eighteenth century engraving.

The Arts and Crafts of Syria

Collection Antoine Touma and Linden-Museum Stuttgart

Johannes Kalter   Margareta Pavaloi   Maria Zerrnickel

with contributions by: P. Behnstedt, A. Gangler, H. Gaube, P. Pawelka, A. Touma

Thames and Hudson

First published in Great Britain in 1992
by Thames and Hudson Ltd, London

First published in the United States of America in 1992
by Thames and Hudson Inc., 500 Fifth Avenue, New York, New York 10110

By arrangement with Edition Hansjörg Mayer, Stuttgart/London

Translation: Sebastian Wormell

Field photographs: Anette Gangler, Heinz Gaube, Chris Heinrich,
Niko Heinrich, Johannes Kalter, Margareta Pavaloi, Antoine Touma,
Maria Zerrnickel, Marieluise Zöllner

Studio photographs: Niko Heinrich

Printed and bound by Staib+Mayer, Stuttgart/Germany

Contents

Dedicated to the people of Syria

2 Nomad playing the *rebab*.

Preface

Writing a book about the arts and crafts of Syria is above all writing about Syria's peoples. Their ethnic and cultural diversity, over centuries of shared history, have shaped Syria to make it the country it appears today: a land of fascinating cultural diversity and one of the interesting areas in the Arabian Peninsula for its ethnology and ethnography. Until recently, however, this part of the Arab world has been greatly neglected by ethnographers and researchers into material culture.

In geographical terms this book concentrates on the material culture of present-day Syria. Culturally the term "Syria" covers the areas the Arabs usually refer to as "bilad esh-sham", i.e. the "northern territories" of the Arabian Peninsula, which, apart from Syria, include Lebanon, Palestine and Jordan.

Our curiosity and interest in Syrian arts and crafts were triggered by Antoine Touma, when we met in Damascus in 1989. By profession a journalist and by vocation a passionate collector of ethnographic material of his country, at great expense both in money and energy he built up a beautiful collection of Syrian costumes and handicrafts, which the impact of modern life has brought to the verge of extinction.

The Linden-Museum Stuttgart itself was able to make a considerable contribution, including Bedouin material brought to Germany by the well- known scholar and explorer Euting in the 1870s, on his return from his journey to Arabia. Between 1986 and 1989 the curator of the Linden- Museum's Department of the Near and Middle East collected rural and Bedouin household goods from southern Syria and the north of Jordan with the kind assistance of colleagues from the Institute of Archaeology and Anthropology of Yarmouk University at Irbid, Jordan.

As we started our work on the collections we soon realized how clearly the ethnic and religious traditions of Syria's peoples are reflected in the richness and wide range of their costumes and dress codes, in types of jewellery or in preferences for particular colour schemes and designs. There are distinctive styles and tastes in dress for men and women depending on whether they come from an Arab, Kurdish or Turcoman background, or follow the Muslim, Christian or Jewish faith (not to mention the numerous splinter groups). This ethnic and religious diversity of traditions not only shaped politics, public life and private attitudes, but also the historical landscape of Syria.

The classical threefold economy of the Near and Middle East – the urban, agricultural and pastoral mode of produc-

3 Peasant threshing in the Alawite Mountains.

tion – results in different ways of life, to which dress and household goods were adapted. The latter provide us with ample information concerning the conditions of everyday life of nomads, peasants and the people living in the towns.

The greater part of the material in the collections mentioned above, and of the objects presented in this book, is typical of urban craftsmanship. Indeed, it was in the cities that most of the luxury goods were produced, as well as the more ordinary items catering for the needs of the towns-people, villagers and Bedouins alike. Jewellery, as a rule, is a typical urban product, even when it is worn in the countryside. But the cities supplied not only the local markets. In particular the beautiful fabrics made in Damascus and Aleppo were already centuries ago being traded to areas outside the "bilad esh-sham", as far as Yemen, Africa and Europe. Household goods made of copper, and furniture embellished with intarsia work were exported to the Arabian Peninsula, and even to Europe, when in the second half of the last century interior decoration "à l'orientale" became the fashion.

The publication of this book would not have been possible without the support and advice of many colleagues and friends.

We would particularly like to thank M. Antoine Touma, who not only let us use his collection but also helped us with his knowledge and his many contacts in and outside Syria. For advice and encouragement while preparing the book we owe much to Dr. D. Hopwood, St. Antony's College Oxford, and to Mrs S. Weir, Museum of Mankind, London, who gave valuable assistance and support.

For organizational support during our survey in Syria we would like to thank H.E. Dr. Najar Attar, Ministry of Culture of the Arab Republic of Syria, H.E. General Mustafa Tlass, Ministry of Defence and Vice-President of the Arab Republic of Syria, H.E. Suleyman Haddad, Ambassador of the Arab Republic of Syria in Bonn, and the Directors of the National Museum and the Azam Palace in Damascus, and of the Archaeological Institute at Palmyra. We are indebted to Dr. Abdul Rahman Attar and Dr. Osman Aiydi for their hospitality and to M. Saeeb Nahass, who helped us with transport during our stay in Syria. Without the interest and energy of Prof. Talal Akili many doors in the Old Town of Damascus would have remained closed, and M. Byassam S. Kalawajy shared his knowledge with us. We would further like to express our gratitude to Mme. Hala Chehade, Dr. Mahmoud Khretani

and M. Adli Qudsi for their friendship and assistance in Aleppo.

In Germany Frau Gisela Dombrowski, Museum für Völkerkunde, Berlin, kindly permitted us to publish some rare objects from her collection dating from the last century and Prof. Eugen Wirth, University of Erlangen, helped with his maps. Prof. Heinz Gaube, University of Tübingen, an Dr. Dorothée Sack, Frankfurt, supported us with advice and information. Thanks are also due to them and to all the authors who contributed articles to this book. The catalogue benefited greatly from the work of Chris and Nico Heinrich. Herr Heinrich took all the studio photographs, and both accompanied us to Syria at their own expense, thus enriching our selection of photographs taken in the field.

Our thanks go to the staff of the Linden-Museum, especially to Frau Ursula Didoni for the photographic reproductions and to Frau Ina Schneider who diligently typed the manuscript.

And finally we thank Sebastian Wormell for the translation.

Unfortunately it is not possible to mention by name all those who helped and supported us in the completion of this book. To them we would like to express or sincere gratitude, most of all to Syria's people, to whom this book is dedicated.

Stuttgart, May 1992

Johannes Kalter
Margareta Pavaloi
Maria Zerrnickel

4 Chan Asad Pasha el-Azm in Damascus.

The Long Way to Self Identification

Antoine Touma

„Yet people call me the African, but I am neither from Africa, nor from Europe, nor from Arabia. I do not come from any country, any city or any tribe. I am a son of the road. My home is the caravan and my life is among the most unexpected one of the wanderring.“

Hassan al-Wazzan (Leo Africanus).
An arabian historian and traveller.
16th century

Striving for a social identity is probably instinctive. Human beings have sought security handed around clan chieftains and kings, discovered prophets and united in new religions, battled with each other for domination or survival, and have distinguished themselves from others through emblems, language, and custom.

The symbols themselves are just elements of a code, and the language spoken through them is not much more mysterious than the messages conveyed through the elements of other codes: a Muslim women's scarf, a Sikh man's turban, a prestigious university diploma, flags, and coats of arms.

Occasionaly, symbols are commandeered: European heraldry originates in part from objects and animals depicted on the shields of Arab warriors. These shields were harvested as trophies in war during the 12th Century Crusaders in Syria. Their images became the signs of European nobility: the English lion, the German eagle and French Fleurde-Lys are originally Mamluk emblems.

Racial and ideological identification underlines the more serious conflicts in the world. Some groups identify themselves with a book of tales and wisdom called the Bible, or of proverbs and civics like the Koran, and look down with pity – or even contempt- upon the uninitiated. Fights over The Book's interpretation can last centuries, like the schism between Sunnis and Chiites or the hostilities between Protestants and Catholics that started in the 15th century.

But to be the Christian or Muslim was not enough when I began to hunt for an allencompassing cultural identity. In my youth, as a boarding student in a French school in Lebanon, I faced my first troubles with the problem of identity. My schoolmates called me Shami, the Arabic word for Damascene as well as the ancient word for Syria. I felt that I did not belong to their community: I was neither French, nor Beiruti, nor Lebanese, just „other“. Looking through the windows of my study room onto the blue Mediterranean I started searching for my cultural roots: who I am really? A Middle-Eastern in an indefinite way, am I an Arab, a Syrian, a Christian, or a Levantine? I began at home in Damascus to explore my world as a tourist would see it. Wandering around in my summer holidays I latched on to the architecture of the city believing then that architecture was the mother of all arts. I wanted to absorb more than just an instinctive sense of what made my world unique. This was to arm for the challenges at school: the Shami could begin to focus on his own national identity.

Sadly, each time I returned to Damascus it seemed as though another set of centuries – old buildings or a milleniaold quarter was being bulldozed for the new boulevards and office buildings. With the old buildings, my heart crumbled. Now the trend is to restore – practically to rebuild – the old town, and I don't know which has been more painful: watching the architectural treasures being flattened three decades ago, or witnessing the current „facelift“. In many corners, Damascus has come to have the charms of a Hollywood backlot.

The changes made in the old town triggered my curiosity and panic: I read books, maps and anything I could find about Syria, from romantic European traveller's stories to Arab and Western histories of the area.

The urgency to get a grasp of my sense of self, place, and culture became more pronounced when I attended Humboldt University in Berlin. There I was perceived as someone vaguely Middle-Eastern. But Syria? What did that mean? I plunged myself again into reading, this time to sharpen my ideas for a more academic audience.

Regardless what political trends are now challenging Syria's identity I found that the traces of a once vast and rich civilization are most immediately accessible in the arts, handicrafts, and traditions still practised in the region. I have devoted myself to a sort of private national identity project by digging into folklore and looking for artifacts that explain some part of Syria's cultural bonds. I have been hunting for what makes Syria's whole. The scientific and ethnographic approach used by Dr. J.Kalter, which is to focus on the objects of daily life, the simple materials and improvised adornments that give so many of the objects in this collection their personality, allowed me to discover how embroideries, jewelry, coffee mortars and printing blocks can be united in design and purpose, however diverse they may appear at first. These simple objects absorbed me and gave my quest for identity the rudiments of a language. Several of the pieces in the collection narrowly escaped melting down, dismemberment or mutilation by greedy merchants. Ms. Margareta Pavaloi would recall the Damascene tailor who massacred thousands of Bedouin dresses in order to export the embroidery strips.

Among Syrians, I felt alone in my passion to preserve elements and symbolic objects originating in both the nomadic and sedentary cultures found in Syria, found among the BILAD-ES-SHAM, among the hodge podge of Syrian renegades, traders, migrants, farmers, intellectuals and merchants whether Arab, Armenian, Kurdish, Circassian or Turkoman. At the end of many years of foraging, when I handed my work and collection over to the Linden-Museum Stuttgart, Dr. Kalter commented that perhaps I had overdone it. With true collector's passion, my aim was to gather as many examples as possible of every design in each material or technique. I wanted to amplify all the whispers of creative craftsmanship.

While Syria is essentially a geographic idea, containing different languages and enveloping cycles of various religions, ways of thinking, and ethnicities, it is full of the warmth amd quest for knowledge associated with the richest periods of most civilizations. Because of the continuous stream of caravans, the patchwork of ethnic groups, and the adventurism of its neighbours, there is a predisposition in the region to absorb the new, and synthetize what is useful or pleasing. The first agricultural settlements were probably in Syria and some of the most famous selfsufficient citystates like Ebla, Mari and Ugarit made Syria into more than a highway or nomad's herding ground thousands of years ago.

The recently discovered Ebla state archives have provided us with the first documents on this area written from a Syrian point of view. We assume that Syria was not a secondary arena of conflict between the big powers of Mesopotamia and Egypt. It might have been the third big power. It controlled an immense territory from Mesopotamia to the Mediterranean coast. It had direct commercial links with Egypt and – astonishingly – diplomatic relations with the faraway kingdom of Khamazi in Eastern Persia, and that in 2250 B.C.

Extensive trading encouraged acceptance of foreign ways of life, symbolized in some handicrafts (one of the examples that persists is IKAT weaving that came into the area from Afghanistan or Jemen and gradually became one of the most wellknown techniques among the weavers of Northern Syria). The ancient city of Aleppo, last Asian stop on the Silk road and still famous for its beautiful and sophisticated production of silk fabric.

Even the printed patterns of simple scarves have changed little since their introduction. The scarf is still worn proudly by the village and Bedouin women, distinguishing them from urban dwellers.

Syrians wear all their history on their backs, like layers of the ancient towns that lie buried under the Tells (hills) of the Syrian desert. They have known luxury and poverty, power and servitude, and absorbed it all in their traditions and crafts.

The Syrian culture is especially alive and vivid among the nomads, and I've held strongly to the task of documenting as much as I could find. This collection is not quaint: I have tried to keep it an honest depiction of the threads of culture that have survived time are still sewn into daily life.

Some inventions still in use in much of the world can trace their origins to Syria. The first alphabet to transcribe individual sounds into letters, not relying on figurative symbols, comes from the Phoenicians around 1500 B.C.. The Phoenicians then spread the Ugarit alphabet throughout the Mediterranean to the Greeks, Etruscans and the Romans. Centuries later, Arabic numerals inaugurated a new era af mathematics. Finally, the twelve zodiac signs that are so popular in the modern west, have their roots in Mesopotamia and Syria as well.

Around 1000 B.C., Aram of Damascus had become the first Syrian king to try and unite the region into a resilient kingdom able to resist incursion of King David in the south and repell the Assyrians in the east. After a couple of hundred years, the Aramean kingdom was defeated by the Assyrians (who also deported the tribes of Israel) but its language Arameic, known to us as the language spoken by Christ, provided the basis of modern Arabic syntax and is still the vernacular used in a few villages just outside contemporary Damascus.

Syria has constantly had to adapt to the political and cultural power that have crisscrossed through the area over thousands of years. For example, the resistance of Tyre to Alexander the Great became a model of heroism. Yet, years after, under the Seleucids, Syria became not only integrated into the Greek empire, but also, its then capital city of Antioch became a Hellenistic center of enlightenment whose influence reached as far as India. Antioch ranked third in importance after Athens and Alexandria.

Once the Romans invaded, the resistance of Queen Zenobia was far more legendary and led Emperor Aurelian to comment, „Those who say I have only conquered a woman do not know what that woman was, nor how lightening were her decisions, how persevering she was in her plans, how resolute with her soldiers.". Nevertheless, thirty years before, an exgovernor of Bosra had become the Roman emperor Philip the Arab. A Syrian empress Julia Donna from Homs and the wife of the Roman emperor Septimus Severus, refused to kneel before the Roman deities until sculptures representing the Syrian ones had been placed alongside them in Rome.

Byzantine art owes several of its principles to the fundaments of early Syrian architecture, iconography and concepts of the new faith. The earliest basilicas have been traced back to the period of the Dead Cities of Qalb, Lozeh and St-Simeon the Stylite in Northern Syria.

Against the Byzantines, the Syrian Arameic population, allied with the incoming Arab groups, encouraged the governor of Damascus, Muawiya, to lead them. They helped him build an empire that stretched from Spain in the west to China in the east. The Omayyad dynasty continued to rule over Spain for five centuries.

When the Mongols of Tamerlan destroyed all that had been left behind from previous invasions, they carefully kidnapped the highly skilled Syrian craftsmen – swordmakers, weavers, potters and glassmakers – and settled them in their capital Samarkand.

Examples of how Syrian cultures spread throughout the world are legends. Scholars are starting to establish indisputable links between European and Syrian literature. One highly controversial case compares Dante's Divine comedy to the writings of Al-Maari, „The Socrates of the Arabs", who lived two centuries before Dante. It would appear that Dante, through intermediate Latin translations, copied some of his best known poetry from the earlier work.

Another area of study looks at the origins of Old Testament stories. Elements of ancient Syrian mythology, carved in the Ebla tablets, bear a striking similarity to some of the most famous tales recounted in the Bible.

Finally, it is fair to say that some of Syria's most charming culture is found in the courtyards of the private homes built in the cities of Damascus and Aleppo. Architectural scholars who have spent lifetimes documenting and highlighting great achievements in momumental buildings, can also find enchantment in the peace and simplicity of dwellings crafted around the seasons and the custom originating in Syrian nomadic societies of welcoming anyone who shows up at one's home. Within urban centres, the high walls surrounding a private house contained fruit trees, a water fountain, and a building of two to three stories: the ground floor for cooking and life close to the garden in summer, and the upper floors for life in the winter. It is remarkable, even for someone who has grown up in Damascus, to be able to enter the oldest homes which retain this architectural design and provide the same, timeless comfort they have provided over hundreds of years.

Other dimensions to Syrian culture, like the musical repertoire which continues to forge an uninterrupted signal of gathering and garanties the identity of societies, is still alive and vivid among nomads and needs to be documented before it disappeared in the sands of history.

Having said all this, I wish to stress that I've tried to find examples of traditional inspiration in every object selected for the exhibition. It is my hope that these objects will reflect a certain quality of forms and colors speak to the visitor of its ancestral patrimony.

Bless the hands of thousands of anonymous artists who have left behind them an open letter of love and affection to all humanity.

5 Camp of the Roualla bedouins.

Landscapes and People –
Landscapes and Ways of Life

J. Kalter and M. Pavaloi

From whatever angle one looks at it, Syria has always been a land at the periphery of the centres of power. Western Syria not only has a Mediterranean climate, it has always culturally been a part of the Levant, i.e. the eastern Mediterranean. From Phoenician times onwards it had links with the whole of the North African littoral, and with North-West Africa and Spain. In the 2nd and 3rd centuries AD Syria produced four Roman emperors. To the north Syria had access to the mountainous regions of eastern Anatolia. Syria maintained relations with the Armenian Empire, and, during the Ottoman period, with the whole of present-day Turkey as far as Istanbul and beyond into European parts of the Ottoman Empire. Movements of populations in the nineteenth century and the first third of the twentieth, led to the influx of a large number of Circassians, Abkhasians and Armenians to Syria. Southern Syria merges into the vast desert of the Arabian Peninsula. To the south Syria was also linked to Anatolia via the Incense Road which started in Yemen. To the east it was open to Mesopotamia. Through the valley of the Euphrates goods and ideas from China, India and Iran were transmitted to Syria along the ancient trade routes of the Silk Roads.

Syria was thus a bridge between East and West, a land through which passed the long-distance trade which enriched the great Syrian cities. It was also a land which saw the clash and fusion of religions and cultures.

At the mountain ranges of the Lebanon, Antilebanon and its foothills three climatic zones meet: the Mediterranean, the subtropical and the arid. The valley of the Euphrates which runs through the desert of Syria from north-north-west to south-south-east has always been a vital line of communication and the route preferred by caravans. It was only towards the end of the 1st millennium that the domestication of the dromedary made it possible to cross the Syrian desert by the shortest route, from Deir ez-Zor on the Euphrates, via the oasis of Palmyra, to Damascus. The significance the of long-distance trade can be demonstrated by just two early examples. Excavations in eastern Syria at Mari, show that around 1800 BC the town, then the capital of a state, was trading in copper from Cyprus and tin from Persia, as well as other goods. Timber, precious stones, oil, wine and spices were traded as far as Crete and the Persian Gulf. Excavations at Palmyra, the capital of a short- lived state that rose to importance through trade in the 2nd and 3rd centuries AD, have revealed fragments of Chinese silks and Egyptian cotton textiles.

6 Stele with representation of a camel, Palmyra, second century AD.

7 & 8 Roof and interior of the dome of the Chan Asad Pasha ed-Azm in Damascus.

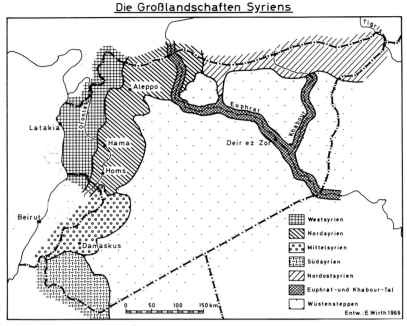

Die Großlandschaften Syriens

⊞	Westsyrien
⧄	Nordsyrien
∷	Mittelsyrien
⊟	Südsyrien
⧅	Nordostsyrien
▦	Euphrat- und Khabour-Tal
☐	Wüstensteppen

Entw.: E. Wirth 1969

The main landscapes of Syria

Distribution of the major linguistic and religious groups (a general overview)

The geographical setting and nature of the land prevented Syria itself from ever becoming an imperial centre. It simply lacked the resources. Characteristic of Syrian history are city states, which fought among themselves, entered into ever-changing alliances, and – depending on their individual strength or weakness – dominated a greater or lesser area of the land around them. The most important of these historically were Damascus and Aleppo – and they remain so today.

Syrian history is characterized by a constant conflict between foreign domination and self-determination. Every one of its powerful neighbours at some time or other made an attempt to gain control of the territory. In the first millennium BC Syria was part of the Babylonian Empire, then became part of empire of Alexander the Great and his successors, the Seleucids. From 64 BC to 395 AD it was a Roman province, and then a province of Christian Byzantium, which assumed the inheritance of Rome. It

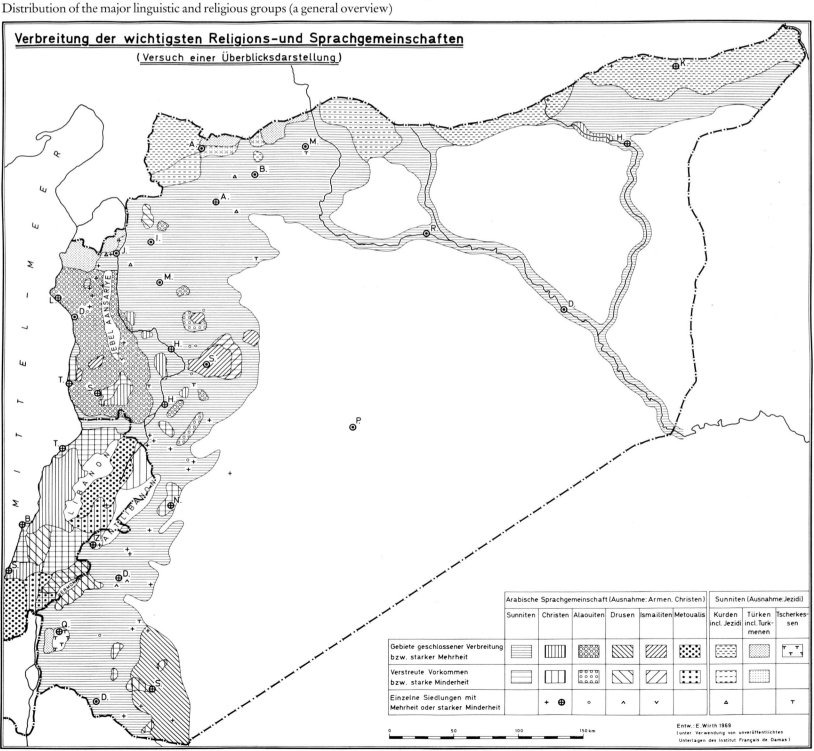

Verbreitung der wichtigsten Religions- und Sprachgemeinschaften
(Versuch einer Überblicksdarstellung)

	Arabische Sprachgemeinschaft (Ausnahme: Armen. Christen)						Sunniten (Ausnahme: Jezidi)		
	Sunniten	Christen	Alaouiten	Drusen	Ismailiten	Metoualis	Kurden incl. Jezidi	Türken incl. Turkmenen	Tscherkessen
Gebiete geschlossener Verbreitung bzw. starker Mehrheit									
Verstreute Vorkommen bzw. starke Minderheit									
Einzelne Siedlungen mit Mehrheit oder starker Minderheit	+	⊕	o	^	v		△		T

Entw.: E. Wirth 1969
(unter Verwendung von unveröffentlichten Unterlagen des Institut Français de Damas)

was at Damascus that Saul became the Apostle Paul. After the fall of Jerusalem in 70 AD Syria became a centre of Christian missionary activity. In western Syria, especially on the slopes of Antilebanon, the most ancient Christian monasteries in the world are to be found. One of these monasteries, at the village of Malula (whose population is still 70 per cent Greek Catholic and 10 per cent Greek Orthodox), preserves the relics of St. Thekla, a disciple of St. Paul, who is venerated as the first female Christian martyr.

In 635 AD Damascus was captured by Muslim armies, and Syria became part of the Arab empire. In the period from 661 to 750 Syria moved from being at the periphery of affairs to the centre. From Damascus the caliphs of the Umayyad dynasty ruled over an Islamic world empire extending from the Atlantic to the Indus. But after the removal of the caliphate to Baghdad under the Abbasids, Syria was relegated once again to provincial status. The period of the Crusades in the 11th and 12th centuries was of very great cultural significance – though more so to Europe than to Syria. Together with Andalusia and Sicily, it Syria which was a major conduit to the West not only not only for the collected wisdom of antiquity, which had been saved by Muslim scholars, but also for a sophisticated lifestyle. The crusader knights adopted, for example, the oriental culture of bathing, oriental musical instruments such as the lute, the tradition of love poetry (which influenced the troubadours and minnesingers) and the game of chess. One of the most eloquent reminders of the crusader period is the fortress known as Krak des Chevaliers, which stands on the 755-metre-high Jebel Kalil dominating the surrounding countryside in the valley of Homs. This fortress of the emirs of Homs was captured in 1102 by crusaders and until 1270 was a distant crusader outpost. During this period Syria provided wide range of high-quality goods for the princely courts and nobility of Europe – enamelled Aleppo glass, damask and brocade fabrics from Damascus, damascene blades and inlaid metalwork.

To understand Syria today it is necessary to familiarize oneself, at least in broad outline, with these important periods in Syria's past. Generally speaking, the history of Syria is characterized by continual conflicts with the imperial powers of the time, as well as by permanent internal tensions. The peasants in the mountains, who generally formed very coherent ethnic or religious groups, were in conflict with the plains and the towns which were striving for dominance. The peasants of the plain and of the towns found themselves in constant conflict with the bedouin of the desert. There was permanent tension between all of these and the central power, which attempted to remain master of the situation by making treaties with changing alliance partners, by demanding payments of tribute, and by exerting military force. Syria was open to repeated invasions, either from the Mediterranean or from the Arabian desert. This helped give Syria its variety and cultural richness, but it also resulted in a difficult balancing act during times of peace and an unstable political structure.

9 Hall of the Knights at Krak des Chevaliers.

10 Inner courtyard of the Tekiye Suleimaniye, Damascus.

11 Monastery church at Zednaya.

12 Date palms in the oasis of Palmyra.

13 View of the Euphrates near Zenobia.

14 Camels in the basalt desert south-east of Damascus.

15 Girls from a group of sheep nomads with their flocks in north-eastern Syria.

16 Farmstead of sheep nomads who have become sedentary.

17 An old olive tree in the Alawite Mountains, western Syria.

The tangible evidence surviving from Syria's seven-thousand-year history means that it is possible to make journeys through a variety of different periods and cultures. But one is always aware of the determining influence of the landscapes, of towns whose role is determined by their location on trade routes or their strategic position in the control of those routes; the dominance of either Mediterranean or the Arab-Oriental cultural influence; constantly changing peoples and languages. Besides the Arabic-speakers, there are also about 5 per cent of Syrians with Kurdish as their mother tongue, and Turkish, Turcoman, Circassian, as well as Aramaic and Hebrew are spoken. Around 75 per cent of the Syrian population belong to Sunni Islam, but there are also splinter groups of the Shi'ite branch of Islam, Alavites, Ishmailites and Druzes in the mountain regions. The largest Christian community is made up of the Greek Christians, i.e. Greek Catholic (Melkites) and Greek Orthodox, who comprise 7 per cent of the population. They are followed by the Armenians (Armenian Catholics and Gregorians), Syrian Christians (Syrian Catholics and Jacobites) and small groups (less than 0.5 per cent of the Syrian population according to Wirth) of Maronites, Protestants, Latins and Nestorians (Assyrian and Chaldaean). As we have mentioned, there are still a few Christian villages, and nineteenth-century accounts mention considerably more villages with an entirely Christian population. Today, however, the Christian population is mainly concentrated in Syria's six largest towns, Damascus, Aleppo, Homs, Hama, Lataqiye and Deir ez-Zor. According to Wirth (1971), just over a quarter of all the Moslems of Syria were living in these towns in 1947, but more than half the Christians. Since the 1967 War between Israel and Syria the number of Jews in Syria has declined to a few thousand, who are concentrated mainly in Damascus and Aleppo, though some of these are very wealthy.

All of these peoples, linguistic groups, members of the widely varied religious groups, have contributed to the kaleidoscope of cultures in Syria. But because their basic attitude is characterized by tolerance, and because – over and above the often confusing variety – there are shared historical experiences and the same forces in the natural environment which have shaped them, it was possible to make Syria a cultural entity.

18 Ruins of the pilgrimage church of the St. Symeon monastery, Qalaat Samaan, north-western Syria, fifth/sixth centuries AD.

19 A row of old residential houses and shops with typical balconies made of wooden grilles, Aleppo.

20 Family photograph: Circassian men at the beginning of the century.

21 Sheikh of a fraternity in the courtyard of his house in Aleppo.

22 A dancer outside the Citadel in Aleppo.

23 Village in north-western Syria with domed mud houses of the type recorded since the third millennium BC.

24 Granaries and dovecote of a farmstead in north-western Syria.

25 Peasant's house and granaries at the same farmstead.

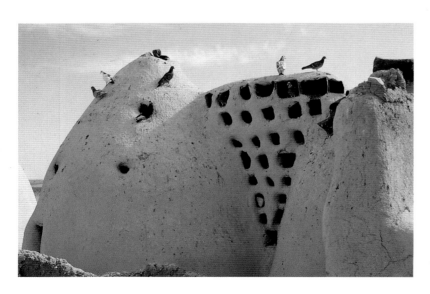

26 A flock of sheep between Palmyra and Damascus.

27 Spring landscape in the southern Jebel ed-Druz.

28 Flocks of sheep on the terraced slopes of the old farmland of western Syria in the Alawite Mountains near Krak des Chevaliers.

29 Han in Akka.

Syria on the Eve of the Modern Age

Heinz Gaube

1. Syrians – Arabs

The notion of 'Syria' (Suriya) as a political idea originated in the nineteenth century in the minds of a few intellectuals. This idea of Syria was, however, geographically confused, and for a long time it overlapped with the idea of Arab unity.

The idea of Arab nationalism – not a militant nationalism, but a cultural one – also had its roots in Syria. The centre of these intellectual, cultural and political movements was Beirut, then Syria's most important port. It was at Beirut in 1866 that American missionaries founded the 'Syrian Protestant College', from which the 'American University of Beirut' was to develop, and few years later, in 1875, Jesuits established the predecessor of the 'Université St. Joseph'. These two institutions not only exerted a considerable influence on the intellectual life of Syria, they also had an effect far beyond Syria in the rest of the Arab world and beyond to Iran and Pakistan.

Young Arabs/Syrians came into contact with the circles of foreign teachers, their pupils (soon to become teachers themselves) and others connected with these institutions. These young Arabs were eager to learn, soak up western education, understand their own culture and language better, and create new forms of thought and new artistic forms. Their first concern was the language. In Beirut the first modern Arabic-Arabic dictionary was produced, new literary forms were tried out, and in many circles there were discussions about culture, nationhood, human freedoms and politics.

Cultural renewal and a sense of Syrian identity were soon the subject of a variety of conflicts. Often these had to do with basic questions that were difficult to answer: how far can a Syrian be an Arab and yet still be a Syrian? – and what is a Syrian anyway?

The Arabs of the middle ages knew Syria as 'Bilad esh-Sham'. This can be translated as 'the Syrian Lands'. But what does the 'Syrian' ('esh-Sham') in this mean? Literally it is the 'northern region' of Arabia, as opposed to the southern region, el-Yemen.

Bilad esh-Sham = the Syrian Lands = (in Western terminology) Greater Syria, extends from the Red Sea and Gaza in the south to the Euphrates, and culturally beyond these into the regions that are now Iraq and Turkey. Faced with this division the intellectual pioneers of the idea of a Syria around the turn of the century thought they could be people of the large historically and culturally varied region of Bilad esh-Sham, and at the same time be Arabs. The same people were also the pioneers of an Arab consciousness – and were closely linked with a network of inter-related families, Muslim and Christian, which extended across the country, as well as having contacts with exiles outside Bilad esh-Sham, especially in Egypt, where many Syrian intellectuals had found refuge from Turkish-Ottoman despotism.

Two main political tendencies therefore emerged in the intellectual circles of the cities of Bilad esh-Sham: the Pan-Arabists and the Syrian nationalists. A third, weaker tendency was represented by the Ottomanists, who sought a sensible political order for their region within the framework of a reformed, modernized and constitutional Ottoman Empire.

The Pan-Arabists saw in an Arab state the opportunity to be sufficiently detached from the Ottoman Empire to defy both the Ottomans and the Western Powers. For them it was indispensable that Syria with its Mediterranean coastline, its educational potential and its economy was part of an Arab state.

The Syrian nationalists argued the opposite. In their view the inhabitants of Bilad esh-Sham formed a separate nation with its own culture and history – and not part of an Arab nation. They saw the role of Syria as a Mediterranean state, and therefore as a link and buffer between Western imperialism and Arab nationalism. They also wanted to be a means of cultural contact between Europe and the Arab lands. Many of them had little faith in the desire of other Arabs to introduce comprehensive social and economic changes.

In the event, the dream of the Syrian nationalists – a separate Syrian state (even if not within the borders which everyone had hoped) – became reality. Yet Syria is also an active part of the Arab commonwealth of states, though this too is different from what the Arab nationalists at the turn of the century had wished for. Syrians are Arabs, but they are primarily Syrians. They have their own history and culture, though because of the common language these are part of a wider Arab history and culture, just as Germany's history and culture is part of European history and culture.

The peculiarity of Syria (from now on I shall often use the word "Syria" to refer to Bilad esh-Sham – Greater Syria or the Syrian lands – but this should now be clear from the context) is already clear from the medieval term "Bilad esh-Sham" which means "the Syrian *lands*": its unity and

30 Above: View over the roofs of houses built of basalt blocks in the old town of Bosra.

31 Waterwheels on the Orontes in the old town of Hama.

32 Top left: Yezidi sheikh of a northern Syrian village.

33 Bottom left: Peasant women in the *suq* of Hama.

34 Top right: A man praying in the Great Mosque of Aleppo.

35 Centre right: Iranian women in the court in front of the Umayyad mosque in Damascus.

36 Bottom right: Peasant woman from the Qalamoun Mountains, in Damascus.

37 Bottom right: Street seller in "African" costume in Damascus.

variety since antiquity, when Syria was the classic land of ancient oriental city states, hardly any of which ever promoted imperial interests. Its history and culture were determined by its role as a mediator between Mesopotamia, Egypt and the Arabian Peninsula, and many of its sons (and daughters) also rose to prominence and power in Rome and other cities of the Roman Empire.

Syria is like a cut gemstone: it has many facets, but it is still a single stone – and the light of every facet is the same light.

2. The First Period of Ottoman Rule over Syria 1516-1831

Bilad esh-Sham can be roughly defined as comprising modern Syria, Lebanon, Jordan, Palestine and parts of present-day Turkey. The Turkish conquerors ousted the Mamluks, who had driven the crusaders and Mongols from Bilad esh-Sham in the 13th century. Ruling from their capital, Cairo, they had brought a long period of internal peace and, for a time, prosperity. Most cities of Bilad esh-Sham have many Mamluk buildings.

The Ottomans arrived as reorganizers. They were responsible in the first period of their rule for a detailed tax register, which is a remarkable source of information about what was "really" there. Soon, however, the Ottoman state moved along the same track as its predecessors, the Byzantines and the Persians, whose system of taxation and rule it also largely retained. Corruption, court intrigues, the buying of offices became usual. Once the Ottoman governors had created some order in Bilad esh-Sham, and divided it up into provinces, they soon followed the example of the Roman consuls, and the Byzantine and Persian governors – and took to lining their own pockets.

Nevertheless the Ottoman provincial administration was based on rationality. It was, however, no guarantee of efficiency, since it overlapped with itself and impinged on an old principal of the Eastern rationale of government: "quis custodiet custodes?" ("who will keep watch over the guardians?") This caused constant insecurity at all levels of government and more than once cost the sultan his life.

The all-powerful authority in the Ottoman Empire was the sultan, who resided in Istanbul. His empire, which extended from the Balkans to North Africa, was divided into provinces. In Syria the number of these varied during Ottoman rule, but the most important provinces were Aleppo and Damascus. Each of them was ruled by a governor (*wali*) with almost unlimited powers. He held the highest political power, was responsible for taxation, for the defence of the province, the security of the roads and so on. The civil jurisdiction lay in the hands of the senior judge (*qadi*). The governor had a deputy (*mutasallim*), and the senior judge's deputy was the *mufti*. The senior judge also supervised the chief of police (*muhtasib*), who commanded the police force (*shurta*). Taxes were collected by a special

official, the *muhassil*, and each of these holders of high offices had below them an apparatus of subordinate officials and scribes. In the larger provincial capitals infantry troops from headquarters were stationed. These were janissaries and others, under their own commanders, while the governor often had his own separate troops.

Alien representatives sent by the central power could not of course govern a province by themselves. We often find a mixture of high officials sent from the centre and those recruited on the spot. The governor and senior judge were usually sent, while their deputies were appointed from among the local nobility.

The Ottoman system of government, sketched here in a very superficial and idealized way, seems to have functioned relatively well in Syria in different areas for various lengths of time, until the 18th century. But even in these "good" times of Ottoman rule, Syria was by no means entirely under the control of the central power. Around the cities, where the governors and their apparatus ruled, the old power structures remained unbroken. Here the leaders of feudal clans were in charge, and in the desert and mountain regions the Ottoman administration was only able to extend its power in a very sporadic way. The expense of military operations against nomads and mountain-dwellers was usually out of all proportion to the usefulness of such undertakings; as soon as the troops were withdrawn everything reverted to what it had been.

The Syrian Wilajets and Sandschaks around 1900.

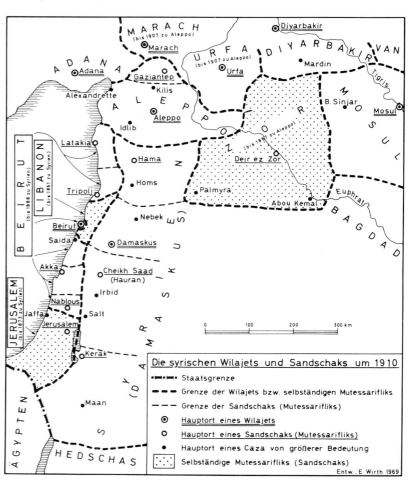

28

38 *Iwan* at the entrance of the Palace of Beshir II, Beit ed- Din.

The Druze emirate of Maan, for example, was soon able to develop as a *de facto* independent state in the mountains of the Lebanon. Its chief leader, Fahr ed-Din (1590-1613 and 1618-1635) developed agriculture, built up close trading relations with Europe and was able to rule far beyond his ancestral region, the Lebanese mountains south of Beirut. He is even credited with building a castle at Palmyra. Eventually, in 1613, the Ottomans moved against Fahr ed-Din, with a large army supported from the sea by warships. He escaped on a European ship to Tuscany, only to return five years later and continue his old policies. Within a few years he was able to build up such power that the Ottoman sultan was forced to appoint him regent of the rural districts between Aleppo and Jerusalem, that is, of all the regions between Aleppo and Jerusalem over which the provincial governors had no direct control.

This occurred in a period of weakness at the Ottoman centre of power. By 1635 the centre had regained its strength. Another army was sent against Fahr ed-Din, who was taken prisoner and brought to Istanbul. At first he was treated as a "guest" of the court, but finally executed.

His successors were able to rule over a considerably reduced territory until 1697, when the last of Fahr ed-Din's successors (one of his sons lived in Istanbul) died. At a local assembly the notables of the southern Lebanese mountains elected a new leader, Beshir I of the Shehab family. The early Shehabs continued the weak policies of the late Maan. Internally there were great clashes between various Druze factions, who instead of carrying the interests of the inhabitants of this part of Syria to the outside world, tore each other apart. These disputes came to an end in 1711 in a great battle, after which the defeated party migrated from the Lebanese mountains and found a new home in the basalt hills south of Damascus, a region which had been uninhabited since late antiquity, and now was called after them the Jebel ed-Druz (or Jebel el-Arab).

Not until the time of Beshir II Shehab did the Shehabs produce a leader who had a firm grasp of the complicated politics of relations between the mountains and the coast, and between the Ottomans and his own interests. During his long period of rule (1789-1840) the inhabitants of the Lebanese mountains and the neighbouring areas enjoyed relative stability and prosperity. At first the great threat to his power was Ahmed el-Jazzar, the Pasha of Akka (Acre – the port on the north coast of Palestine, which had been the last bastion of the crusaders in Syria). The end of his rule

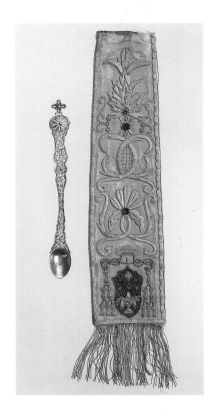

39 Torah scroll from Damascus. Black ink on antelope leather with turned and painted wooden support.

40 Spoon for celebrating the Holy Eucharist, silver filigree with fire-gilding, and a fragment of the stole of a Christian patriarch. Damascus, nineteenth century.

41 Chased silver mount for an image of the Madonna, and chased silver votive gifts. Damascus, nineteenth century.

42 Glass-painting with a calligraphic inscription of the name of God (Allah). Damascus, nineteenth century.

43 Scourges for Shi'ite Moharram processions. Iron, wood; the one on the left with mother-of-pearl inlay. Damascus, nineteenth century.

44 Chased silver medallion for sewing on to a Muslim processional banner.

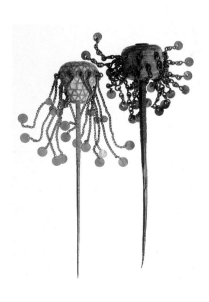

led to the Egyptian invasion of Syria in 1832, which opened a new era in the history of Syria.

But it was not only in the mountains and more inaccessible parts of Syria that the local rulers were able to establish themselves almost independently of the central power in Istanbul. On the Mediterranean coast too, at Akka, for instance, it was possible for rulers, who were only nominally under the Ottomans, to assert themselves. Ahmed el-Jazzar ("Ahmed the Butcher" – so called because of his cruelty), whom we have already mentioned, is a good example of this.

A Bosnian by birth, he had already lived a turbulent life, spending time in Istanbul and Egypt, and as governor of the Syrian coastal town of Sidon, before becoming governor of Akka in 1775. His predecessor was Zahir el-Omar, who since 1746 had ruled Akka and its hinterland almost independently and had been killed in a military campaign in that year. Unlike Zahir, who was satisfied with ruling Akka and its hinterland, Jazzar had greater ambitions. We have already mentioned his constant attempts to bring the Lebanese mountains under his control. Here he was opposed by Beshir II Shehab. Ahmed el-Jazzar was able to use governors dependent on him to gain control of the coast as far as Tripoli to the north, and then attack Damascus.

Before becoming the actual governor of Damascus in 1785 (though he governed it from Akka), Jazzar successfully withstood the siege of his city by the French under Napoleon. Until his death in 1804 Jazzar held the governorship of Damascus four times. The fact that it had to "reward" the renegade governor of a strip of the Syrian coast with the second most important governorship in Syria was a clear indication of the weakness of the Ottoman central power in Syria.

But in Damascus the situation did not seem very different from that on the coast and in the Lebanese mountains. Here too – even before Jazzar - one family, the Azm family, had established itself as governors with a very great degree of independence. In 1725 the first Azm, Ismail, became governor of Damascus, and for a long period other members of the family held governors' posts of other Syrian cities, at Tripoli, Hama and Maarat en-Numan. The most important of the Azm, Asad el-Azm, had been governor of Hama, before he took up his post at Damascus. Asad's fourteen-year rule over Damascus brought the city relative peace and prosperity. His palace in the middle of the old town of Damascus (now the Folk Museum) and the prominent *khan* (caravanserai) nearby with its domes rising above the surrounding buildings and its fine masonry in black and white layers ("*ablaq*" technique), are reminders of the period of Asad's rule in Damascus.

So it was not only the small coastal cities that followed Akka's example: things were no different in Tripoli, where again one family ruled for a long time, and the same was true in the mountains, where the hand of the Ottoman

45 & 46 Courtyard and prayer hall in the eighth-century Umayyad mosque in Damascus.

47 Courtyard of the Great Mosque in Aleppo, eighth to nineteenth centuries.

central power could never gain direct – if any – control. The weakness of the Ottomans was also apparent in Syria's second most important city, Damascus. Here government was made difficult mainly because of struggles between two factions within the city led by two opposing groups of janissaries.

The janissaries had been the elite infantry of the Ottomans, made up of boys who had been taken from the Christian parts of the empire (the Balkans) and given a thorough military training. They were well paid and enjoyed special privileges, such as their own jurisdiction, and had contributed much to the expansion and safeguarding of the Ottoman Empire. By the 18th century, however, they had become a badly paid (though still privileged) and disorderly group of old campaigners, forced to earn their living in business in the towns. Not all these janissaries had been taken as children; some were recruited from native marginal groups (Turcomans, Kurds, nomads).

In Damascus, where the janissaries mainly lived in the southern part of the city, in the street by which grain and animals to be slaughtered entered the city, the "genuine" janissaries and the local recruits vied with each other mainly over control of the staple foodstuffs and their prices. By manipulating these prices they (and others) were able to enrich themselves.

At that time Damascus was only the second city of Syria. Aleppo, the old metropolis of foreign trade, was far bigger. Even before the Ottoman conquest Aleppo had enjoyed an economic boom, and it prospered still more after the invasion brought about the fall of the Mamluk-Ottoman frontier, which had been an obstacle to Aleppo's trade with the East, in particular with Iran. In the first two centuries of Ottoman rule the *suq* (bazaar) was considerably extended. Ottoman governors and high officials built great *khans* (caravanserais) and shopping streets connected with them.

48 Deir el Qamar: the capital of the Druze prince Fakhr ed-Din. In the background is Beit ed-Din, the palace of Beshir I.

Aleppo was worth investing in because it was one of the most important trading cities of the empire. It was through Aleppo that the profitable trade in Persian silk reached Europe. Many European states had trading posts or consulates there. Consequently Aleppo was the only Syrian city to remain under direct Ottoman rule throughout the whole Ottoman period. Any attempt to build up local rule was opposed by the Ottomans with all the means at their command. In the eighteenth century such an attempt was made by the Jumblats, but they were forced to flee into the mountains of Lebanon, where they still play an important role today. The Ottomans were thus unable to put their claim even to Aleppo beyond dispute.

As a result of this instability a new Ottoman governor appeared at Aleppo almost every year. Many of these governors were among the most important officials of the empire, and some of them later rose to the rank of Grand Vizier, the most senior office in the empire. The rest of Syria received no profit – or relatively little – from trade with Europe and the East. Aleppo was exceptional because of it profits made from trade, which were accompanied by a highly developed craft and manufacturing sector and a flourishing hinterland. Circumstances like those in Akka were unthinkable in Aleppo – but conditions similar to those in Damascus arose in Aleppo after the collapse of the Safavid empire in Iran in 1722. As Iran sank into chaos and then into stagnation, the Iranian silk production as an export-orientated branch of the economy collapsed and Aleppo lost its most important trading commodity.

Aleppo thus became a city like Damascus. Henceforth its most important trade was not the great caravans going from and to the East, but, as in Damascus, grain and meat. Aleppo also became as riven by factional strife as Damascus. Economic interest groups within the city competed for control of the profits from basic foodstuffs. They formed into two parties, which took the struggle onto the streets. In Aleppo these were not two factions of janissaries as in Damascus. Here the janissaries were a closed group which opposed the *ashraf*, who were supposedly descendants of the Prophet Muhammed – and apparently a better sort of lumpenproletariat. The governors and the other high officials changed frequently. Sometimes they were able to keep the city under control, but at other times they would be forced to flee and return with reinforcements to regain control.

Syria's ethnic, geographical, religious and tribal variety did not enable the Ottomans to govern Syria as we understand it. Opportunism, loss of orientation, self-seeking and ignorance, and – by the second half of the eighteenth century at least – the imperceptiveness and selfishness of the officials from Istanbul, had in every province brought ruin to an economy based primarily on agriculture.

In the countryside taxes were not collected by regular state bodies but by tax farmers, who acquired their right to collect taxes by devious methods, by open defiance or though bribery. But whatever the means they used to become tax farmers, their aim was always the same: to squeeze as much as they could from the peasants by force. These short-sighted profiteers had little interest in whether the peasants then still had seedcorn for the following year, or whether they would be able to survive to sow it; they had other concerns.

The tax farmers had to rake in as much as possible as quickly as possible, since they lived in a state where they could lose their head and their fortune overnight. The injustice from above was passed on downwards - the "classic" Oriental dilemma. In this way the basis of Syria's economy, agriculture, was almost destroyed.

Eighty per cent of Syrian peasants (those who had not starved to death or been killed by the tax collectors) saw no alternative to escaping to the towns, where they only added to the already existing problems. They fell in behind one or other of the town factions, often risking their lives for the interests of the very people who had directly or indirectly threatened their existence before. Eventually they themselves also contributed to bringing the Ottoman administration of Syria to the edge of collapse at the beginning of the 19th century.

The precariousness of the situation which the Ottoman Empire found itself in was recognized by some, even in Istanbul. On the Arabian Peninsula the Wahabites, a fundamentalist Islamic movement, on whose surge the Saudi royal house of Saudi Arabia was to come to power, had risen in revolt; a little later the Greek uprising broke out, and in Egypt Mohammed Ali was striving for independence.

The reform-orientated circles in Istanbul found a patron in Sultan Mahmud II, who came to the throne in 1808. Against much opposition he attempted to strengthen the central power and weaken local forces by means of administrative reforms. His government is associated particularly with the decision to disband the janissaries, who consistently sought to hinder reforms and had taken the Ottoman Empire from one military disaster to the next.

3. The Egyptian Invasion of Syria in 1832 and its Effects During the period up to the First World War

For Syria, however, the decisive impetus for reforms came not from Istanbul but from Cairo. Mohammed Ali had become governor there in 1805, three years before the accession of Mahmud II. His great influence on the history of Egypt was to last until after the Second World War. In 1841 the Sultan in Istanbul granted him hereditary governorship over Egypt, making Egypt a state with *de facto* independence from the Ottomans, and it was not until the Egyptian Revolution of 1953 that the rule of his descendants came to an end.

Mohammed Ali was born at Kavalla in present-day Greece, and rose after a relatively short career to the important post of Governor of Egypt. Napoleon's Egyptian expedition had left a deep shock in the country. Its success had been made possible by European technological superiority, discipline and organization. This was recognized by many Egyptians and the call for modernization of the state and the economy became louder and louder.

Mohammed Ali became the enforcer of ideas for modernization by systematically changing Egypt's administrative, military, law-making and economic structures on European lines, with the assistance of European advisers. Indeed his aim was to turn Egypt into a state which would equal the European states. The fact that in the end he did not succeed was due less to any failing on his part than to the intervention of the European powers, whose interests were not served by the emergence of a modern state on the other side of the Mediterranean.

This is not the place to discuss this attempt by an Arab country to free itself from the fetters of European hegemony, and how the attempt was frustrated by the European powers, above all Great Britain. Here we shall concentrate on Mohammed Ali's Syrian policy.

In order to implement his policies in Egypt without Ottoman interference Mohammed Ali needed a shield against the Ottomans. This shield was Syria. His son Ibrahim began the conquest of the country in 1832. Ottoman power in Syria collapsed within a few months, and by the end of the year Ibrahim and his troops were already at Konya, deep inside present-day Turkey.

With the cooperation of the European powers a treaty concluded between Egypt and the Ottoman Empire the following year gave Mohammed Ali the governorship of all Syria for his lifetime. He introduced two far-reaching reforms, which were to have a decisive influence on Syria until after the end of the First World War.

Syria (i.e. Bilad esh-Sham) was made a single province governed from Damascus. Each provincial town was now given a vice-governor. Ibrahim, as commander-in-chief of what was for that time a very large army (between 1832 and 1840 it grew from approximately 300,000 men to approximately 900,000), stood above the vice-governors and the governor.

Ibrahim deprived the leading families in the towns of their power and disarmed the population. He secularized the legal system and left the *qadis* with responsibility only for family and property law. The tax system was reformed and regulated tax collection was organized, compulsory military service for Muslims was introduced, and equality before the law for Muslims and non-Muslims. (Under traditional Islamic law non-Muslims are second-class citizens.) Ibrahim brought security to the countryside; peasants were again able to settle without fear, and merchants could lead their caravans from one town to another without risk.

All these reforms and measures for bringing order were imposed by Ibrahim with firmness and with the backing of his huge military apparatus. This went against the interests of many: the urban bourgeoisie which was now deprived of power and had to pay taxes regularly; the Muslim population, who suddenly had the Jews and Christians as their equals, – and the European powers, who found the "sick man on the Bosphorus" more congenial than an Egyptian-Syrian state orientated towards modernization.

At the Convention of London in 1840 England, Russia, Austria and Prussia imposed a diktat on the Ottoman sultan and Mohammed Ali – against the opposition of France, whose anti-British stance led it to take the side of Mohammed Ali. According to the diktat the sultan was to grant Mohammed Ali hereditary governorship over Egypt, but he had to withdraw from Syria (except Akka). British and Austrian ships appeared off Beirut and Alexandria to add weight to the demand.

The Egyptians withdrew from Syria. Although Ibrahim's regency over Syria had been appreciated by many as a period of peace and order, for others it had brought too much order and change, and some, especially the Druzes of Jebel ed-Druz, rose against him.

However, the wheel of time could no longer be turned back. In Istanbul Mohammed Ali's success had strengthened the hand of the reformers around Mahmud II and his son Abdul Mejid, who succeeded him in 1839. If the Ottoman Empire wanted to survive, then reforms were the only way of doing so. After 1829 the janissaries were abolished and replaced by a modern army on the Western model. A decisive step to reform was taken in 1839, when the sultan signed the "Hatti Sherif" ("Noble Decree") giving force of law to extensive reforms in administration, the military and in civil law. It ushered in a new era in the history of the Ottoman state, called the "Tanzimat" ("Reform") period. Despite many setbacks and opposition in the court and in the population, which gave rise violent Muslim riots in Aleppo (1850) and Damascus (1860) against Christians and Jews, who were now all guaranteed equality before the law, these reforms marked a new phase in the history of Ottoman rule over Syria.

The central power became stronger and the countryside safer. The land laws of 1858, although their results ran counter to the intentions of their creators who sought to spread property among the peasants, led to clear and productive conditions in rural areas. Henceforth these were controlled and recultivated by rural and urban notables who formed a new land-owning class.

The policy of the Ottoman state towards the nomads had been on the one hand to make them sedentary, and on the other to force them out of the parts of Syria which could be used for agricultural purposes. This encouraged the recolonization of more agricultural regions of the country, which was also helped by the settling of Circassians in fortified settlements. Muslim Circassians migrated to the Ottoman Empire in several waves between 1864 and 1890. Since the Crimean War of 1853-1856 their homeland in the northern Caucasus had become Russian and so was ruled by Christians. Most of the new Circassian fortified settlements stood on the sites of ancient settlements, which had been uninhabited since the middle ages – or even since late antiquity. This policy regarding the nomads and new settlements was seen most clearly in the region that is now Jordan. The capital, Amman (Philadelphia in antiquity), had been depopulated since the early Islamic period and was now resettled by Circassians. The same was true of Jerash (ancient Gerasa) to the north of Amman. In what is now Syria Circassians were settled at Quneitra on the Jaulan, in the regions west of Homs and Hama in central Syria, and east of Aleppo as far as Raqqa on the Euphrates.

In the towns too the Ottoman policy of reform yielded results. Trade and industry flourished again, there was an enormous amount of building activity, and Damascus, which had already been the capital of Syria under Ibrahim, increased in importance. So did the port of Beirut, which as we have seen was to become the intellectual centre of the country in the second half of the nineteenth century and an important centre of the Syrian nationalist and Arab nationalist movements.

The development made rapid progress in all areas and Western influence increased with Western educational institutions – or educational institutions founded on Western models – and with the ever-growing trade with Europe. Railway lines and modern roads were built, and as goods arrived from Europe, the influence of European ideas became ever stronger in the country, and the call for democracy, political parties and freedom of conscience became louder.

This was the situation on the eve of the First World War. What had begun in 1832 with the Egyptian conquest of Syria, the modernization of all areas of life and an openness to western ideas at all levels, had led to a new self assurance and an economic boom, which strengthened Damascus and Beirut at the expense of Aleppo.

The entry of the Ottoman Empire into the First World War on the side of Germany and its allies heralded the end of the last great Eastern empire. Nothing seemed more welcome to the British, French and Russians. Each had already chosen its own portion from the ruins of the Ottoman Empire, though after the Russian Revolution only Great Britain and France were left to put their intentions into practice. In December 1914 Great Britain declared Egypt its protectorate, which meant that, as well as the Persian Gulf and India, Britain also controlled Egypt, through which ran the Suez Canal, the sea link to India.

The local *sherif* Husein, the ruler of Mecca, who was dependent on the Ottomans, became a tool in the hands of the British in their struggle against Ottoman rule in parts of the Arabian Peninsula and in Syria. He had adopted Pan-Arab ideas and hoped through his revolt against the Ottomans, which started in 1916, to gain an Arab empire for himself and his descendants, an empire whose borders had been outlined for him in a deliberately vague manner by the British a year before. According to the British promise, the regions west of the line running through Damascus, Homs, Hama and Aleppo were to be outside the empire, as were the provinces of Basra and Baghdad.

Almost at the same time as this promise made to the *sherif* the British entered into negotiations with the French. The outcome of these negotiations was the "Sykes-Picot Agreement", which still stirs emotions today. It divided up Syria and the adjoining territories between the French and the British, and, with several later modifications, forms the basis for most of the present frontiers in the region.

To exacerbate still further the misgivings of the Arabs and sow the seed of the present troubles and the Arab mistrust of the West, the British now had the effrontery to make the "Balfour Declaration" part of their "New Order" in the Middle East. This gave consent to the creation by the Zionists of a national homeland for the Jews in Palestine, which later led to the establishment of the state of Israel.

Unwittingly betrayed many times, the Arabs helped the British to drive the Turks out of Syria and on 1 October 1918 the victors entered Damascus. Aleppo was captured almost a month later and shortly afterwards the armistice of Mudros brought the Ottoman state's part in the First World War to an end.

This had been preceded by years of brutal oppression, famine affecting whole regions and the last rearing of Ottoman arbitrary rule in Syria. The public executions of Arab nationalists represented only a small part of the violence; countless Armenians also became victims of this terror. T.E. Lawrence's *Seven Pillars of Wisdom* and Franz Werfel's *Die Vierzig Tage des Musa Dagh* vividly describe this period.

Supported by false promises and hopes, an Arab state was proclaimed in Damascus on 1 October 1918. Its hoped-for frontiers were large, but in reality nonexistent, and this was soon to become apparent. There was haggling between the British and the French, and President Wilson of the United States brought his own ideas to this despicable game of old European diplomacy around the Mediterranean, a game which in all probability he did not really understand.

At the Versailles Conference in April 1919 Syria and Iraq were divided into British and French mandates. The British received Palestine, Transjordan and Iraq with its oil wells, the French Syria, and what was to become Lebanon, as well as the region of Antiochia in the north-west of Syria, which was to be annexed by Turkey in 1939.

Sherif Feisal, the son of Husein, who had led the Arab troops against the Turks, returned from Versailles disappointed, and sought with all means at his disposal to save the Arab state as a constitutional monarchy under his leadership. He believed he could negotiate, and still believed in the British – but they had long since disowned him and their promise. The French, who had used no military force, carved out for themselves the best parts of old Syria (present-day Syria and Lebanon), while the British had to pay for their dishonourable policy in Palestine by subsidizing the non-state of Transjordan, though they were able to take advantage of Iraq-Iranian oil.

On 23 July 1920 the French General Gouraud defeated Feisal's poorly armed Arabs at Meisalun on the road from Beirut to Damascus, and the dream of an Arab state under Feisal with Damascus as its capital came to a sad end. Feisal was given the "consolation prize" of a royal title over a British-governed Iraq. His brother Abdallah became the emir of Transjordan, a state which could not survive on its own.

The British had thus achieved their peace in a manner which showed contempt for people. The structure they established was swept away in Iraq by the revolution of 1958. The grandsons of Abdallah, both educated in England, now rule the "Hashemite Kingdom of Jordan", which in the late nineteenth century was the least populated part of Syria. The imperial power of Great Britain and France has collapsed. Syria has decolonized itself. There can be no question that a contribution to this was made by a third phase of reforms, the reforms in the period under the French mandate.

4. Between Feisal and Independence in 1946

An Arab historian wrote after a critical discussion of the mandate period in Syria and Lebanon: "Yet there were some things which Lebanon owes to the mandatory power. Among them was the introduction of a relatively modern administrative system and modern customs and excise, a land register, an administration of antiquities and the construction of many roads. Public order was maintained... In Syria the same policy was followed. But since resistance was stronger, the punishments were more severe and the losses greater. In Syria few roads were built... and there was less public investment."

So there is not much good to be said about this period. It began with éclat. After the conquest of Damascus one of the first actions of General Gouraud was to visit the tomb of Saladin, who is regarded in Europe as the man who drove the crusaders from Syria, though in reality he had precursors and successors.

Gouraud did not go to Saladin's tomb to honour the tolerant Saladin who appears in Lessing's *Nathan der Weise*. This was made plain by the words he spoke there: "Ma présence ici consacre la victoire de la croix sur le croissant." The sentiment expressed here was to characterize the ensuing period: this was revenge at last for the defeat of the crusaders.

After the end of the First World War France quickly took measures to put the Sykes-Picot Agreement into effect. On 15 September 1919 a meeting took place between Lloyd George, the British Prime Minister, and Clemenceau, his French counterpart, at which it was agreed that British troops should be withdrawn from Syria and replaced by French troops. It was on the basis of this agreement, which was made far from Syria and without any say from the Syrians themselves, that Gouraud captured Damascus. This marked the beginning of French mandatory rule.

On one side was the humiliation of the Muslims, which Gouraud instigated at the tomb of Saladin, on the other the basic conditions concerning the duties of the mandatory powers, as laid down shortly afterwards by the League of Nations:

"Towards those colonies and regions which as a consequence of the late war are no longer under the rule of the state which ruled them previously and which are inhabited by people who are not yet in a position to rule themselves in the challenging conditions of the new era, a principle should be applied in which the welfare and development of these people is a sacred duty of humanity.

"The best means of realizing this is to transfer the care of such peoples to developed nations, which from their resources, their experience or their geographical situation are best able to take on this responsibility and are willing to bear this responsibility. This responsibility shall be

49 Akka, view from the mountains.

assumed in the form of a mandate of the League of Nations."

From the very first this noble idea and the actual business of ruling proved to be irreconcilable opposites. The reasons for this lay not only in the mandatory powers' craving for territory, there were also internal factors at work. While the population of Palestine and present-day Syria were in favour of a united Greater Syria, which would be assisted preferably by the Americans, or, failing that, by the British, other forces were at work in Lebanon. The Uniate and Catholic Christians, for whom France had already been the protecting power for some time under Ottoman rule, demanded an independent state under French protection.

Their wish was granted. On 1 September 1920 Gouraud proclaimed the "independent" state of "Greater" Lebanon (as opposed to historical Lebanon which only included the mountains) with the coastal strip between Tyre in the south and Tripoli in the north and the Beqa, the high valley between the mountains of Lebanon and those of Antilebanon.

Three years passed before this coup was sanctioned by international law. In July 1920 Gouraud had occupied Syria, and in September of the same year he created Lebanon – but it was not until September 1923 that the League of Nations recognized the French mandate over Lebanon and Syria. Thus, against the opposition of the majority of the inhabitants of historical Syria, the future state of Syria was only a fragment of the old cultural unit.

The French took their time to make the first steps towards turning Lebanon and Syria into "states". In 1926 Lebanon was given a constitution - formulated in Paris. But in Syria the French had to act with more caution. In 1928 elections were hold for an assembly to create a constitution. In 1930 a draft constitution was presented, but the French rejected it because the assembly had defined Greater Syria as a political unit and conceded too many rights to a future president of Syria.

After Lebanon had broken away from Syria and become a separate state, the rest of Syria was split up into individual "états". In 1920 the French established the Alawite "state" in the north-west of the country. This was followed in 1922 by a Druze "state" in the south-east, and what remained of Syria was split into "states" of Damascus and Aleppo. At first sight this was an excellent solution for the French, since they were able to play with the sectarian feelings and old animosities between Damascus and Aleppo. They were exercising their power in the classic tradition of "divide and rule".

But it did not prove as easy as Gouraud may have imagined. His successors were not satisfied with this solution, and the dividing up and reuniting of the country continued up to 1939. As the policies changed so did the French high commissioners in charge of the administration of the mandate regions.

The French did not get much joy from their colonial rule in the guise of a mandate. They were unable either to rule or to bring the various interests in the country together in the way they wanted. The Syrians united against them in the revolution of 1925-1927, when there was bitter fighting on both sides. Parts of Damascus were bombed and new national heroes emerged, such as the Druze leader Sultan el-Atrash, whose revolt in the Druze region had been the starting point for the revolution. The leader of one of the smaller states that the French had created in order to facilitate their rule, now rose against them for a unified Syria. The Druzes who had migrated here two hundred years earlier had learnt to become Syrians.

In reaction to the revolution of 1925-27 the French sought to set their dealings in Syria on a more legal basis. After the dissolution of the controversial constitution-making assembly of 1930, the French simply altered the constitution to suit themselves. It came into force after the election of a parliament in 1932. After the parliament had been constituted, it elected the first president of Syria, Ali el-Abid, and then the arguments began on a different level. The French high commissioners dissolved parliaments and changed administrations. But whenever and wherever the French built a barrier, they found that ultimately they could not withstand the will of the Syrians.

On 9 September 1936 a meeting between the French Popular Front administration under Léon Blum and a Syrian delegation agreed that the imposition of French authority should be replaced by cooperation. This represented an unambiguous step towards independence. The agreement found approval among the anti-colonialists in France. They saw it as a genuine fulfilment of the instructions of the League of Nations to France as a mandatory power. In Syria parliamentary elections were held. The new president was Hashim el-Attasi, and the new administration set about successfully turning Syria into a state. The representatives of the Druze and Alawite states gave way and Syria took shape within its present borders. Multiplicity thus reached agreement over unity.

In France, however, the Franco-Syrian treaty was not ratified. Negotiations in which the Syrian government conceded more and more of the contents of the original treaty led to increasing opposition in Syria; and in France the influence of those who wanted to exercise power directly in Syria grew. In 1939 the first phase of relative Syrian independence came to an end. The president resigned, the parliament was dissolved by the French high commissioner, the constitution was repealed and an administrative council was set up. The separation of the Alawite and Druze regions from the central state created conditions similar to the period before 1936. The power of the French administration had increased again, but important posts were also occupied by Syrians. It amounted to half a step backwards, and France's weakness in the Second World War was soon to open the path to real independence.

The behaviour of the French in the Second World War was less brutal but just as confused as that of the Ottomans in the First World War. Despite France's early capitulation. On 27 June 1940 the new high commissioner Mittelhauser declared: "There is no change in the status of the mandatory power... The French flag continues to fly in these regions. France will continue to carry out its task in the Levant." The flag was of course the flag of Vichy France.

Free French troops with British and Iraqi support began an attack on the Vichy troops in Syria and Lebanon in June 1941. A few months later the Vichy forces were defeated. General Catroux, the commander of the Free French forces had declared at the beginning of the offensive: "Inhabitants of Syria and Lebanon! At the moment when the troops of 'Free France' together with the troops of the British Empire, their allies, enter your land, I assume the power, responsibility and duties of the representative of France in the Levant. I do so in the name of 'Free France', which is the true France.... In this role I come to prepare the end of the mandate and to declare you free and independent..."

After the Allied victory Catroux proclaimed on 28 September 1941: "In the name of 'Free France' and of its leader, General de Gaulle, I accord recognition to Syria as a sovereign and independent state."

It was another two years before parliamentary elections were held in Syria in September 1943, and Syria obtained its first independent government. It was, however, independent only on paper. Pre-Vichy France, Vichy France, 'Free France' – all were imperialists. The more secure 'Free France' became, the less inclined it was to turn its promises fully into deeds. On grounds of "security" France continued to exercise control over Syria.

But in 1944 by a new agreement the country was given the most far-reaching independence yet. British and American pressure on France led to further progress. There were even military confrontations between the British and the French in Syria. On 15 April 1946 all foreign troops had to leave Syria. Henceforth the Syrians held their destiny in their own hands.

World Market and State in the Near East
The Political Economy of Syria

Peter Pawelka

Although historians and sociologists use different methods to investigate and interpret historical processes, they generally agree that since the beginning of the nineteenth century the Near East has been exposed to a continual procress of modernization. It is true that this socioeconomic transformation happened at different times and in different ways in the various parts of this region, and that it sometimes came to a standstill, but in the long run contact with the European capitalist world brought economic innovation and social class struggle, and so changed the structure of the Near East once and for all. In Syria modernization is said to have begun with Ibrahim Pasha in the 1830s and to have continued through many stages of stagnation and dynamism up to the present day. I do not share this perception of a linear development. Instead I shall present the history of modern Syria as a contradictory process, with a cyclical recurrence of traditional and modern elements, both of which have their problematic and progressive sides. In my view the formation and development of modern Syria are marked by the conflict between two opposing forces: on one side the expansive world economic system with its political protagonists and mechanisms, and on the other the power of resistance of the Oriental bureaucratic state with the social forces that supported it. While the great trading centres of the world economic system, with help from the indigenous upper classes, sought an ever more complete integratation of Syria economically, socially, politically and culturally, various groups of bureaucrats struggled to restore the controlling power of the state over this process of transformation which was being directed from the outside. We can distinguish three phases in this process:

– The period until te First World War saw a systematic economic penetration of Syria by the capitalist world market. This brought with it the creation of a new "bourgeois" upper class, trade and finance capital, and the ownership of large estates. The oriental state strove in vain to prevent these forces becoming independent, but it did manage to block their rise to political power.

– After the First World War imperialism transformed Syria into a dependency of the world economic system. The new "bourgeoisie" established itself, though not without conflicts, as the ruling class in the political system too, and guaranteed the integration of Syria into the world economic system. Resistance to this double rule was organized among the rural masses by politicized sections of the modern educated middle classes (Ba'th), and this forced the political system into self- dissolution.

– Syria was freed from this chaos by a "revolution from above". The military bureaucracy of the Ba'th liquidated the rule of the old bourgeoisie, renewed the controlling power of the state and endeavoured to integrate the peasant masses, who had been completely neglected, into a state-guided concept of development.

In this chapter I shall attempt a more detailed and nuanced interpretation of these controversies between the forces of the world economic system and the oriental state.

1. Classic imperialism and the oriental reform state

In the seventeenth and eighteenth centuries historic Syria (present- day Syria, Lebanon, Palestine and Jordan) experienced the socioeconomic decline of the once flourishing Near-Eastern civilization within the framework of the Ottoman Empire. This decline can be traced back to the collision of two quite different modes of production (sociopolitical organization of economic processes): one related to tribute, and the other the capitalist method. Internal crises and external intervention in the circulation of finance and goods of the oriental economy undermined the traditional socioeconomic controls of the Ottoman State, and led to a decentralization of political power and economic stagnation. While the state was no longer able to guarantee any internal security and the collecting of taxes was privatized in the hands of urban notables and tribal leaders, the economy declined to a permanent standstill. The exhausted capital was not invested, and the artisans, strictly regulated and controlled by the guilds, were unable to introduce innovations in the organization or technology of the production process. Under constant pressure from high-quality industrial goods from Europe the "industrial" production withdrew into niches; the export of raw materials increasingly surpassed that of finished products. Added to this was the external weakening of the empire, so that the once-lucrative transit trade to the European powers was lost. The Near East only survived the eighteenth century because during the Napoleonic Wars the trading powers in Europe and overseas were engaged in bitter competition between themselves. But at the beginning of the nineteenth century under the leadership of Great Britain Europe turned again to the

Near East. This marked the beginning of the collapse of the old structures.

With the help of direct governmental and military intervention European trading interests were systematically imposed in Anatolia, Syria and Egypt. Syria developed into a supplier of agricultural raw materials (grain, cotton, silk, wool and fruit) and a market for European industrial goods, above all textile products. This stimulated agriculture, since the cultivation of export products changed the local agrarian structures and concentrated the interest of the prosperous urban classes on the control of land. While the notables were able to accumulate ever greater portions of the agricultural profits by tax-farming, the peasants experienced ever- increasing exploitation. Their traditional ties with their patrons were broken.

Because of its manoeuvrability in the low price range Syria's textile industry was still able to adapt to market conditions, but other branches of craft industry folded under the pressure of European goods. By the middle of the nineteenth century Syria was so integrated into the world economic system that its was becoming directly affected by the world trade cycle directly. At the end of the 1850s a European recession brought a fall in the price of wheat, which reduced the credit available to the Syrian upper class and resulted to contraction in the textile industry and social unrest. On the other hand a recession in the 1870s put an end to imports of French textiles and led to a boom in the Syrian clothing industry. The main places to profit from this were the inner Syrian cities of Aleppo, Damascus, Homs and Hama.

The 1890s saw the opening up of parts of the Ottoman Empire by the introduction of transport technology financed by foreign capital (railways); Syria was also part of this process. As the infrastructure expanded, the areas under cultivation grew. Increased export opportunities (and greater security) allowed businessmen, notables and tribal leaders to invest in the cultivation and repopulating of long- neglected tracts of land. In the last two decades before the First World War Syrian agricultural exports (silk, grain, cotton, tobacco, wool, skins and citrus fruit) expanded considerably. By far the biggest part of the agricultural profits flowed into the hands of the rich urban upper classes. Nevertheless, the remainder that was left for the poor rural population was sufficient to stabilize the home textile industry at the lower end of the market. The traditional Syrian clothing industry kept its place in the oriental market until the First World War through a cautious manipulation of fashion and hard efforts in production field. But despite this achievement it was unable to break out of the traditional technology (mechanical looms) and organizational structure (family-based workshops with minimal division of labour). As a rule handicrafts and manufactures could only survive where they had no foreign competitors. Consequently the rich upper class concentrated its activities on agriculture and trade. The only exception to this was the silk industry in the Lebanon

mountains (the hinterland of Beirut). There the interests of the French silk industry had brought about the foundation of a capitalist silk production as early as the 1850s. Its growth influenced the formation of a special socioeconomic system, which in the long run divided the coastal region politically from the Syrian hinterland. But even in Lebanon industrialization was ultimately so subordinate to trading interests that it was unable to achieve a self-supporting economic development.

The integration of Syria into the capitalist world economy led to an extremely unequal exchange of goods. True, the country exported raw materials in increasing quantities, but ranged against it were even bigger - and above all cheaper – imports: European textiles, intermediate products (cotton yarn, metal, wood), tropical agricultural products (e.g. sugar) and luxury consumer goods. The balance of payments was balanced, however, by the proceeds of exports with oriental neighbours, transit profits, and above all by credits, endowment investments by religious and political movements (missions, Zionism), and money sent by guest workers overseas.

The economic penetration of Syria also changed the social structures of the country. New social groups arose, the power relationships between the social classes shifted, social unrest and class struggles began. On the Lebanese coast a massive social restructuring between the Druzes and the Maronites took place. In Syria too there were social revolts, usually characterized as conflicts between religious groups. Central to our consideration, however, is the formation of a new social upper class, which owed its existence to the world economic system. In an Ottoman Empire shaken by crises the system of tax-farming (*iltizam*) was the business that brought the biggest income, although it was the least productive. Groups of notables and tribal leaders in the provinces of the empire had been able to use this income to make themselves independent. The intrusion of the interests of foreign capital gave dynamism to these classes. Trade and commercial ownership of large estates opened up undreamed-of opportunities for enrichment, but also changed the traditional social power relationships. Cooperation with the Europeans gave privileges to the businessmen among the minorities (Christians, Jews, Armenians, Greeks etc.), who had previously been discriminated against as non-Muslims. The members of these minority groups were culturally closer to the Europeans, to whom they therefore appeared to be more trustworthy, and since they had multicultural expertise, they established themselves as the conveyors and representatives of European capital in the coordinating points of imperialist expansion. The Muslim businessmen were restricted to internal trade within the Ottoman Empire and external trade with Asia. Because of the privileges received by the minorities in the form of European protection and access to European credit, even in times of crisis, they drew upon themselves the hatred of the broad classes of the Muslim population. This erupted in the unrest in

Damascus in 1860. But the Muslim merchant class was also able to consolidate its position in the slipstream of imperialism. They used their control of agriculture (land, means of production, credit) to commercialize agricultural production and cream off excessive profits from this area (by leasing, taxation, protection measures, profiteering). The peasant producers were left with barely enough to live on. Thus in the nineteenth century a "ruling class" (minorities, trading and finance capital, commercial ownership of large estates) in cooperation with the foreign capital was established within the Ottoman Empire. This class, "extracted" from oriental society by the trading centres and made the instrument of outside forces, represented for the first time in oriental history the socioeconomic independence of a section of society from the state.

In the following decades this "modern" upper class in Ottoman society pressed for political power. But until the First World War they were opposing an oriental state in the process of reforming itself, which although it was not able to set up anything to equal the European interests, was still capable of blocking the ruling class politically. The traditional oriental state had not tolerated any independent social dynamism and had always prevented the formation of such a dynamism as long as it had power to do so. This was true also of the reform state in the nineteenth century.

The first state resistance to imperialism came not from the Ottoman state but from Egypt. Mohammed Ali, a former representative of the Ottoman bureaucracy, attempted to built Egypt up as the industrial centre of the Orient (1805-1848). This experiment in development was strikingly similar to the Japanese example (the Meiji Restoration). Before Great Britain put a stop by force to the complex economic development he instigated, Syria took part in this development as part of the Egyptian state unit. Mohammed Ali's son, Ibrahim Pasha, sought to build up an effective state administration in Syria as well, and endeavoured to turn the whole of the Syrian silk trade and some other export sectors into state monopolies. The profits expected from these were to finance industrialization, though this was to be predominantly in Egypt, not in Syria. This monopoly system went against the British principle of free trade and was vehemently opposed by the Europeans. It also threatened the interests of the Syrian merchant class and drove it into coalition with Great Britain and the Ottoman Empire. By means of political and military interventions by Great Britain, the European powers first thwarted the economic policy of Ibrahim in Syria and eventually brought the downfall of Egypt too. In the history of Syria this period of strong state control is regarded as the beginning of modernization. Syria was effectively managed, and the creation of security and order encouraged economic growth. But this short flowering symbolizes something more: the oriental reformist state, which intervened actively in the economy to encourage productive sectors (manufacturing crafts) and was attacked by both imperialism and the indigenous trading bourgeoisie.

50 Portrait of Ibrahim Pasha in a contemporary engraving.

When the Ottoman administration came back again in 1840, Syria sank once more into the chaos of intercommunal strife, and it was to be more than two decades before the reforms of the Ottoman state had progressed far enough for it too to begin to affect the social conditions in Syria. The Ottoman reform state did not have the economic ambitions of Egypt. Caught in the vice of European financial and economic interests, it attempted only to renovate its political and administrative system. For this it needed higher revenue from taxation and it therefore sought to make its administration of Syria more effective. This policy had contradictory results:

– First, the strengthening of the Syrian administration (military control, administrative reform, colonization) increased security and order, and thus fostered the growth of the economy to the advantage of the ruling class and of foreign capital. The Ottoman state achieved higher revenue, but this was far from being sufficient to make the Ottoman administration independent of the tax farmers of the ruling class. The state therefore had (unwillingly) to share its power with the notables and the tribal leaders in provincial councils.

– Secondly, the state continued to block the establishing of a private ownership of land. True, the Syrian big land-owners were able to make claims over much wider areas than was the case in Anatolia or in the Iraqi provinces, but the resistance from the patrimonial state bureaucracy to the ruling class, who were influenced by external forces, kept open the consolidation of large-scale private landownership.

This state of suspense between state and ruling class, between pre-capitalist structure and dependent capitalism, was intensified still further under the Young Turks by the ideological conflict between Turanism and Arab nationalism. For the Syrian development this stalemate was unsatisfactory. The surplus production of the Syrian economy was creamed off, but it was not invested in capitalism, nor was it used by the state for productive purposes in Syria. One portion went as profit to foreign firms, while another helped the Ottoman state to survive, and yet another part was consumed by the indigenous bourgeoisie (in luxury goods and house building).

2. Colonial rule and bourgeois state

The Ottoman Empire's miscalculation in allying itself with Germany in the First World War, gave the Western trading centres the opportunity to get rid of the last remnants of this hostile state power in the Near East. The dividing up of the empire among the victorious powers was to lead to an uninterrupted capitalization of the Arab societies. Under the League of Nations Mandate (San Remo 1920) Great Britain appropriated Iraq and Palestine, the most important regions economically (because of oil) and strategically (because of the Suez Canal), while France received agricultural Syria. Under direct French rule a systematic privatization of Syrian agricultural land began (state land and tribal land, in many cases common land also). By the end of the Mandate period 75 per cent of land used of agricultural purposes was in the hands of the big landowners. The commercialization of farming (cotton) led to a reduction in the cultivation of cereals and an increasing dependence on imported foodstuffs. The extreme impoverishment of the peasants, who as tenants were now allowed to keep barely 30 per cent of their harvests, ruined the Syrian textile industry, since it lost its most important class of customers. In Aleppo alone the number of textile workers declined from 68,000 in 1914 to 25,000 in 1926. The silk industry fell victim to the world economic crisis. French industrial goods dominated the Syrian market at all levels. All the industries of the infra-structure (railways, water, electricity, and the rest) were in the hands of foreign businesses. French financial institutions controlled the currency, insurance and credit market of the country.

This economic penetration was matched by a social structure which encompassed both those who reaped benefits from the socioeconomic structure and those who were marginalized. The favoured groups were the indigenous trading bourgeoisie and the commercial big land-owners; Syrian financiers were also involved in the lucrative credit business. Craft and industry on the other hand had no opportunities for development. It was only during the Second World War, when foreign trade collapsed, that industrial production of goods in various fields could develop in Syria for the first time. However, after the war its protagonists were soon forced back into their niches by American industrial goods. The industrial workforce was correspondingly very small and constantly threatened by unemployment. Around 70 per cent of the population worked in agriculture. The total neglect of this sector again formed a structural barrier to any industrial development, since there was no internal market for bulk goods and the well-to-do classes in society bought high-quality goods from industrialized countries. This social framework already indicated social conflicts to come, but for now these were outweighed by the problem of the colonial administration.

In Iraq Great Britain soon managed to impose indirect control with the help of the ruling class, but France was not prepared to use such a strategy. The bourgeoisie in Syria was much more developed and had imposed more severe limits on the scale of imperialist exploitation. France attempted to control Syria by means of a French administrative apparatus (bureaucracy, law courts, police, armed forces), regional fragmentation (separation of Lebanon, division of Syria into five units) and communal structuring (representation of ethnic and religious groups). The exclusion once again of the economically privileged class from political power led to a war, lasting for decades, between the colonial power and the ruling class. This conflict of attrition (Colonial War 1925-1927, political and diplomatic conflict between parliament and the administration) resulted in Syria's independence in 1946, but it caused lasting damage to the political capacities of the bourgeoisie. The bourgeois regime in the 1950s was incapable of reorganizing its own socioeconomic base, nor did it have the political mechanisms to hold back the incipient class struggle.

The parliamentary system of the bourgeois regime was created by veterans of the independence movement (el-Jabiri, el-Quwatli and others). But the political parties established by these representatives of the ruling class were merely clubs for dignitaries, with no ideology, programme or organization. Regionally aligned (the National Party with its centre at Damascus, the Popular Party at Aleppo and Homs), the politician-notables mobilized their electorates on the basis of client structures: the local bosses of the town districts (abadayat) told their people whom to vote for. As well as the 76 representatives of these parties, 31 independent representatives of the ruling class also took

51 Camel corps of the colonial army.

52 Sultan Atrash.

their seats in parliament. Ranged against them were half a dozen deputies split into tiny insignificant parties (including the Ba'th). Despite its absolute dominance the ruling class remained politically incapable of action. Concerned with their local problems and inter-regional conflicts, they had no national political or economic concept. Most marked was their dispute over external cooperation with Iraq or with Egypt. As representatives of ancient trading interests the citizens of Aleppo saw their connections with Mosul and Baghdad cut off, while Damascus was deprived of its links with Palestine, the Hejas and Egypt. The opposing commercial and political interests of the two poles of Syrian trade were reflected in countless parliamentary controversies over foreign policy and multiple intrigues.

The four military interventions in politics which took place after 1949 (ez-Zein 1949, esh-Shishakli 1949, 1951 and 1952) were intended to counter this backward-looking status quo in socioeconomic relations. Their aim was to eliminate the party system and parliament. The authoritarian rule of the military took as its model Atatürkism in Turkey, but it rested on a completely different socioeconomic basis. In Syria the "dictatorship" of al-Shishakli reflected an attempt to modernize bourgeois rule with the help of the state. It strove for a more effective state organization on a national basis for the first time (reform of bureaucracy, support for education, homogenization of society, separation of the administration and the particular interest groups in society). The influence of foreign capital was restricted (nationalization of some infrastructure industries, criticism of the conditions attached to foreign aid programmes, nationalization of credit, and the development of a central bank), and state assistance was given to the expanding indigenous entrepreneurs. It was only towards France that the regime had a positive attitude, since France's weakened economy offered favourable conditions. This policy was in the interest of the national industry (cotton processing, cement, sugar refining, soap, glass and paraffin) which was now emerging from its niches, and the modern agrarian capitalists ("merchant tractorists"), who used mechanization of production to expand especially the cultivation of cotton on an enormous scale. Both groups represented a new and innovative party in the Syrian bourgeoisie. This alliance between the state and national bourgeoisie was also matched by cooperation with the growing radical forces (Arab Socialist Party, Ba'th), whose attacks on the "parasitic and feudal" big landowners were encouraged, since they could only strengthen the agrarian capitalist party. Moreover the industrial bourgeoisie had to take an interest in the raising of peasant living standards for the sake of the internal market. However, such a coalition between antagonistic classes could only be temporary. It was more useful to the radicals and strengthened their position among the Syrian political parties.

The progressive bourgeois-bureaucratic regime of esh-Shishakli was toppled in 1954 by a broad coalition. Its members were the traditional parties of the bourgeoisie (Popular and National Parties), the minority elites who were averse to homogenization, the radical parties, for which a strong bourgeois state was too dangerous (Ba'th, Communist Party), and pro-British Iraq. Above all Great Britain feared that Syria's nationalist bourgeois tendencies might spread to Iraq, which would have affected the West's oil interests. In esh-Shishakli Syria lost a national leader who had rejected all external demands, and a representative of national capitalism who had striven to reorganize and modernize the bourgeoisie.

The resurrected party rule with its parliamentary system was paralysed from the very outset. The new parliamentary elections (1954) brought a political stalemate between the ruling class and the new radical forces. The bourgeois had superiority in numbers, but they remained split, disorganized, with no developed programme and also received few votes. The radical forces (Ba'th and Communist Party) were able to form a breakaway liberal progressive block (el-Azm) out of the Independents, and so set against the bourgeoisie a potential force which was far superior in its ideology and propaganda. The first great breakthroughs into the traditional classes of electors took place around Hama, in the Jebel ed- Druz and at Damascus.

The mechanization of agriculture, slow industrialization and educational progress in independent Syria had resulted in great social changes in the 1950s. In the countryside

53 Colonel Adib al-Shishakli.

54 Akram al-Haurani.

55 President Shukri al-Quwatli.

"proletarianization" released the peasants from their traditional loyalties and self-identification. Many peasants found new jobs outside agriculture. In the towns the administration and business were not longer able to absorb the middle classes, who now had modern education. When they found their opportunities for development blocked in this way they became increasingly radical, as did the disorganized peasants as they came into contact with modern education and radical ideas. It was against this background that the amalgamation took place between the Ba'th (Aflaq and Bitar), then a party of urban intellectuals, and the social-revolutionary peasant movement of el-Hourani (Arab Socialist Party). This united movement strove for a reorganization of the political system at the expense of imperialism and the ruling class. Within the framework of a Pan-Arab structure, it was intended that a strong secular state should emerge based on a high level of social involvement, which would actively intervene in the economy (land reform, nationalization of banks and major industries, industrial laws) and be committed to a balanced social system (welfare state).

Although this programme was the product of urban, westernized intellectuals, it first made progress among the rural middle classes, especially among the minorities (social revolutionary, non- denominational). Only in the wake of the anti-Western eruptions following the Baghdad Pact and Suez Crisis did it gain a foothold in the towns. For the first time in the history of Syria a broad alliance of social forces (intellectuals, officers, peasants) prevailed over the old conflict between town and countryside and the regional splits along community lines.

Released by the radical middle-class forces, the class struggle (socioeconomic problems) increasingly overlaid the internal conflicts within the bourgeoisie (coalition with Iraq or Egypt, national or Pan- Arab, modernization of the capitalist base). An additional element in these internal Syrian conflicts was the Arab confrontation between social- revolutionary innovation (Egypt under Nasser) and the conservative neo- colonial powers (Iraq under Nuri es-Seid). Behind them also stood the superpowers. The political system of Syria was only held together on the surface by necessity through a Grand Coalition of all (antagonistic) powers, in the cabinet of Sabri el-Asali. At its heart it was split into groups who were linked as clients to various Arab and world political powers. All political parties and movements accepted material support from external sources, and the "struggle for Syria" thus became internationalized. The main factor which drove the Syrian state into the anti-imperialist movement was the many naive attempts at intervention by the United States to ward off a supposed Communist seizure of power. In this climate the Ba'th party, which was still politically weak but was better organized than the rest, was able to break the political stalemate. The leadership of the Ba'th did not, however, seek a revolution from below. Rather it saw in an alliance with Nasser's revolutionary Egypt the opportunity to outplay the still over-powerful ruling class of Syria in a supra-national context, while on the other hand controlling the revolution by bureaucratic means. To this end the Ba'th leadership systematically (by their own diplomatic manoeuvres and by mobilizing the masses) drove the Syrian state into union with Egypt. In so doing they had various aims: they themselves would assume the role of an ideological and programmatic elite, while the Arab world would experience a political renaissance, and Syria a social revolution. The conservative forces hoped instead for protection against radical changes. In reality the United Arab Republic (1958-1961) was entirely dominated by Egyptian interests in foreign and economic policy, and Egyptian bureaucratic organization.

3. The Revolution and the modern bureaucratic state

Although the Syrian bourgeoisie was a product of a dependent capitalist development and owed its socioeconomic strength to imperialism, it was only after a prolonged struggle against the French colonial power that is was able to gain political power. The bourgeois state as it emerged after the Second World War reflected for the first time in Syrian history the legitimate rule of a social class. The institutions of the political system consistently represented the interests of the ruling bourgeoisie, but they had not grown to suit the socioeconomic and political change in the fifties. The reorganization of capitalist base of the state was unsuccessful. A revolution was looming among the peasant masses. In this situation the Ba'th leadership again entrusted Syria to the oriental state. Ironically it was once again Egypt – just as it had been under Mohammed Ali – that was striving for a bureaucratically regulated renewal of the Arab world in a period of imperialist restraint in the Near East, and which again took Syria under its "protection" as part of this scheme. This experiment quickly came to grief because of the Egypt's "occupation policy" (Secession Coup 1961), but the bourgeois state of Syria was no longer capable of regeneration. A second coup, in March 1963, brought a final end to the regime of the bourgeoisie. A "revolution from above" headed by a military bureaucracy, broke the urban bourgeoisie's monopoly of power in favour of the peasants. How could this have come about?

The voluntary abdication of the Ba'th leadership had left the whole party in disarray and thus made the revolutionary movement incapable of action. The dynamics of change therefore shifted to bureaucratic circles. An alliance of young officers with a nucleus of former Ba'th functionaries took the initiative. The great majority of the others came from the rural population and the minorities, and their approach to the social problems was more radical than that of the original Ba'th intelligentsia – but it was also more realistic and straightforward. Confronted with bourgeois reaction, a split revolutionary movement and a variety of political and ideological rivals, the new bureaucratic leadership group concentrated on consolidating its power and establishing a revolutionary social federation.

The officer corps, which until then had reflected all political forces, was systematically purged and filled with young Ba'th supporters. The rebuilding of the party strengthened the rural element and the minorities at the expense of the urban membership structure. The expansion of the Ba'th into a party of the masses outflanked the urban party intelligentsia and led to a massive struggle for power. After a lengthy stalemate the new regime under Salah Jedid (1966-1970) backed a radicalization of Ba'th ideology. Henceforth it was to concentrate on the Arab revolution in one country, Syria, which was to claim leadership and so rival the Egyptian model of development. There was to be a one-party system and a transformation of society (land reform and nationalization of the major businesses). At the centre of this approach stood the peasants. With their help the power of the big landowners was broken. A radical land reform did away with the latifundia, halted the proletarianization of the peasants and levelled out the agricultural structure with a mixture of small and medium-sized landownership. The state assumed a large number of the tasks with which "feudal" big landowners had exercised control. It was concerned with the infrastructure, the means of production, credits, marketing and the organization of production (cooperatives). But it stopped agricultural reform in the interests of the medium-sized landownership and traditional outlook of the peasants as a whole before the dynamics of social experiments (purging of leftist party cadres). In this way it restricted capitalist development in the countryside, but it did not destroy either the forces behind this development, or its methods. Above all it did not create any autonomous cooperative sector, which could have become the basis for the countryside taking on a dynamic of its own.

In its economic policy the Ba'th regime strove for a complex development which a bourgeois state was incapable of, because of its capitalist market rationalism. In contrast to the trend until then, the agricultural sector was orientated towards the internal market (production of raw materials for indigenous industries, foodstuffs), while the industrialization was carried out by the state. The two sectors were to be integrated. At the same time the state supported its social base though the expansion of service sectors and the state apparatus in favour of the rural middle classes, again at the expense of economic efficiency. It thus undermined important elements of a progressive dynamic of development. This radical programme, however, was matched not only by unusually high social mobility, but also by social conflicts, which were equally intense and discriminated above all against the urban classes. In foreign policy Syria's concentration on itself and on the transformation of society combined to lead to exaggerated rhetoric

and a dangerous overestimation of the countries capabilities. In this way Syria was not only brought to a deep socioeconomic crisis, but at the same time it recklessly exposed itself to the superior military machine of Israel in the June War of 1967. This resulted in intense conflicts within the new state class. In 1970 the army intervened to take control of the crisis, and it was from this military intervention that the present regime of Hafiz el-Asad emerged.

On a broad social base, once again integrating the urban sections of the population into the development process, the political leadership brought about a pragmatic adjustment to the existing economic structures, which received new impulses in the context of increasing Arab petrodollars. The building of a strongly patrimonial state in the 1970s marked Syria's return to those traditions of the Near East, which gave the state the role of controlling all social and economic processes, and protecting the peasants from aggressive economic private interests. At the same time, however, the privileged integration of the Near East into the world energy system through OPEC marked the beginning of a new phase of imperialist penetration. And the contradiction between on the one hand aggressive capitalist economic powers and their agents in society, and on the other state's resistance and steering in the opposite direction broke out again at new levels and in new forms.

The Syrian Mohafazats 1967.

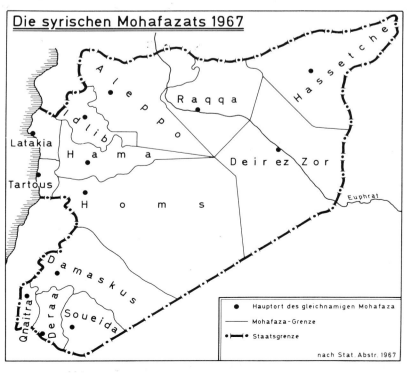

The Town

1. Origins and Geography

Heinz Gaube

Most of the geographers of classical antiquity treat Syria as a unit, similar to the Great Syria (Bilad esh-Sham) of the later period. However, the classical geographers always look inwards from the coast, and so see Syria as a border region of the Mediterranean world. Their information becomes thinner as they move from the coast towards the interior, and only those places in Inner Syria that can be connected with specific historical events, mythical characters or great figures in history are mentioned. Beyond Inner Syria lay the frontier with the Arabs and the frontier with the Persians marked by the Euphrates. In these works, however, there is no concept of "Syria" as such, a fact that becomes particularly clear in the long treatment of the region by Strabo (died c. 25 BC).

Not until about a thousand years later did the geographical study of the Orient, which until then had been mainly anecdotal and from the point of view of scientific accuracy was often plain wrong, become a scholarly discipline freed from classical models and able to describe the Orient from inside with a sense of empathy and abstraction.

A late tenth-century Arab geographer, al-Muqaddasi, who was born in Jerusalem, laid out on a map the towns of Syria – or rather, the part of the province of esh-Sham, which today is Syria – on three lines (= roads) running north-south. The eastern connection runs from the Euphrates, from the town of Balis (Meskene) through Khanasir (south-east of Aleppo), Palmyra, Selemiye (east of Hama) to Deraa and thence on to the Gulf of Aqaba. This is a route which roughly follows old Roman roads, and so probably never existed, also Palmyra and Selemiye have been interchanged probably by a copyist. The geographer's purpose in drawing this line was rather to express an idea: these are the places which lie at the edge of cultivatable land; to the east of them the world of the nomads begins.

On the middle line, between Aleppo in the north and Damascus in the south, lie Qinnesrin, Kafr Tab, Sheizar, Hama, Homs, Baalbek; while on the coast Lataqiye and Tartus are shown. Eight other cities then follow along the coast as far as Gaza.

This arrangement of big and fairly big settlements in three zones running north-south corresponds to the pattern of settlement in Syria that is determined by nature. Only on the coastal strip and in Central Syria (as seen from west to east) is dense settlement possible. East of these only scattered settlements are found. These have strong links with the world of the nomads and fluctuate between prosperity and decline to a far greater extent than do the settlements in the coastal region or in Central Syria. They become the victims when the central state becomes weak, but are the gainers if a strong state is able to keep the nomads away from regions which peasants can use.

Just as the relations between the Inner Syrian towns and those on the border of the Badiya (Syrian desert steppe) fluctuated, so also did the relations between the Inner Syrian towns and those on the coast. For many centuries Tripoli had been an important port. There was no great difficulty in gaining access to it through the break between Lebanon and Antilebanon and the mountains of Lataqiye. For centuries the route through this break, via Homs, had been the most convenient connection between inner Syria and the coast for the towns between Aleppo in the north and Damascus in the south. As increasing modernization brought the ability and willingness to build roads suitable for wheeled vehicles, this old link between the towns of inner Syria and the Mediterranean was superseded by others: from Aleppo to Iskenderun (Alexandretta) and from Damascus to Beirut. From the eighteenth century onwards these roads were continually increasing in importance. For long stretches the route from Aleppo followed an old Roman road, and there are still many kilometres of large stone blocks which remain from the road built by the Romans. However, the road from Damascus to Beirut, which crosses the transverse valley of Antilebanon and Lebanon, has no such impressive reminders of an ancient route.

Between the towns on the coast, whose ups and downs were determined by the general situation in the Mediterranean, and the settlements on the eastern edge of Syria, whose culture was subject to constant fluctuations, lie the cities of Central or Inner Syria, Aleppo and Damascus, Homs and Hama, four cities which first and foremost made up, and still make up, Syria's urban culture. All of them have been continuously inhabited for about five thousand years, a remarkable fact even among the towns of the Orient.

Where else can towns be found with such a long continuous history? Not in Europe, nor to the east or west of Syria. Babylon was once more splendid than these towns, but it is long since dead. The same is true of Susa, Persepolis and Assur – name after name might be listed. On the Syrian coast in the second millennium BC the city of Ugarit flourished. It was there that alphabetic script was invented. It is now Ras Shamra, the 'Fennel Hill', which was excavated by French archaeologists almost half a century ago, and now forgotten among eucalyptus and fruit trees. Lataqiye to the south of it was already important in pre-Roman antiquity, but in the middle ages the ruined remains of its buildings served as a quarry for distant cities that were newly founded – and subsequently died, towns such as Samarra in Iraq. Only in the modern period has Lataqiye flourished again.

Seen in anthropomorphic form, the region around the line between Aleppo and Damascus is the trunk of Syria, with one arm embracing the coast, and the other the desert steppe, the Badiya. Inner Syria owes its continuity to the way it links together the Mediterranean and the world of the nomads – the world the Arabs call "Badiya", where life is impossible if one stays continually in one place and nomadism is a necessity.

But the fact that Inner Syrian towns have been able to exist for millennia is not only due to their favourable situation between two worlds, the Mediterranean and the Badiya. The wet and fertile coastal strip is shielded on its eastern side by mountains, where agriculture is also practised, and the Badiya is the source not only of the threat from the nomads, but also of the products of the nomads: camels providing meat, wool and transport, and goats and sheep providing meat and wool. Without the Inner Syrian cities as mediators and consumers these products could not have been marketed profitably.

Whenever the route to the West via the Mediterranean was open, the wool produced by nomads, as well as raw silk from the western mountains were processed in the cities, packaged for the market and exported across the Mediterranean. Fluctuating proportions of these raw materials were processed in the towns to make end products for changing markets. Today each of these four cities – Aleppo, Hama, Homs and Damascus – still has its own specialities in the processing and working of wool and cotton (a raw material which has been produced in the country only in recent times). The cities are favoured in other respects too. They are surrounded by olive groves, vineyards, fruit plantations and vegetable gardens, around which are regions where the excellent Syrian hard wheat and other cereals are grown.

Syria is a land of cities – but it is not the land where the city originated. There are many models for the origins of the city and the state, which are very closely related phenomena. As far as we can tell from our present knowledge, city and state first appeared in southern Iraq, in Babylonia. Recent theories, for which there is good archaeological evidence, have reverted to a "post-diluvian" idea – though it is not formulated in these scriptural terms. Southern Iraq, which had been flooded with fertile sediment, became accessible for settlement because of a lowering of the sea-level and a reduction of precipitation in regions that fed the Persian Gulf. Since the ground water level was still high and the soil was still moist, the "early high cultures" were able to emerge here around 3000 BC.

It was probably not quite as simple as that, of course. It is certain, however, that writing was invented in Babylonia – and that shortly afterwards writing emerged in Syria and was used for local needs. The script was thus not simply adopted in Syria but changed so that it could be used to write the local language.

Archaeologists found this at Ebla, south of Aleppo. Towards the end of the third millennium BC a city state was in existence there and was flourishing culturally, structurally and economically. Besides texts connected with business there were also literary texts, which show that the creative muse was already to be found there. This then was a very sophisticated society in which people were already concerned with things beyond simply earning their bread.

Seen through our somewhat foreshortening historical perspective, in which in the early period the passage of a few centuries counts for little, the phenomenon of the town went through Syria like lightning. Excavations have been possible at Ebla, which today lies deserted between fields, and were also carried out at Hama some decades ago. In my opinion it is only by chance that no texts similar to those found at Ebla have been found there. At Homs, whose ancient centre has been a military zone for decades, no excavations have yet been possible. Damascus and Aleppo have always been so continually and so densely settled that *tells* with no settlements could not arise there. (*Tells* are the thousands of artificial hills found in Iran, Iraq, Turkey and Syria and the adjoining regions, which are evidence of settlements usually going back thousands of years, though at certain times they were abandoned or destroyed.)

Nevertheless, even in Damascus and Aleppo there are indications of *tells*, which are situated in the middle of the urban area and have therefore not been excavated (though there is also a surprising lack of interest in them on the part of archaeologists). Thus the history of the origin of the town is to be seen in the contrast between Iraq and Syria. There are many indications that this decisive step in the history of mankind was made in Iraq. But how far steps made in the neighbouring regions, Iran and Syria, were influential in this, we do not yet know. Our confusion over the question is the same as that of the Old Testament: one section of the Syrian population, the Jews, created for themselves a picture of history, which included Iraq (Abraham) and Egypt (Moses). This is a legitimate view and does not lack profundity.

Syria is the land of ancient cities which have survived and still survive today. Their neighbours, the Mesopotamian states and Egypt (which was so very different), had problems with them from the third millennium BC onward. Even then the Syrian individualists, linked together by family ties and shared ideas, were free and yet not free – but they had an openness to external influence, and not just intellectually. They were a commercial people, as is shown by the Phoenicians (i.e. coastal Syrians) who influenced the whole Mediterranean area from the second millennium BC. Hannibal, the Carthaginian who launched an attack on Rome, was a "great- grandchild" of Syria, descended from coastal Syrians.

2. The Form of Cities

Historians believe that around 6000 BC individual settlements developed out of loose settlements. In the course of time centres were formed among these individual settlements. There may have been various reasons for this: a convenient location on roads or water, for instance, or some religious significance. From among these centres in the period up to c. 3000 BC central centres (i.e. cities) took shape.

We are still very far from being able to trace this development step by step. However, it is reasonable to apply the "centre theory", which was first developed in a geographical dissertation in 1932 and is today accepted by a variety of different academic disciplines, to the historical development of the early systems of settlement. A city is after all a centre, and if centres are not just small subcentres or markets, but also fully developed cities, then they differ considerably from their surroundings in socioeconomic terms.

The city is the place of non-agricultural production, commercial centre, centre for services and seat of the administrative power. It could not be all of these if it did not have an agricultural hinterland. This produces what the city does not produce: food, and it buys what the town produces. It provides the urban industries with raw materials, and urban trade with goods. It makes use of the services provided by the town, whether they be those of the priest, the hairdresser, the mountebank, the notary or the scholar, and through the taxes it pays it finances the administration, which is centred in the city. Furthermore it provides part of the urban upper class, the landowners who live in the city, with capital which they can use to invest, produce and speculate in the town.

The surrounding countryside and the city form an indissoluble unit; the one cannot function without the other. If the surrounding land is the body, then the city is the brain. Here all the nerves come together, here things are planned and controlled, and from here come the investments and innovations, and into the city flow the profits.

If the surrounding land is the producer of animal and vegetable foodstuffs and raw materials, the city is the place where all those engaged in non-agricultural production, in trade and in a variety of services, do their work. In the city various sorts of businesses and dwellings have to be joined together in an organized whole, combining the greatest efficiency with the least expense.

In the Islamic-Oriental city this has been largely achieved, and this means that – regardless of the various historical roots (whether Hellenistic-Roman or even earlier in the Islamic West, or Ancient Mesopotamian-Iranian in the East) – there is a high degree of uniformity as regards its organization and appearance. We can therefore speak in general terms of an Islamic-Oriental city. Its essential elements, i.e. the functions mentioned expressed in concrete form, can best be seen in a schematic model.

The city wall, the external landmark of almost every Islamic-Oriental town, usually has an irregular plan reflecting the growth and shrinkage of the town. The number of gates varies. Enclosed in the wall, but usually having a direct link with the outside, is the citadel, the seat of government power. Several of the gates provide entry for overland roads into the city. On the busiest of these there develop suburbs, in which the secondary economic centres are formed, usually near the gates.

Within the city walls the overland roads form the main axes of communication. The Great Mosque is located as a rule on one of these main axes. In its vicinity there are often administrative buildings and schools (*medrese*). The never-ending stream of passers-by on the main axes of the inner town attracts trade and industry, and so these main axes are lined with shops and workshops, forming the city's *suq* or bazaar. To shield customers and the shopkeepers/craftsmen from sun and rain, the parts of the *suq* on the main axes are provided with roofs made of wood or stone – or are spanned by tarpaulins. The greatest density of passers-by is at the centre of the *suq*, usually near the Great Mosque. Here the most expensive goods, fabrics, jewellery and suchlike are sold. Shops with less expensive goods are situated on the periphery of the *suq*. Near the gates there are generally shops and workshops whose stock is geared to the requirements of a rural clientele.

The *suq* or bazaar (one word is Arabic, the other Persian) is the most characteristic feature of the Islamic-Oriental city. Nothing comparable is found in pre-Islamic times – or in other civilizations. It is the economic control-centre for the city and its hinterland. Wholesale and retail trade, crafts and manufactures, credit and brokerage, are brought together here into an organic whole within a single architectural framework. Behind the shops and workshops are the *khans* or caravanserais, the headquarters of wholesale and export trade, trade courts, warehouses and offices.

In Syria, as in a number of other Islamic countries, there are generally no residential houses in the *suq*. Residential and business areas are strictly divided. However, residential quarters are to be found spread throughout the town, inside and outside the walls. In the past these quarters were shut off from each other by gates. Larger residential quarters had public facilities as a necessary complement to the houses: mosque, bath (*hammam*), bakery, public fountain, school and a small market (local *suq*) for everyday items which it would be too extravagant to buy in the central *suq*.

Access to the residential houses was from the inner-town main axes via secondary axes, alleys and cul-de-sacs. The cul-de-sac formed the town's smallest unit of organization above the house. As a rule from the cul-de-sac only a few houses are built. Formerly the cul-de-sacs could be shut off by gates from the rest of the quarter.

56 The Azem Madrasa, Damascus.

57 Damascus *c.* 1900, schematic plan: 1. City Wall, 2. Great Mosque, 3. Citadel, 4. *Suq* / Bazaar.

3. Concrete Examples: Damascus and Aleppo

Let us now turn to real examples the two biggest cities of Syria, Damascus and Aleppo, of what has so far been examined in historical and theoretical terms. Here we shall deal with the cities in broad outline; the details will be filled in by the following chapters.

Illustrations 57 and 59 show schematic plans of the two cities in the nineteenth century. Both the old town centres are now of course surrounded by extensive areas of new building, which do not interest us here. At Damascus the town wall with seven gates surrounds an irregular area roughly rectangular in shape. For nearly the whole of its course it follows the line of a town wall which already surrounded Damascus in Roman times, and may rest on even older foundations. Within the wall are the Great Mosque and the Citadel and the *suq*/bazaar which stretches between the two. Other important public buildings – schools, hospitals and holy tombs – are situated in the north-western sector of the walled town, which has a close-meshed grid pattern that contrasts with the suburbs to the north and south, and is characterized by a layout of alleys and streets based on lines running north-south and east-west. This layout has its origin in Hellenistic-Roman town-planning laid over an older arrangement of space, which was probably centred on the south-west part of the walled town. It is not known whether the principal sanctuary of the pre- Hellenistic town, probably a temple to the Aramaic god Haddad, already occupied the site of the Great Mosque, but this is likely, since the Roman temple and the Byzantine cathedral stood on the same site.

58 View over the old town of Damascus from Jebel Qasiun.

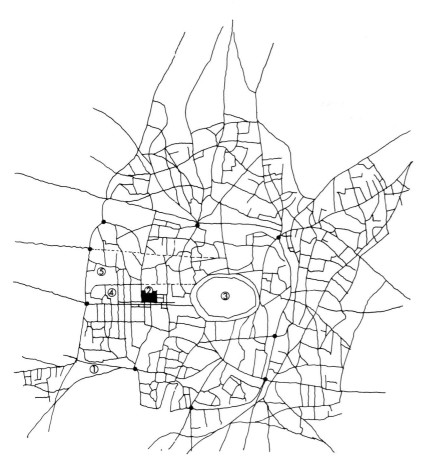

59 Aleppo *c.* 1900, schematic plan: 1. City Wall, 2. Great Mosque, 3. Citadel, 4. *Suq* / Bazaar.

The system of alleys and streets oriented to the points of the compass which is found in the walled old town is also the basis for the plan of the old-town quarter *extra muros* to the north. They are the oldest parts of the city outside the walls and merge into the town *intra muros* to form a single piece. These parts of the old town of Damascus probably already had their structure in the tenth century AD. There is an important old mosque here. A local *suq* runs along the main axis running east-west and a southern branch links this suburb with the walled town.

The quarters in the south-east are different. They extend along the road which links the cereal-growing Hauran region in southern Syria with the city, and their layout is determined by the course of this ancient route.

The features we have described above in theoretical and schematic terms are found in Damascus in a characteristic form reflecting its particular situation and history. The same is true of the shape of Aleppo, which is not as extended as Damascus. The town wall in its present form dates from the fifteenth and sixteenth century AD. At that time it was extended eastwards, thus depriving the citadel of its "classical" peripheral position, which it had retained until then, and bringing it within the walled town.

Here too we see traces of regular Hellenistic planning in the western part of the walled town. The former colonnaded street, now the main axis of the *suq*, links the western gate with the citadel. North of this main axis is the Great Mosque, which stands on – or near – the site of the former Byzantine cathedral. Around the Great Mosque is the centre of the *suq*.

60 The Citadel of Aleppo.

The regular pattern of streets and alleys of the Hellenistic town skirted a hill in the northern part, which was probably the centre of pre- Hellenistic Aleppo. How far the parts of the old town to the east of the citadel, both *intra* and *extra muros*, are pre- or post-Hellenistic, cannot yet be determined. But they were certainly inhabited in the pre-Islamic period, while the northern suburbs did not attain their present structure until the fifteenth century.

All suburbs and the non-Hellenistic inner-city areas are characterized by a radial system of main axes spreading outwards from the centre around the citadel. These axes extend beyond the walls into the surrounding countryside. In the western part of the town, too, a radial arrangement of the main axes overlays the Hellenistic planning scheme and forms a basis principle of organization linking the centre through nine gates with the suburbs, the surrounding country and the long-distance trade routes.

Urban Life
Building and Dwelling: the example of Aleppo

Annette Gangler

1. Urban Forms of Buildings

The basic form of the peasant houses of Inner Syria has much in common with the basic form of the town houses. This is not surprising since the town house is built for the same climatic and social conditions as the traditional peasant house. In the course of time, however, the town house developed its own forms, and was increasingly assimilated to foreign influences, while the rural house remained to a greater extent attached to its original forms.

A. Russell's *The Natural History of Aleppo*, published in 1794, gives detailed information about the form of building of Aleppine town houses at that period. Russell's description of the palaces of Ottoman officials and the residences of wealthy merchants is still applicable to the houses of the old town of Aleppo, and is also valid for houses in Damascus of the eighteenth and nineteenth centuries.

After briefly mentioning the seraglio of the pasha of Aleppo, and the seraglio of former governors, Russell describes "modern" palaces, i.e. buildings probably erected in the late eighteenth century and characteristic of the architecture of the following decades.

First he divides the houses into three categories: "seraglios", palaces or great houses, the houses of rich merchants, and the simpler residential houses (he distinguishes between Muslim, Jewish and Christian houses). He emphasizes that in the Christian houses the separation of private and public spheres is of hardly any importance. Like the simpler Muslim houses it generally has only one large courtyard, whereas rich, elegant Muslim houses have a three-courtyard plan comprising a guest courtyard, a larger living courtyard and an office or kitchen courtyard.

Russell's "modern" palaces seem to have been large, three-courtyard complexes of this kind. According to Russell they are composed of an asymmetrical ensemble of individual buildings, but they have a certain elegance and are suited to the climate. After passing through a first, unpaved courtyard – a forecourt with stables – we come to a second courtyard, the reception courtyard. Persons of rank would enter on horseback as far as the foot of a stairway leading up to a colonnade, roofed in wood and with painted and gilded decoration, behind which lie the reception rooms. All the individual elements in these magnificent reception rooms are described, and they are also typical of the reception rooms of more modest palaces and houses. The main room is long, with a richly painted and gilded ceiling. There are views of towns and gardens painted above the doors and inscriptions above the windows and wall niches. The space is divided into a *divan* (seating area) raised about 45 cm and a lower *ataba* (waiting area for less important visitors and servants, as well as a place for removing shoes) which is decorated with marble inlay.

The *divan* consists of a wooden bench, which is more than a metre wide and about 10 cm high, running round the three sides of the room. It is covered with mattresses, which have covers embroidered in gold with fringes. Velvet-covered cushions lean against the walls. The two corners of the U-shaped *divan* are both raised by the addition of another mattress, provided with soft brocade cushions and reserved as places of honour for whoever is the highest ranking person in the room. The floor of the *divan* is covered with Persian and Turkish carpets. Such reception rooms may also have a wooden projecting bay with windows. Reception rooms on the ground floor have windows only on one side of the room with corresponding wall niches opposite. Sometimes the rooms are cooled by the water of a fountain in the *ataba*.

The dwellings of higher officials and servants are also located around this second courtyard, while the third courtyard, usually the biggest, is reserved for the *harim*, the private living area. This courtyard is linked with smaller courtyards, around which the bath and private kitchen are located. Trees and flowering shrubs, vines climbing over wooden trellises and jasmine give cool and shade, and the

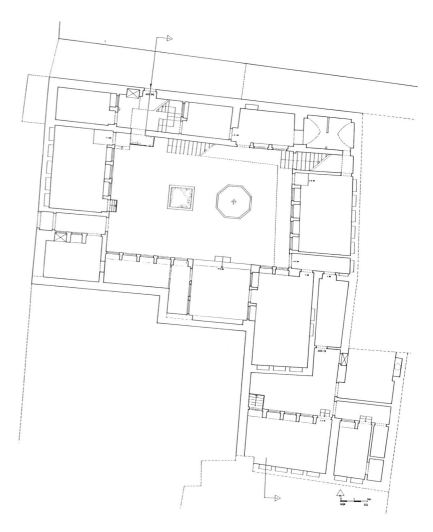

61 House in the north-east of the old town of Aleppo.

62 The Basil House in Aleppo.

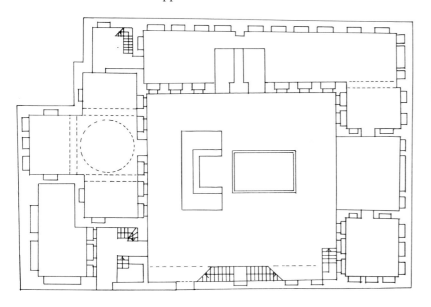

63 The Jumblat House in Aleppo.

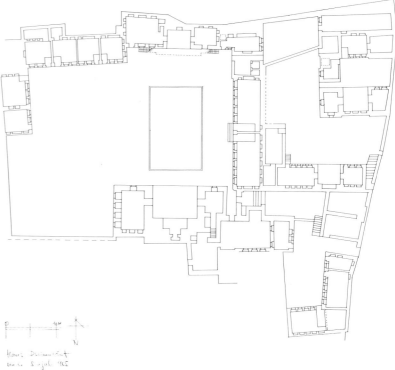

53

scent of the jasmine mingles with that of roses in full bloom and other fragrant plants. A water basin in the middle of the courtyard, running water in little marble channels and fountains cool the air, reflect the light and give a pleasant murmur; beneath a pavilion, on a raised platform (*mastaba*) a *divan* is occasionally set up.

The southern side of the courtyard is dominated by an alcove (*iwan*), raised about 45 cm higher, open to the courtyard and spanned by tall arch. This is furnished with a *divan* of mats and cushions for the hot summer months. The small side-chambers adjoining the *iwan* are used for resting and are called "*kubbe*". At times of day when the rays of the sun are reflected too strongly, one can shelter from them in the *qaa*, a large square domed hall on the north side of the courtyard. The marble-paved area under the dome (*ataba*) is linked though arches to separate, raised *divans*, while in the corners are two smaller rooms, also called *kubbe*, behind wooden trellises. The *iwan* and the rooms reached from it are used a living area in summer, while the *qaa* is used in the winter.

The other rooms facing the courtyard on the ground floor are used as bedrooms. They are richly decorated, and cooled by air channels (*badinj*). The beautiful, spacious rooms on the first floor (*marubba*), which sometimes have bay windows, are reached up external stone steps and are only used for festive occasions.

The façades of the courtyard are of different heights, and some parts of the building have vaulted cellars (*mughara*), while an even deeper cellar is used as a large reservoir of water (*sahrej*). The palace complexes described by Russell resemble the Azem Palace in Damascus (*c.* 1750) and the seventeenth-century Jumblat House in Aleppo. The original form of the Jumblat House is difficult to reconstruct exactly because of its many later additions and alterations, but the north-east courtyard was probably the centre of the reception area, while the south-eastern part was reserved for family living and was dominated by a high *iwan* on the south side, opposite which was a smaller, raised north *iwan* (ill. 61).

According to Russell the *harim*, the large family courtyard, with the adjoining *qaa* and *iwan*, is also found in smaller palaces and rich houses. There is no unpaved forecourt. The reception courtyard is smaller and less magnificent and is used for entertaining visitors. When there are special festivities, however, the whole *harim* is used as a reception courtyard.

Such houses, consisting of a reception courtyard with direct access from the street, a large living courtyard and an adjacent kitchen courtyard, are found in many traditional Muslim quarters in Aleppo and Damascus. Examples from Damascus are the Sibei House, in which there is another smaller courtyard besides the reception courtyard, and the Nisam House, which has a large reception courtyard reached through an entrance with several turns (*dihlis*), and a smaller family courtyard with kitchen between them. Russell's description of the more modest houses with only

64 Wall hanging for decorating a wall niche. Geometric appliqué work and inscriptions. Aleppo, *c.* 1890. (Museum für Völkerkunde, Berlin)

65 Water spouts from a Damascene fountain, cast bronze, seventeenth-nineteenth centuries.

66 Detail of a fountain, opus sectile with cypress motifs, Damascus, nineteenth century.

one courtyard, and more rarely with a *qaa*, but almost always with an *iwan* and a "best" room (reception room), which has simple painted decoration, also accords with many examples in the old city.

On the other hand, published examples of large one-courtyard houses in Aleppo are not necessarily representative of Islamic forms of dwelling. They are mostly Christian houses and seldom have several courtyards. An example is the Basil House in Aleppo (ill. 62) with its small kitchen courtyard with a separate entrance, and a large living courtyard with no special guest quarters. The arrangement corresponds very closely to the account given by Russell (ill. 63): the division into summer and winter quarters and the individual architectural elements, such as the three-part *qaa*, the south *iwan* with its adjoining rooms, which can be entered from there, the separately built rooms with windows looking onto the courtyard and wall niches on the facing wall, and the division into the lower *ataba* and a raised sleeping and sitting area, as well as a fountain and a *mastaba* on the *iwan* axis in the middle of the courtyard and one external stairway leading to the roof terraces and rooms on the upper floor. Russell's descriptions are therefore typical of the architecture of Muslim houses in the eighteenth and nineteenth centuries. The buildings in Damascus are distinguished from those in Aleppo less by the organization of their ground-plan than by the use of building materials and the form of the façades.

In Aleppo even the simplest buildings are built entirely of grey limestone, while most Damascene houses consist of a stone base with an upper storey, usually overhanging, of half-timbering filled with clay bricks and rubble stone.

This difference in building technique, with the narrower and taller building in Aleppo, affects the appearance of the towns and streets. The high, smooth walls of Aleppo radiate an air of respectability, clarity and enclosed-ness, while the alleys of Damascus are low and their overhanging upper storeys make them seem more twisting, more picturesque and less elegant.

The ground floor has no openings apart from small windows for light and ventilation, but the rooms on the upper floors have windows opening onto the street. The wooden oriels (*surfa*), mentioned by Russell in his description of the main reception room, are found in both Aleppo and Damascus. In the late nineteenth century the oriels in Aleppo were often joined together to fill the whole breadth of an overhanging storey on the façade and this feature determines the character of whole sections of streets (for instance, Bab en-Nasr Street).

The courtyard façades of the big palaces and rich houses in Damascus are characterized by their use of *ablaq* technique, i.e. layers of stonework in different coloured stones (limestone and basalt). The inner courtyards of the Damascus houses have a stronger horizontality in the articulation of their façades, and are more colourful, with more *riwaqs* than their Aleppine counterparts. They therefore appear wider and lighter than the narrower courtyards

67 Candlesticks in Ottoman style, left sixteenth century, right seventeenth century, with snuffers, Damascus.

68 Bowls with epigraphic decoration; used as soap-dishes in the bath, left bronze, right silver with traces of gilding.

69 Divan of a house in Damascus.

of Aleppo, which radiate peace and severity. The impression of overloaded ornament, created by the frequent use of elaborate and varied paste decoration, hardly ever appears in Aleppo, since the façades there are almost exclusively shaped with faceted and relief decoration. The decoration of the interiors is similar in both cities, except for the use of paste decor in Aleppo.

Examples of such urban houses are also found, for example, in the old-town quarters in the eastern part of Aleppo, where building activity increased suddenly in the mid-nineteenth century, after a long period of crisis towards the end of the eighteenth century, when the city was hit by epidemics and earthquakes.

The old-town quarters in the eastern part had an important mediating function between the surrounding country and the city, since the trade in agricultural products from Aleppo's hinterland had become one of the most important elements in the economy, together with the trade in home-produced textiles. High profits could be made, for instance, from trade in grain, which arrived in the north-eastern part of Aleppo and had to be stored. Large *hans* for this purpose were constructed in the north-eastern part of the city in this period with large investments from Aleppine merchants. The families, who came from the agricultural regions to the east of Aleppo, established themselves in the eastern part of the old town in the mid-nineteenth century, when Ottoman law made it possible to register landownership, thus creating a new class of urban big landowners.

The new wealth was displayed in intense building activity in the eastern quarters. This can be seen from the large number of inscriptions dating from the period after 1850. In this part of the city a quarter of the houses are built in the style of the period between 1850 and 1900.

Houses of this period generally have smaller courtyards, unlike those rural houses and those built in an earlier phase of prosperity, and the surrounding building is more compact. This means that the built-over area increased as a proportion of the total area of the site, and that therefore the density was greater and the character more urban.

The cellars beneath parts of the buildings became an essential feature of almost all buildings. The first, fairly deep cellars we come across have small, shapeless windows for light and ventilation. The cellar vaults consist of simple barrel vaults with intersecting vaults over the windows. In the north section, and on the other sides of the building, they are at a level half or a third of a storey below the level of the courtyard, but they may be deeper on the south side, if there is a south *iwan*. When such vaulting appears on the ground floor it supports an upper storey, which in earlier houses consists of a smaller guest section open to the west – in the direction of the wind. Upper floors extending across the whole side of a courtyard are only found as a rule in larger complexes of buildings and date from a later period. An impression of several storeys is created by the upward-thrusting façades with small, high windows and cellar windows, both of the same shape, as well as the large windows of the rooms above the cellars, the *ataba* of which may be as much as half a metre above the level of the courtyard. These brightly and beautifully decorated rooms are the living rooms and bedrooms. One room is used as a reception room. In some large houses this reception room is a simple *qaa* on the north side.

Much more common than the *qaa*, however, are south *iwans* about six metres high and raised about half a metre above courtyard level. They have marble inlay, and canopies (*tiwan*) for shade. The clear north-south orientation adopted in buildings after 1850 is suited to the climate. This "classical" form of building changed around the turn of the century.

The medium-sized buildings from the period after the turn of the century, unlike the buildings of the period before, rarely consist of two, let alone three courtyards. They are built as smaller units within the earlier structure based on larger land plots, or else built over existing houses. At first the reception courtyards developed into independent buildings, then the large living courtyards were transformed into smaller one-courtyard houses.

The built-over area increased still further in proportion to the area of the plot. The courtyards become narrower and in buildings after 1900 two storeys become the norm. In large complexes the ground floor came to be used as a *khan*, above which traditional inner-courtyard houses rested on heavy piers.

2. Urban forms of dwelling and lifestyle

The development of forms of building is affected by climatic conditions, the building material available and the location within the city, while the interior organization of the house is determined by the family's way of life. If we compare the customs of the Muslims in the late eighteenth century, as described by Russell, with the present-day ways of life in the old town, we find they are surprisingly similar. Then as now the separation of private and public life, of men and women, is a determining factor in communal living and daily life, affecting the way the house is organized – and hence the form of the dwelling.

We find great differences between the forms of dwelling of the simple population from the rural districts and the richer urban population. Russell describes the daily life of rich and less rich "Turks", i.e. urban merchants and craftsmen, and shows the traditional lifestyle of Arabs, Turcomans and Kurds, who live in the suburbs and whose manners and customs are still strongly attached to the nomadic and peasant life.

The Arabs, who are called Bedouin, though the "real" Bedouin live in tents in the summer and in caves near the city in the winter, dress differently from the "Turks" and do not marry outside their circles. The women work in the rich houses as servants. The Turcomans, who distinguish themselves from the Bedouins, also live in simple houses and work in agriculture or as camel-drivers.

As prosperity increases these more nomadic-peasant ways of life and dwelling become overlaid by an urban life-style, which Russell describes in his detailed account of the course of a day in rich families: the men rise at dawn, drink coffee and smoke a pipe, then partake of their breakfast, consisting of bread, fruit and laban, in the courtyard or the reception area. If they do not leave the house to work or pay visits, they receive guests, who are offered coffee and the hookah.

The midday meal is served at about eleven o'clock at a round table on which stand small dishes with salt, salad, laban and preserved vegetables. For the first course soup is brought, then come other bowls containing dishes made of lamb, poultry, kibbe, stuffed vegetables and rice. When the eating is over, the people drink water and wash their hands. The meal does not last long, and the men eat separately from the women. After a midday rest lasting one or two hours, they go about their work.

The main meal generally takes place in the early evening and consists of the same dishes as the midday meal. Then comes the time to make family visits, when coffee is again drunk and the hookah is passed round. Bedtime is between nine and ten o'clock. The mattresses, which are piled in the *divan* in the day time, are spread out and a cotton sheet is laid over them. A silk cloth, which may be thin or thick depending on the time of year, is used as a blanket. A lamp burns the whole night, and a charcoal brazier provides heating in winter. In the summer people sleep in the court-yard or on the roof.

The women bring up the children, keep the house tidy, and practise handicrafts such as spinning wool, sewing and embroidery. Above all they are concerned with the prepa-ration of food. In grander houses the food is always bought by the men, or else the women buy from itinerant female sellers, who come to the door.

Women do leave the house, however, to make family visits or to go to take a bath at the *hammam*, where on special occasions, such as the birth of a child, recovery after an illness or before and after their marriage they meet and celebrate. When the women visit their female relatives, they leave the house early in the morning and return home before sunset, or else they stay the night with the family. Another pretext for leaving the house is to visit the family graves, usually on Thursdays. Messages are sent in the form of flower arrangements, which carry a secret meaning in their colour and combination.

The women live together communally in the house, but the first wife of the father has certain privileges. If men have several wives, which is rare, each of them has a right to her own room. The children of different wives all have equal rights. When a son comes to marriageable age, the mother looks for a bride among her female relatives. When the son marries, a room is made available to him as a bridal chamber. On the death of his father the privileges of his first wife pass to the wife of the eldest son, and the migra-tion of the younger members of the family – or the dividing up of the house – begins.

According to Russell several generations lived in one house, and this is still true of about a third of the house-holds of the lower middle class. This means that the fami-lies consist of a nuclear family and the parents of an adult son of the nuclear family. On marriage the wife leaves her parental home and moves in with her husband in the house of her parent-in-law. As a rule the eldest son marries first.

For financial reasons a number of married sons together may keep a household in the house of their parents, but on the death of the head of the family this form of communal life is generally broken up. The eldest son then takes over the role of father in the parental house, and the extended family reproduces itself again.

The father and mother generally have one room, while the children as they grow up share the other rooms for sleeping. A married son and his family have a room provided for their own use. In houses of earlier periods with large courtyards, which often have two sides with one-storey buildings, any extra room could simply be built on when it was needed. In richer urban houses of the mid-nineteenth century there was provision for such an additional room from the start, and an additional storey could be added later. All these rooms used by various members of the family have the same basic furnishings and contain the same basic elements as peasant houses and the simpler rooms of earlier houses, and the individual rooms are still used in this way today. However, the rooms used for special purposes, such as reception rooms and guest rooms have lost some of their importance, and the *iwan* and *qaa* are hardly used at all. They are consequently not kept in good repair, let alone built from scratch. On the other hand, bathrooms have become an established feature of all houses.

As Russell mentions, baths were only found in the large houses of the wealthy. Men and women of all social classes used regularly to visit the *hammam*, which were to be found in all districts of the city. The visit to the *hammam* is still an important event in social life and for women espe-cially provides an opportunity to meet, to talk about family matters and celebrate on special occasions.

Like the baths, the kitchens with an open fireplace, chimney and a cistern or well with a pump in the wall to the courtyard, were an established feature of the large houses. Nowadays the open hearth has been replaced with a gas cooker, the cistern is filled in, and the pump in the courtyard is no longer used.

Social life too has changed. It is true that it is still the privilege of the men to do the shopping, but the coffee-houses, where once music was played, shadow plays performed and stories told, hardly exist any more. The rearing of racing pigeons, described by Russell, is now only found in a few houses, since this form of amusement seems to have been supplanted by television. Indeed the television set has become a status symbol in every household.

Even today most of the every-day life of women at the lower end of the social scale is spent among themselves in the house, which as a rule they leave only to make visits to the family, the *hammam* or the graves. When the men are out at work, they run the household. They use a hosepipe to clean the stone floors of the rooms and the courtyard, prepare the food and do work at home such as sewing and embroidery to earn extra money.

Family life still seems to follow the traditional rules, though people have become accustomed to televisions, radios, refrigerators, ventilators and European furniture, such as beds, tables and chairs. But in fact it seems that under the modernizing pressure of western influence the nuclear family is replacing the extended family as the social norm, and the traditional family bonds are being dissolved both from within and without.

70 Upholstery covering for a chair. Woven silk, Damascus, *c.* 1890.

71 Reconstruction of a men's reception room in the Azem Palace, Damascus.

72 Reconstruction of a women's reception room in the Azem Palace, Damascus.

Urban Material Culture

Johannes Kalter

The history of urban culture in Syria extending back over thousands of years has been described from a various points of view: the significance of the cities as administrative centres and the focus for the interrelation of the urban population, peasants and nomads, as well as their significance as religious centres, as centres of crafts and trade. The structure of the two most important cities, the great rivals Aleppo and Damascus, has been described, as well as the development of urban architecture in the nineteenth and early twentieth centuries. Another chapter deals with examples of urban craftsmanship, in so far as they are specifically related to Syrian urban culture. Many aspects mentioned so far could only by described or illustrated with photographs as no material evidence exists which could display them. In this chapter specifically urban artefacts will be discussed using examples from our collection in the Linden-Museum. In this context "specifically urban" does not mean to say that urban luxury goods were not also sometimes found in exceptional instances in the houses of well-to-do peasants, or even – if they could be easily transported – in the tents of noble and well-to-do bedouins.

73 Detail of a painted wooden ceiling with plaster relief in the Azem Palace.

74 Lamp, cast bronze, Azem Palace.

75 Courtyard of the Azem Palace, Damascus.

76 Detail from the courtyard façade of the Azem Palace with a carved and inlaid mirror glass.

The exceptional importance of urban culture in Syria is also evident in the proportion of town-dwellers in the total population. According to Wirth (1971) town-dwellers made up at least 25 per cent of Syria's population around 1950. The census of 1960 identified 42 per cent as urban, and since then the urban proportion of the population has risen steadily. The specifically urban artefacts which will be discussed below were, however, always the property of a relatively small upper class consisting of landowners living in the city, the owners of urban manufacturing businesses, rich merchants, high administrative and military officials, and scholars. The possessions of the ordinary people living in the town, as far as household equipment and objects for personal use were concerned, did not differ essentially from that of the peasants. The household goods and furnishings belonging to the urban upper class were distinguished from these by their quantity, the materials used, the quality of their workmanship and by the finish suited to the requirements of urban life. Besides the specifically Syrian elements strong influences the urban Ottoman culture had been absorbed from Istanbul. In addition to this, European elements found their way to Syria either via Istanbul or – between 1830 and 1840, during the reign of Ibrahim Pasha – through Cairo or through direct contact between the Syrian cities and France, in particular Lyon and Marseille.

The Linden-Museum collection contains objects exemplifying all areas of urban life. The collection includes items from the purely private sphere, as well as personal utensils, which can be divided into male and female categories. Objects used in a more public context also exist. These are objects used in the mosque and the *medrese* as places of religious and intellectual life; the citadel as the seat of administration; the *suq* as the centre of crafts and trade, and the centre of economic management for a region and the centre of foreign trade, which was of great importance particularly for Syrian cities; the coffee-house as the principal leisure facility for men; and last but not least the bath, probably the most important meeting place for women, besides serving the needs of both sexes for ritual cleanliness, relaxation and hygiene.

The intermixing of Oriental and European household goods and style is very apparent in the furnishings of the men's and women's reception rooms of the large town houses. Much depends, of course, on the personal preferences of the inhabitants. The *divans* with brocaded cushions, and later covered with imported English fabrics, were replaced by folding chairs with intarsia work or by upholstered armchairs in the middle of the last century. The silk material used for covering these armchairs in the 1880s and 1890s has motifs very similar to European art nouveau. A typical oriental piece of furniture was found in the women's area: a great chest of precious wood inlaid with mother-of-pearl. In the men's and women's areas trays with supports of turned wood served as tables. Typical of higher quality urban furniture were heavy, brass trays with

silver inlay, scroll-work decoration and text cartouches, and those with a brass alloy preserved from tarnishing by an admixture of gold; the latter trays had a shine similar to gold. Towards the end of the century, however, tables imitating European models with folding sides became popular. Details of the craftsmanship, such as turned grilles made of coloured wood, carved decoration and mother-of-pearl inlay, are typical of Syrian products in the last quarter of the nineteenth century. Often, however, it is difficult to decide whether the products of Syrian craftsmen were made for the home market or for export. Another example of luxury furniture must not be omitted: mirrors in carved frames with mother-of-pearl inlay. The looking glass is usually niche-shaped. The cresting of the mirror consists of candelabra-like interlaced scrollwork. The upper termination is formed from *mukarnas*. Masonry wall niches contain the typical luxury goods of the upper class, such as lead crystal glasses from Bohemia with red, blue and gold painting made specifically for the oriental market, Chinese porcelain, and also ceramics from Çanakkale in Turkey. Boxes with intarsia work in bone or precious wood and mother-of-pearl are found in every living area. The larger ones were used by women for keeping their toiletries and jewellery. In the men's and women's areas were boxes for offering typical oriental sweets, while in the men's section were also smaller boxes used as cigarette boxes. In the houses as well as in the mosque or *medrese*, boxes made of copper or bronze with rich silver inlay, or tables were used to keep the Koran in Mamluk style. Also used were Koran-stands with mother-of-pearl intarsia work and/or carved ornaments. In addition to the chased, openwork ceiling lights found throughout the Near East with glass holders for oil – replaced towards the end of the century by electric bulbs, candlesticks cast in bronze in a very uniform style existed. Their style changed only very little from the late Mamluk to the end of the Ottoman period. Washing sets, consisting of basins and ewers, were just as decorative as they were indispensable for generous hospitality.

The guest was greeted on his arrival by the master of the house, who would place the basin in front of him, hand him soap, pour water over his hands and pass him a towel of fine, absorbent cotton. Then bottles of rose-water would be passed round. Depending on the taste and the wealth of the owner these were made of gold, silver, copper gilt (a typical Ottoman technique) or silver gilt. Then incense burners were passed round to delight the guest with fragrances and drive away evil spirits. Incense burners of the eighteenth century were usually cast in bronze or brass and are distinctive for their clear-cut forms. Those dating from the nineteenth century are very Baroque in appearance and are made of gilded copper or silver. After this greeting ceremony, which is very elaborate by western standards, Turkish mocha was poured from richly decorated jugs, which were made of brass or silver, or silver-plated. The meal consisting of many courses was then served either on imported Chinese porcelain or on tin-plated copper dishes with engraved floral ornaments. After the lavish meal tea was offered. Teapots, tea jars and sugar containers were also made of silver or were silver-plated. Then the pipes were lit by servants holding pieces of burning charcoal taken from the brazier in the middle of the room using tongs, which were often lovingly decorated. Everyone brought his own mouthpiece with him. Generally these were made of silver with engraved or niello decorations, and often they had amber tips. No self-respecting coffee-house would lag behind prosperous private households when it came to the quality of its hookahs. Since the middle of the last century cigarette-smoking has become increasingly common, in addition to the use of hookahs. The cigarettes were smoked in holders which have even more varied decorations than the mouth-pieces of the hookahs. The Linden-Museum collection contains examples made of amber and imitation amber, with and without silver inlay, bone, silver with filigree or niello decoration. The most valuable cigarette-holders were thought to be those made of black coral with silver inlay. In the 1890s black coral was often imitated in bakelite.

Typical examples of urban artefacts – which at the same time were a sign of being a member of a particular class: that of scholars and calligraphers (and therefore artists) – are writing implements cast in bronze, and occasionally silvered. These consisted of a cylindrical container for quills and an ink pot, as well as paper scissors, with elaborate openwork handles and gold inlay. They usually indicate the workshop where they were made. The steel edges of the scissors may be burnished.

Also typically urban are containers with several layers and a handle, which are made of bronze or tin-plated copper and were used, for example, to bring lunch to merchants in the *suq*. Most of these containers were imported from Istanbul, but some were also produced in Damascus.

Confusing similar to these containers are boxes with with a lid and openwork base. They were used for taking the locally produced soap (usually based on olive oil) and flannels to the *hammam*. The openwork base was intended to allow the water to drain out. Some small factories in Aleppo still produce this very pleasing local type of soap which is also imprinted with a stamp. Heavy plates cast in bronze or silver with a floral edge reminiscent of Timurid models in the fourteenth century, and engraved scrollwork decoration and inscriptions running round them, were used to hold flannels and soap in the *hammam* itself. One object in the Linden Museum's collection, made of heavy silver with vestiges of wash- gilding, gives an idea of the luxury of some of the bathing equipment. Eye make-up was carried in chased, cypress-shaped silver cases. These were often fastened by means of the same stick used for applying the cosmetics, often surmounted by a bird. The most striking part of the ladies' bathing outfit were high-heeled sandals made of precious woods with bone and mother-of-pearl inlay and a velvet band with silver embroidery in relief. The extensive set of washing utensils was carried behind the master or the lady by a male or female servant respectively. This set was enveloped in large, square cloths, usually purple or dark red, with silver embroidery in the Ottoman style.

Since the end of the Second World War urban life in Syria has undergone even more radical changes than the life of the peasants or the nomads. With the exception of a few pieces of furniture, which are still used for their proper purpose, and hookahs (now found more often in coffee-houses than in private homes) the articles described in this chapter, if they can be found at all, are used merely for display.

77 View through the rooms of the *hammam* (bath) in the Azem Palace).

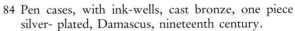

78 Top left: Washing sets, brass, and brass with silver and copper inlay, Damascus, nineteenth century.

79 Incense burners; back row: cast bronze, seventeenth/eighteenth centuries; front row: silver and copper, gilded. Damascus, nineteenth century.

80 Coffee pots; left: brass, right: silver. Damascus, nineteenth century.

81 Flasks for rose-water, brass, silver, copper, gilded, Damascus, eighteenth/nineteenth centuries.

82 Food container, brass and copper tin-plated; vessel with lid, copper tin-plated. Damascus, nineteenth century.

83 Sugar hammer, cast bronze with glass inlay, Damascus, nineteenth cent.

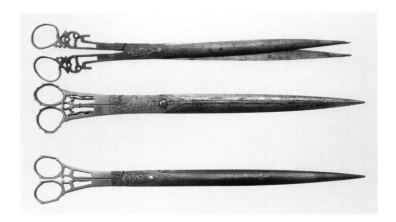

84 Pen cases, with ink-wells, cast bronze, one piece silver-plated, Damascus, nineteenth century.

85 Paper scissors, steel with bronze handle and workshop signatures inlaid in gold. Damascus, eighteenth/nineteenth centuries.

86 Velvet bag with silver embroidery in relief, for bathing utensils, Damascus, nineteenth century.

87 Bath sandals, cedar-wood with bone and mother-of-pearl inlay, Damascus, nineteenth century.

89 Coffee house at the foot of the Citadel of Damascus.

90 Bent-necked lute with mother-of-pearl intarsia; small kettle drums.

91 Long-necked lute and tambourine, both with rich mother-of- pearl inlay.

88 Containers for eye make-up (*kohol*) with sticks for application, brass and lead, painted wood, Damascus, nineteenth century.

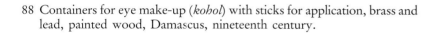

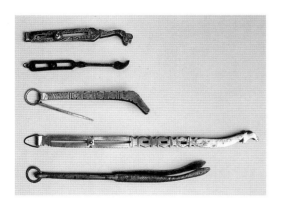

92 Tongs for lighting water pipes, cast bronze, one with applied nielloed silver. Damascus, nineteenth century.

93 Water pipes: water containers made of Bohemian lead crystal, with chased silver tops.

94 Two bases of water pipes, Bohemian glass, painted; left: eighteenth century; right: nineteenth century.

Urban Handicrafts

Johannes Kalter

The observation made by the great Arabic philosopher of history Ibn Khaldun (1332-1406) regarding the conditions under which handicraft can develop is still applicable to Syria in the nineteenth and early twentieth centuries:

> "The mind does not cease transforming all kinds of crafts including the composite ones, from potentiality in actuality through the gradual discovery of one thing after another, until they are perfect. This is not achieved all at one stroke. It is achieved in the course of time and of generations. Things are not transformed from potentiality into actuality all at one stroke, especially not technical matters. Consequently, a certain amount of time is unavoidable. Therefore, the crafts are found to be inferior in small cities, and only the simple crafts are found there. When sedentary civilization in those cities increases, and luxury conditions there cause the use of crafts, they are transformed from potentiality into actuality. And God knows better." (Ibn Khaldun, *The Muqaddimah, An Introduction to History*, ed. F. Rosenthal, New York 1958, 3 volumes.)

As far as the range of different crafts and the quality of the products are concerned, the two largest towns in Syria, Aleppo and the capital, Damascus, are accordingly the most important centres of craft production.

The rise and decline of urban handicrafts between the beginning of the nineteenth century and today reflects the chequered history of the region, the success of competition from cheap European mass-produced imported items, and the progress made in the industrialization of Syria and its integration into modern world trade. On the other hand, when "Orientalism" was in vogue in Europe towards the end of the nineteenth century, it breathed new life into almost extinct crafts producing luxury goods such as inlaid metalwork and furniture with intarsia decoration. But between the two World Wars, even the production of such luxury goods declined. Since the oil boom in the 1970s the craftsmen of Damascus have found new markets in the Gulf States. The manufacture of goods for the tourist market and for export to Europe (mainly, it seems, to France, Italy and Spain) is increasing, and among sections of the Syrian upper class and the rising middle class it is becoming chic to furnish one's home in the "traditional Syrian" style. Craft skills are still available. Expensive raw materials which are hard to obtain, such as precious woods and bone, have sometimes been replaced by plastics or materials that are easier to work, such as wood paste made of sawdust, and bone paste composed of powdered bone. The working methods which we have observed make it clear that, despite the continued low wages for craftsmen (approximately 150-200 DM a month), the production processes are being rationalized in the face of increasing pressure from competition. But this can only be ascertained where modern machinery has been introduced, since there are no descriptions of production processes in an earlier period.

Unfortunately most of the travellers' accounts in the nineteenth and early twentieth centuries provide only incomplete lists of the various crafts.

Three travellers' reports illustrate the changing history of Syrian handicrafts. W.G. Browne, who travelled through Syria in 1795/96, found trade and industry booming: "The manufactures are in a flourishing state, being carried on with great spirit both by Christians and Mohammedans; silk and cotton are the chief articles...", whereas after his journey in 1852/53, H. Petermann wrote: "As long as the rule of Ibrahim Pasha continued, trade and industries flourished – now everything is laid low." R. Oberhummer and H. Zimmerer (1899) also described a general decline of handicrafts in Damascus, but, compared with the situation in the middle of the century, production seems to have increased again: "Apart from splendid saddlery, almost the only pieces of art handicraft still crafted were the well-known wooden shoes inlaid with bone and mother-of-pearl, small tables and pedestals, and beautiful brass plates and jugs. In the goldsmiths' bazaar one also finds a wide range of pretty items of jewellery, such as silver brooches and pendants, which are worked with great diligence and are not dear." Oberhummer and Zimmerer go on to say that everything else came from Istanbul or Persia. The same authors also report from Aleppo that (p. 89) "the bazaars are overflowing with European goods; Marseilles in particular is a channel for the import of materials, cloths and colonial goods."

In the years since 1980, especially in Damascus, I witnessed a diverse and at times even contradictory development. Crafts which are regarded as typically Syrian have increased in importance. These include the production of inlaid furniture, small boxes and board games, brass and bronze objects inlaid with silver and copper, and also sword blades inlaid with gold or the application of inlay to old blades. The craftsman uses antique pieces in the museums as a model, besides making use of old catalogues of work produced for the Paris World Exhibition in 1897

95 Street in the Suq Hamidiye in Damascus.

96 End of the Roman colonnade on the main axis of the Suq Hamidiye in Damascus.

97 Decorated mule drawing a water cart in Damascus.

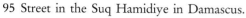

98 *Suq* of the carpet-sellers in Aleppo.

99 Wool and yarn dealer in the *suq* of Damascus.

100 Grocer in the *suq* of Damascus.

101 Glass-blower in the Tekiye Suleimaniye in Damascus.

102 Making opus sectile in Damascus.

103 Turner in Damascus.

(these catalogues are treasured by the proprietors of the firms and jealously guarded) and postcards dating from the turn of the century.

Some pieces come close to forgery. New styles have been developed as a result of customers' demands, and the taste and creativity of the head of the particular firm. The aesthetic merits of some of these are very debatable.

A similar development can be observed in architecture – particularly among stonemasons, who imitate mosaics in the style of the Mamluks, and among specialists who paint ceilings and wood panelling in the style of Damascene houses of the well-to-do of the period between c. 1750 and 1900. Through the initiative of the Society of Friends of the Old Town of Damascus, and private citizens, many old houses have been renovated. This process involves an enormous amount of in-filling, because the houses have been neglected for such a long time and have been ruthlessly gutted by astute art and antique dealers.

Generally restorers do not stop at the restoration of extant or damaged parts. They also create very good copies, if patterns are available or if the motifs can be reconstructed from what survives. If this is not possible then something new is made in an appropriate style.

An increasing demand for handicrafts connected with architecture stems from the Damascene upper class, tourist hotels and authorities in charge of public buildings. The nouveau riche Gulf Arabs create a complete "genuine Arab" identity for themselves, with the help of architectural decoration, furniture, inlaid metalwork, arms for display, traditional textiles and so on. These crafts are supported by the government – mainly because they bring in foreign currency.

The work of coppersmiths and brass smiths – such as trays, pots, bowls, jugs and lamps – once made up most of the furnishings of Syrian households in the cities and in the villages. Trays on turned supports and used as tables, have now been replaced by European-style tables. The old pots, bowls and jugs have been superseded by mass-produced wares, most of them imported. Candlesticks have become unnecessary.

In Damascus there is still a coppersmiths' *suq*, where very large cooking pots and pans are made for rural weddings, and for the requirements of the military, schools and probably also for hospitals. In the coppersmiths' *suq* of Aleppo the whole range of simple, undecorated household utensils is still produced for the apparently still very traditional, mainly rural population of the surrounding countryside.

Nevertheless, the coppersmiths have declined considerably in importance during the period I have witnessed. Almost all the examples of older, good quality metalwork which I saw in 1980 in the United Arab Emirates and Oman were said by their owners to have come from Damascus. But because of rapid economic, social and related cultural changes, this region has virtually ceased to be a customer for simple handicraft products.

104 Brass smith cutting out the base of a vessel.

105 Brass smith punching a tray.

106 Tray with punched and engraved decoration, brass alloy with gold admixture, Damascus, nineteenth century.

107 Copper smith beating out the rim of a tray, in Aleppo.

108 & 109 Workshop and merchandise for sale at a copper smith's in Aleppo.

Also nearing extinction is the craft of the potter, whose most important products were water and oil jars. They have now been almost entirely replaced by metal and plastic canisters.

Chests for peasant households, carved or mounted with sheet metal, have been replaced by chests made according to European models. I do not know anywhere where they are still being made. Joiners in Damascus have specialized in manufacturing pieces in the style of French furniture of the last century.

The traditional leather craft has also become almost extinct. Home- produced factory-made shoes and slippers in European style have taken over almost everywhere. Sandal-makers now produce their merchandise almost exclusively for tourists, though to a modest extent traditional leather shoes, and especially boots, are still made for bedouins.

The effect of the laws of the market can be seen most clearly in a little specialist *suq* supplying the needs of horses, mules and asses, near the Hamediye *suq*. Here riding and pack saddles were sold for horses, mules and asses, as well as bridles and amulets and horse trappings. As a consequence of the improved infrastructure, such as road construction and increasing motorization, animals have lost much of their importance for riding and transport. Correspondingly the number of producers of related accessories, particularly the saddlers, has been in continual decline. An exception to this are the producers of representative horse trappings, which by Syrian standards are extremely expensive, and are made not so much for the home market as for the Gulf States.

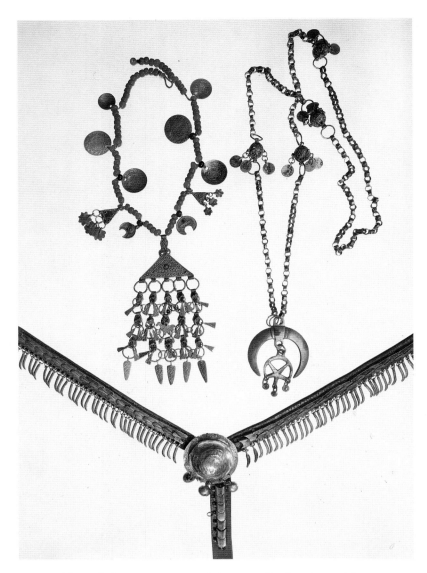

110 Necklaces; below: Ottoman-style breast collar for a horse. The crescent pendant with a star (top right) is found in sculptures of horses in late antiquity. Damascus, eighteenth/nineteenth centuries.

111 & 112 Left: leading chains; right: neck ornaments for horses. Damascus, twentieth century. In Damascus there is a special *suq* for riding- and pack-saddles, bridles and horse trappings. In the last ten years the range of items for sale has drastically diminished.

Craftsmen Catering for the Rich and for Foreigners

The Makers of Metal Inlay

In the Orient inlay is one of the most popular techniques for decorating metal objects. A softer decorative metal (gold, silver or copper) is combined with a harder ground metal (bronze or steel) by being hammered on to a roughened surface or into a lower ground prepared by picking out the pattern with a burin. The earliest examples of inlaid metal objects from the Islamic world can be dated to the ninth and tenth centuries. These are mortars, oil lamps or bowls, cast in bronze with copper inlay, from the area ruled by the East Iranian dynasty of the Samanids and the dynasty of the Ghasnavids who had their residence at Ghasni in what is now Afghanistan. From there this decorative technique spread westwards. The town of Mosul in present-day Iraq, Damascus, and to a lesser extent Cairo were centres of production for such metal goods in the thirteenth and fourteenth centuries. They were highly prized throughout the Islamic world. After the Mongol conquest of Mosul in the thirteenth century the centre of production of inlaid metalwork shifted to Damascus.

The earliest surviving inlaid metal object is now the Louvre in Paris. It was probably made in Damascus for a sultan who reigned between 1237 and 1260.

From the mid-thirteenth century until the beginning of the sixteenth boxes, vases and candlesticks were produced in Damascus for the European market and exported via Venice. A blank space in the shape of an escutcheon was usually left in their decoration so that it could be filled with the future owner's coat of arms. Such pieces served as models stimulating the local production of these luxury objects in Venice in the sixteenth century.

The Linden-Museum's collection contains no examples of inlaid Syrian metalwork from the seventeenth and eighteenth centuries. The knowledge of the technique, however, was clearly not lost, and towards the end of the nineteenth century the production of inlaid work in Damascus revived. The domestic demand from a bourgeoisie whose economic strength was gradually increasing, and the fashion for Orientalism in Europe – especially in France – resulted in deliberate stylistic allusions to the tradition of the Mamluk rulers of Syria in the fourteenth and fifteenth centuries in the case, for example, of the production of Koran boxes, Koran tables and washing utensils and trays. Vase shapes, containers for house-plant pots, cigarette boxes, little bowls and suchlike were orientated more towards the European taste of the time. The end of this development is represented by the large shell cases inlaid with gold and copper, which are used as umbrella and walking-stick stands in restaurants and tourist hotels.

113 Koran table, brass with gold, silver and copper inlay. Work of Jewish craftsmen. Damascus, late nineteenth century.

114 Koran box, brass, silver and copper inlay with floral and epigraphic decoration in kufic and naskhi script. Damascus, nineteenth century.

115–117 A traditional Damascene Jewish workshop for metal inlay. Centre: a craftsman engraving the surface of a table. Right: a woman beating silver wire into the prepared surface.

Metal inlay is a highly specialized craft. The craftsmen use undecorated pieces which have been cast or wrought in bronze or brass by other smiths; only the decoration is applied in the inlay workshops. In Damascus we had the opportunity to observe the work processes and ask the owner of a workshop a number of questions. Maurice Nuseiri is the owner of the company called Omaiyad Bazar. The workshop is situated in the Jewish quarter of the Old Town of Damascus and was founded in 1927 by Sion Nuseiri, the father of the present owner. At that time a large number of businesses of this type were established, producing pieces for the Syrian as well as for the European market – in particular France. In the heyday of the firm his father employed sixty workers; today there are only six workers. Until the 1960s the son produced mainly for the European market, but since then his main customers have been the Gulf States, the big tourist hotels in Syria, as well as Syrian customers for private and public buildings. He provides anything he is asked for, from metalwork for doors to ashtrays, inlaid lamps and flowerpot holders.

The work produced by the firm stands or falls by its "chief craftsman", Musa Seidiya, who is said in Damascus to be one of the best craftsmen in his field. Musa learnt the craft from the father of the present owner. He has been working for forty years in the firm and began his apprenticeship at the age of ten.

The present owner of the firm is not himself a craftsman; he pursued a different career before taking over the busi-ness and has not mastered the craft. His sons, too, receive a different education. It is surprising to learn that Musa's mother also worked for this firm. She made the silver-wire inlays in exactly the way as Musa's own daughter, who has learnt it from her father. (It seems to be quite common in Syria for women to practise craft professions. Annegret Nippa noted: "In Aleppo daughters of Armenian gold-smiths learn the craft as young girls and practise it at home. At Deir ez-Zor, before the emigration of the Jewish gold-smiths, their daughters are also said to have run workshops in their homes.")

Pieces are made to order. The ordering is done by means of a catalogue; the owner has photograph albums with photographs or polaroids showing the range of products and variations of patterns. The customer can bring his own particular wishes and ideas. The owner also "invents" new patterns himself. He often draws inspiration for these from standard works on Islamic art, which are on a shelf behind his desk. It is also possible to order exact copies of old pieces. Musa's great skill as a craftsman guarantees an outstanding quality of execution. The owner of the shop does not give Musa preliminary sketches. Instead, he talks over his new designs with him, and Musa then carries them out.

Maurice considers a design to be new of traditional orna-ments are combined in a manner different from what has been usual up to then. According to Musa and Maurice, there were formerly fairly strict rules of design. Three basic ornaments were used. First, there are vegetable ornaments called *nabati* (flowery), i.e. rinceau ornaments, each with its own name, e.g. *fatimi* after the dynasty of the Fatimids. Secondly, there are strictly geometrical ornaments called *khutut handasiye* (arabesque). Lastly there is what is called the Persian Style, in which figural representations are used to fill the two basic shapes mentioned above.

The use of script can be combined with all these forms of decoration. Preferred are the ductus of the *thuluth* and the *kufic* (usually floral *kufic*). Their severity and monumentality makes them the most suitable for this sort of decorative technique. Smaller cursive scripts, such as the *naskhi*, would be difficult to beat into a metal ground.

In the past – that is, in the time of Maurice's father – the fundamental rule was that a basic pattern had either to be floral or geometric, and the choice then determined the whole appearance of the object. The filling of the surfaces between the basic pattern would then be floral in the case of a geometric basic pattern, or geometric in the case of a floral one. The surface was articulated by means of borders and roundels. The articulation apparently follows strict rules. If Musa receives the instruction from Maurice to make, for example, a tray with a geometric border or central roundel, he can vary the rest of the ornament in accordance with these rules. Musa says, and one can believe him, that he has several hundred designs in his head. There are no pattern books. Complicated and expensive pieces commissioned by important customers are made entirely by Musa himself. In these cases he does not make any preliminary drawings. Simpler patterns are drawn by Musa in Indian ink on the piece and he leaves them to be executed by other workers.

A clear division of labour, such as I have seen at Maurice's workshop, seems to be the rule. The chief craftsman makes the preliminary drawing. One worker lifts out the marked lines with a burin. Another hammers copper or silver wires into these engraved lines. The wire is not cut off but torn off with a powerful blow with the hammer. This part of the production process demands the greatest dexterity, and for this reason it seems that girls and women are preferred. Another craftsman then goes over the lines of the inlay with a very sharp chisel cutting away the edges of the inlay which overlap the surface of the piece. The piece is then finished off by being polished with fine sand or chalk. Pieces made of thin metal are bedded on a base of putty to prevent the ground from springing back and causing a warp in the engraving or inlay. As regards the quality of craftsmanship the pieces produced today can stand comparison with those from the Mamluk period. They differ mainly in their mixture of different styles of ornament, as described above.

118 Tip of a Muslim processional banner with epigraphic decoration, cast bronze. Damascus, twentieth century.

119 Tray with floral, geometric and epigraphic decoration, cast brass with silver inlay. Damascus, nineteenth century.

120 Typical export wares made in Damascus, late nineteenth century / early twentieth century. Vase, rose-water flask, incense burner, box; brass, inlaid with copper and silver.

121 Raw materials for inlays: shells and camel bone.

122–124 Polishing of the mother-of-pearl parts, and their insertion into the foot of a table. Detail of a table top. The mother-of-pearl inlay is set in tin.

The Intarsia Craftsmen

Intarsia is a mosaic-like inlay of contrasting materials such as bone, mother-of-pearl, woods of various colours – and today plastic as well – set into a wooden object. The earliest examples of this technique in the Orient are found in ancient Egypt. Objects with intarsia decoration are known from the tomb of Tutankh-Amun (fourteenth century BC).

The earliest examples from the Islamic period in the Museum for Islamic Art in Cairo can be dated to the ninth century, while Syrian objects with intarsia decoration have survived from the tenth century. These early works are from the religious sphere, such as the panels of preaching chairs (*minbar*), Koran stands (*rahla*), and, more rarely, the doors of mosques, *medreses* and saints' tombs. The technique of intarsia spread westwards from Egypt and Syria to Andalusia and Morocco, and eastwards to Iran and India. Syrian and Egyptian intarsias have retained their unmistakeable style and even today they are technically among the best examples of this ancient craft.

The early works from the eleventh and twelfth centuries show that the cabinet-maker's art was highly developed at a time when woodworking in medieval Europe was still at a crude early stage. This is true both in their decorative elements and in the construction of complicated and compartmented parts, which are worked with unusual precision, and with polygonal frames and fillings.

At first sight this may seem surprising, since compared with the forested regions of northern and central Europe the Orient is very short of wood. On the other hand it should be remembered that several of the precious woods which have since become native, such as cedar, cherry and walnut, were introduced to central Europe by the Romans (Wöhrlin, 1990).

Craftsmen say that their works are in the Mamluk tradition both in their decoration and in the types of furniture made. This, however, is only partly true. In Syria, as in the whole of the Orient, traditional furniture was relatively sparse. People sat on *divans*, cushions with brocade covers, which were arranged round the walls of reception rooms. The use of tables was not common; food was served on brass or copper trays placed on folding supports. In the homes of well-to-do citizens these supports were already decorated with intarsia work at an early period. Household equipment was kept not in cupboards but in wall niches, good examples of which may still be seen in the Azem Palace in Damascus. The only traditional pieces of furniture were chests for storing textiles and possibly jewellery. In the countryside these usually only had carved decoration, but urban chests were generally decorated with intarsia work. Before the eighteenth century chairs and armchairs were only meant for important people. At the end of the eighteenth century and beginning of the nineteenth the growing, western-orientated, "bourgeois" class, following the example of Istanbul and Cairo, introduced a

125 Koran stands, carved and inlaid, Damascus, nineteenth century.

126 Bath sandals, Damascus, mid-nineteenth century (Museum für Völkerkunde, Berlin: Petermann Collection).

127 Box for toiletries and jewellery, wood, mother-of-pearl inlay in tin setting. Damascus, nineteenth century.

128 Box, cedarwood with camel-bone inlay, Damascus, nineteenth century.

129 Sewing-box in the form of a table, wood with mother-of- pearl, Damascus, nineteenth century.

130 Large chest, walnut, mother-of-pearl inlay in tin setting, cypress motifs, Damascus, nineteenth century.

European style in furnishing. Octagonal, round or star-shaped tables were produced, as well as chests of drawers and cupboards, massive armchairs, cradles, sideboards, folding chairs, screens and large mirror frames. It is impossible to say whether all this products were made for the Syrian upper class, for Europeans living in Syria or for export to Europe (again predominantly to France). The only clues are the occasional inlaid inscriptions. Besides these new products the traditional range of wares continued to be made. The most striking and best known of these are the high-heeled sandals, usually called "bridal shoes", though they were also used for visits to the baths.

The ornamentation follows two different basic patterns:
1. A strictly geometrical tradition, modelled on the inlaid stone floors of Mamluk palaces of the fourteenth and fifteenth centuries. These, for their part, had absorbed influences from Roman and Byzantine floor mosaics. This style of decoration is mainly found in intarsia work in wood using various coloured woods, and in bone inlay.
(I would classify the typical early Islamic interlaced star ornament as a sub-group of this style. It is the most popular decorative motif for large surfaces, such as cupboard doors, screens etc., with mother-of-pearl inlay.)
2. A very simple all-over geometrical decoration (usually consisting of rhombuses), is combined with lavish vegetable forms, such as palmettes, foliage rinceaux, tulip, carnation and peony motifs, and vases. This style of decoration is based on the Ottoman tradition. Pieces of this kind are decorated over the whole surface with mother-of-pearl and are therefore particularly expensive. Today this style is predominantly used for furniture intended for export to the Gulf region.

The decoration of the two basic types can be supplemented in rare instances by inlaid inscriptions in severe *kufic* or remarkably fluid and elegant *naskhi*.

In Damascus we had the opportunity to get to know the business run by Hassan Sami Sanadiki in Hariqa. We were able to ask Mr Sanadiki some questions and observe the work there. This is a family business which has been in existence since 1885. According to the owner, it is the only firm which has continued this craft without interruption even during the period of total disruption of this craft tradition between the two world wars. The present owner runs the firm as both craftsman and businessman. He knows his trade well and calls himself a master. The firm employs forty- two workers, who work six days a week, ten hours a day. Their training takes around six months.

The firm restores old pieces of furniture and makes new ones from the catalogue or after consultation with the client. Here again the models are from the catalogue of the Paris World Exhibition of 1897, which is kept under lock and key and is guarded as a trade secret. Only intarsia work in mother-of-pearl and bone is made.

The production process involves much division of labour. The owner transfers the ornaments onto the body of the piece of furniture using work plans drawn up by computer. According to him his father still worked entirely without models. Some intarsia works are made with the pieces outlined with tin strips, and some have no setting for the mother-of-pearl inlays. In a third variant the mother-of-pearl inlays are surrounded by a wood paste coloured brown, which strongly emphasizes the outlines of the ornament. The assistants specialize in various processes. One, for example, beats in the tin strips; the next cuts up the shells into manageable pieces for polishing; another polishes the pieces with precision using an electric polisher in order to make them fit their positions in the inlay; a last assistant then inserts them. In the past the individual processes were performed in separate workshops. The advantage of this was that no worker knew the complete production process, and the master was not training any competition for himself. Today he complains that his well-trained workers move away or set up their own business, precisely because they know the whole production process. A beginner should be able to inlay about ten pieces in a ten-hour shift, while a very good worker can finish up to five hundred pieces in ten hours, after about two years' experience. The grilles made of turned wood for insertion into tables or chests, for example, are made by a specialist workshop. They are now manufactured on electric lathes, and their quality in comparison with older pieces has declined considerably. The most important wood for furniture is walnut, from the countryside around Damascus. For the turned grilles rosewood, lemonwood or beechwood is used.

There are considerable differences in the quality of mother-of-pearl. Cheap mother-of-pearl, with a matt texture, is obtained from Deir ez-Zor and comes from the Euphrates, while shiny, expensive mother-of-pearl comes from Lake Tiberias. Today mother-of-pearl is imported from Japan and the Philippines; it usually has a greenish sheen. The bone inlays were formerly made of camel bone, but today mainly compressed bone powder is used.

Brocades produced in Damascus are used for covering upholstered furniture. The small patterns of these brocades were in fact patterns from textiles intended for clothing. In the past considerably more robust upholstery textiles especially made in Lebanon were used. Their patterns are reminiscent of art nouveau textiles.

The quality of intarsia work has not suffered because of the technical rationalization of the work processes. On the contrary, the introduction of electric polishers has meant a striking improvement in the precision of the polishing of the mother-of-pearl inlays in comparison with similar pieces from the middle of the last century. Despite this the picture of present-day production has changed considerably in comparison with that of nineteenth-century pieces. Mother-of-pearl can now be imported in any quantity needed and is used as a decorative element in a far more extravagant way than it was in the past. The very fine simple geometric and vegetable relief carvings (especially foliage rinceaux and trefoils), arranged in deliberate alternation, can be produced only by painstaking and time-consuming manual work, and have therefore almost completely disappeared.

On close inspection therefore the "typical traditional Syrian furniture" produced today differs considerably from its predecessors in the nineteenth century. The main purchasers of the modern products are the upwardly mobile Damascene middle class, as well as citizens of the Gulf States, and to a lesser extent tourists. Direct export to Europe plays practically no part at all any more.

The Production of Wood Intarsia

We were also able to observe this production process in a Damascene workshop. It has been even more rationalized than the others. Wooden or plastic rods with a triangular, rectangular or rhomboid shape and with edges measuring about 3-8 mm are bundled together in a pattern about 80 cm to one metre in length, and glued together in rigid wooden casings. After the glue has set, these packets, with a rectangular, square or triangular cross-section, are taken out of their wooden casings and cut on motor saws with very fine blades into slices about one millimetre thick. The outline is then incised to the depth of the thickness of the inlay with a chisel on the object to which it is to be applied. The inlay is applied in one piece and glued on. Then the object is rubbed down with fine sand paper and given a glossy coat of varnish. The differences in quality are mainly due to the materials used. Pieces with real wood are more expensive than those made with plastic as a wood substitute, although to the layman they are mostly indistinguishable. Pieces are considered particularly valuable if they have small mother-of-pearl triangles or rhombuses inserted as well as the wood intarsia. This sort of inlay work cannot be included in the rationalized process of producing wood intarsia described above, since each piece of mother-of-pearl has to be polished and inserted individually. This means that, even though most of the workers in this branch of the process are children and young people, it still involves a considerable extra cost. The process described here is used to make boxes of almost any size required. These are mostly sold in the many souvenir shops. For the domestic market and tourists *taula* (backgammon) boards are made. Next to cards *taula* is one of the most popular leisure activities for men in the coffeehouses. Less common is the production of table tops and supports. The use of mother-of-pearl or bone and wood intarsia side by side for the decoration of furniture seems no longer to be common, though they can be found side by side on pieces dating back to the nineteenth century.

131–134 Production of wood intarsia in Damascus, and inlaid wood boxes.

75

135 & 136 Display case of a silversmith and nielloed silver armlets, contemporary craftsmanship, Deir ez-Zor.

137 A silversmith in his workshop, Deir ez-Zor.

138 & 139 Melting down a silver coin, and the finished silver foil.

The Craft of the Silversmiths

The craft of the silversmiths is becoming extinct today. This is because in Syria, to an even greater extent than in other parts of the Islamic world, jewellery is a form of social security for women. Apart from amulets, cheap glass-bead jewellery, which they can assemble themselves, or jewellery made of natural materials, girls and unmarried women wear no jewellery. The basic provision of jewellery is part of the bride price. It is the inalienable property of the woman, who is completely free to do what she wants with it. After marriage women receive jewellery from their husbands, as Annegret Nippa says, not as a gift but as a reward for their contribution to the family income in the previous year. The production of the silversmiths was therefore always very dependent on the seasons. Peasants bought jewellery for their wives after the harvest, for instance. Today almost everywhere in Syria silver jewellery has been supplanted by gold jewellery made in a style no different from that found in other parts of the Islamic world. This may be explained by the fact that jewellery has largely lost its other function as a sign of being a member of a particular regional or ethnic group. Because of the change from a subsistence to a market economy, which has taken place almost everywhere in Syria, silver has lost its importance as a reserve currency; its value on the world market fluctuates much more, whereas gold is thought to keep its value. Nippa says that in Deir ez-Zor goldsmiths buy their raw material in Aleppo at the world market price. The jewellery is sold for the purchase price plus 20 per cent for labour and a further 10 per cent, depending on the relationship between the seller and purchaser, and the bargaining abilities of the purchaser. A large number of silversmiths have therefore become car mechanics, while a few have made the change to become goldsmiths.

Silversmiths appear to have worked only in Damascus, Aleppo and Deir ez-Zor. Even in travel accounts of the eighteenth and nineteenth centuries there is no mention of the activity of silversmiths in Homs, Hama or the Syrian towns on the Mediterranean coast. Judging by the quantity of silver jewellery that still exists, the number of silversmiths must have been considerable. Today there are still a few old masters working in Damascus, but they now only carry out repair work and have otherwise turned to selling silver jewellery and antiques to tourists, or work as suppliers for antique shops. It is not at all easy, however, to assess the actual number of silversmiths, since the terms silversmith and goldsmith were used synonymously by early travellers. Oberhummer, for example, writes of goldsmiths who make many pretty articles of jewellery, such as brooches, pendants etc. in silver. It may be significant that I have come across a large number of pieces of jewellery, which I believe to have been made around the turn of the century or before, whereas old pieces of gold jewellery, which can be dated with certainty to the last century, are

140 & 142 Aleppine silversmith making a nielloed silver ring, and the stages in its production from blank to the nielloed ring before cleaning.

143 Flintlock pistol with leather holster, and Circassian dagger, nielloed silver mounts. Northern Syria or Turkey, eighteenth / early nineteenth centuries.

extremely rare. On the other hand the explanation for this may be that wives, when they are disowned by their husbands (which seems to have been a more frequent occurrence in the past than it is today) supported themselves by selling their jewellery, which was often their only property. It can be assumed that gold jewellery can be sold more easily, and in such instances would usually be melted down and re-worked.

It is interesting to note that from what we were told in Damascus and Aleppo, as well as from our own observations and the older literature, the craft of the silversmith was practised almost exclusively by Christians. In Damascus these are Catholics and Armenians, and in Aleppo the silversmiths and practically all the goldsmiths are Armenians. Deir ez- Zor is an exception; here Jewish silversmiths were working until the 1930s, when they migrated to Palestine, and there are supposed to have been some Armenian silversmiths in the past as well. Today three out of four silversmiths are Muslims and the fourth is Armenian.

It is difficult to discover a specific regional style in silver jewellery. There is a fluid transition to jewellery from present-day Turkey on the one side and to jewellery from Palestine and Iraq – in particular Mosul – on the other. The most straightforward is the demarcation with respect to the jewellery of the peoples of the Arabian Peninsula, where the style of the jewellery particularly of Saudi Arabia and Oman, is clearly influenced by Yemenite, Jewish silversmiths.

We shall look in detail at the range of jewellery produced by the Syrian silversmiths in the next chapter. Here I shall only draw attention to one technical peculiarity of Syrian silversmiths' work.

The most unusual of the many decorative techniques employed by Syrian silversmiths is niello. Niello is an alloy of silver, copper, lead and sulphur with borax as a flux. The constituents of the alloy are washed, crushed and melted onto the ground metal by firing. Depending on the proportions in the mixture the colour of the niello ranges from blue-black to deep black. After firing it has to be cleaned and polished.

This is a very specialized decorative technique and is found in only a few places in the Islamic world. Niello work is known from the south of Morocco (probably the work of Jewish craftsmen from Tagemout and Taroudant), from the Caucasus, from the city of Mosul in western Iraq, from the city of Bukhara in Uzbekistan, from Herat and Kabul in Afghanistan, and from centres of production in present-day eastern Turkey. In the eleventh and twelfth centuries nielloed silver works were also made in the Ghasnavid empire, with its centre in Afghanistan, and that of the Iranian Seljuks. In Syrian objects niello decoration is used on the mounts of the sheaths and handles of daggers of a type that is clearly Caucasian (best known are the Circassian daggers), on silver mounts for flintlock pistols, on cigarette boxes and cigarette holders, as well as on broad armlets of a type strongly reminiscent of eastern Turkish armlets, on silver rings and on disks sewn on to caps. Its style is very strongly reminiscent of comparable material from the Caucasus. From this it can be assumed that the niello technique, called *minnah* by Syrian craftsmen, was introduced by Armenian or Circassian craftsmen. Further evidence is the fact that from the middle of the last century niello work has been produced by Armenians in Jerusalem, and by Circassians in the Jordanian city of Kerak. The fact that niello work regarded even by the people who make it as an exceptional achievement in craftsmanship is indicated by the fact that niello objects very often bear craftsmen's signatures. (According to S. Weir, p. 61, the armlets with niello decoration were called "Circassian armlets" in southern Jordan. She also mentions that Circassians and Armenians were makers of nielloed jewellery.)

Today niello work is still made in Damascus by a craftsman in the Tekiye, in Aleppo by the Armenian Zare Karagoulian in the Khan el Suchne, and in Deir ez-Zor by Abdallah Sultan and Abdeljabbar el Maslavi. Nielloed armlets, made and signed by craftsmen in Deir ez-Zor, with naive representations of mosques or branches of blossom, often appear on the art and antique market in Damascus. It seems that only the demand from tourists keeps this ancient and sophisticated technique of the silversmiths alive.

144 Armlets, silver, nielloed in the Circassian style. Southern Syria, late nineteenth century, *c.* 1930.

145 Armlets with splint fasteners, appliqué and niello, made in Deir ez-Zor for bedouins, twentieth century.

Syrian Folk Jewellery

Johannes Kalter

By "folk jewellery" I mean the traditional jewellery of the urban, rural and nomadic population of Syria conceived as a cultural region. (Syria, as we have already mentioned, is not here restricted to its present-day national boundaries.) In the period which concerns us members of the urban upper class also wore courtly Ottoman jewellery as well as jewellery imported from Europe, but these will not be discussed in this chapter. As already explained in the chapter on handicrafts, jewellery was the most important possession of all married women. It was given to them as part of their bride-price or in return for their contribution to the family income. Among peasants and nomads this payment in jewellery was made after the end of yearly economic cycle, while for the city-dwellers it depended on the results of the family business. If women themselves were active in business they invested their surpluses in jewellery.

Traditionally the most important material for jewellery was silver, but for poorer people copper and bronze were also used. Silver gilt and gold were less common and used only in exceptional cases. Precious stones played no part in folk jewellery, but semi-precious stones occur occasionally. Cornelian, agate, turquoise and amber were the first

146 Female statue, stone, Palmyra, second/third century AD. All the elements of her jewellery are found in Syrian folk jewellery today.

147 Headdress and dorsal jewellery of a nomad woman in Chan Sheichun.
148 Peasant woman from Chan Sheichun.
149 Bedouin woman who has become sedentary, near Mari.

150 Above and below: headbands of a bedouin woman; centre: headband of
a peasant woman. Damascus or Aleppo, twentieth century.

151 Druze fezes with coin pendants across the forehead and head-discs,
silver filigree.

choice, and magical properties were attributed to them because of their colours. Consequently glass beads of the same colours could be substituted.

Jewellery's function as a savings bank and insurance policy is particularly apparent in the frequent use of unaltered coins as pendants, arranged in rows on headbands, in earrings etc. The economic importance of jewellery is further demonstrated by the fact that it was produced in large quantities meant to be worn as an ensemble. Here the quantity of jewellery and its weight were more important than the quality of the craftsmanship. Temple pendants, armlets and anklets were usually worn in pairs. The most important indication of quality was the silver content. Since no silver was mined in the region, the raw material was obtained by melting down worn-out old jewellery and coins. Besides Ottoman coins, Maria Theresa dollars were particularly popular because of their high silver content. In the present century they were still being struck in Vienna specially for the oriental market. Both Mershen and Weir, writing of Jordan and Palestine respectively, note that since the 1940s the production silver jewellery has been largely supplanted by gold jewellery in a rather uniform style. This is basically due to the drastic economic change in the first half of this century. According to Mershen, in the 1960s the production of silver jewellery in Jordan had largely ceased. According to my sources of information, the substitution of gold for silver jewellery probably took place in Syria at about the same time.

As mentioned in the previous chapter, there are very few silversmiths still working in Syria, in Damascus and Deir ez-Zor. I observed that the silversmiths of Deir ez-Zor can only produce a very limited amount of work because the lack of their raw material, silver. The silversmiths still working today therefore basically restrict themselves to repair work.

It is extremely difficult to draw the line between Syrian folk jewellery and the jewellery of the neighbouring regions, as traditions of late antiquity and Byzantium are still just as apparent as those of the Near East. Syrian jewellery, however, also shows influences of Egyptian, Palestinian and Yemenite jewellery, as well as of jewellery from present-day Turkey, the Caucasus, Iran and Central Asia. The folk jewellery of the region thus reflects Syria's extensive trading contacts and the very heterogeneous composition of the Syrian population. The armlets and anklets especially show types similar to those found all over the Arabian Peninsula and beyond as far as the Arab-influenced East African coast – but there is no connection with the jewellery of Arab North Africa. Antoine Touma's collection, which he bought in Syria, contains many objects which have been classified by Weir as typical of the Palestinian bedouins and are described by Mershen as characteristic of the folk jewellery of Jordan. A large quantity of tightly fitting necklaces consisting of elements chased in matrices are described by Mershen as typical of the Kerak/Madaba region in Jordan. They too are found in

152 Head-disc for sewing on to the fezes of Druze boys, chased silver in poussé-repoussé technique.

this collection. Clearly they were worn all over Syria. Chains of the type called "Jerusalem chains" also make up a sizeable proportion of necklaces found in Syria. Other individual parts too, such as crescent-shaped pendants on jewellery, are found in the same form all over old Bilad esh-Sham (i.e. modern Syria, Jordan, Lebanon and Palestine).

Despite differences in detail, the remarkable uniformity makes it possible to speak of a "Syrian" region in jewellery. This is probably due in part to the fact that this jewellery was only produced at a very few production centres. In Syria these are known to be Damascus, Aleppo and Deir ez-Zor, in Jordan they are Kerak and Irbid, while the most important production centre in Palestine was Jerusalem. Another reason may be the mobility of the craftsmen. As we saw in the previous chapter, the craftsmen were mainly Christians, with a high percentage of Armenians, who had immigrated from regions outside Syria, and Jews. The Jewish element may explain the evident Yemenite influence in Syrian folk jewellery. Another important reason for the uniformity of the jewellery most probably is the mobility of the population, particularly of the nomads.

Few pieces of jewellery are signed by the craftsmen. Our collection includes some from Damascus and Deir ez-Zor. By now it should have become clear that any classification of jewellery according to particular tribes or local groups is extremely difficult, if not impossible. It is more feasible to

give information about the places of production, but this by no means indicates that the jewellery was necessarily worn there as well. In most cases it is possible to categorize the jewellery according to the larger economic sectors – urban, agricultural or pastoral- although here too the transitions from one sector to another are as fluid as the transitions between the economic groups themselves. A nomad woman, who had become sedentary, would still wear her nomadic jewellery. Even the perusal of old travel accounts do not help us any further in finding classifications. Even otherwise meticulous observers only state that there were many silversmiths in Damascus or Aleppo, and that jewellery was commonly worn, but their descriptions are not sufficient for any categorization. To some extent this may be because not much importance was attached to folk jewellery, but it is certainly also due to the fact that male travellers had no opportunity to see women's jewellery, which was mostly hidden under clothing. Even old photographs are not much help. The few surviving photographs which show jewellery being worn, such as those of Bonfils, are studio shots. We cannot assume therefore that the jewellery shown actually belonged with the costumes.

Apart from enhancing the female beauty and simultaneously being an important means of investment (frontal jewellery, ear jewellery, temple jewellery, armlets, anklets, earrings and – for bedouin women – nose rings), jewellery

153 Turban pins, urban jewellery in the Ottoman style. Damascus, nineteenth century.

154 Frontal or dorsal jewellery of bedouins in the region outside Hama, gold and glass stones, twentieth century.

155 Frontal jewellery, silver filigreed or chased, top right with the inscription "Mashallah", below with cypress motifs. Aleppo or Damascus, nineteenth century.

 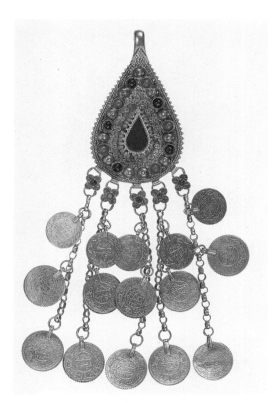 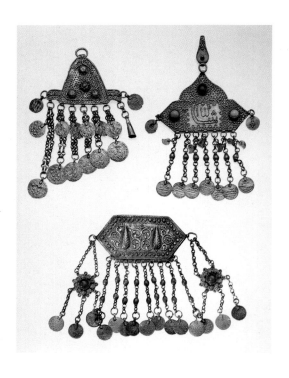

156 Pair of earrings for bedouin women, gold filigree with glass stones, Deir ez-Zor, after 1940.

157 Earrings, silver gilt with coin pendants, corals and glass stones, Damascus, nineteenth century.

158 Temple pendants, gold filigree, said to be the work of Christian goldsmiths from Hama, made for bedouins.

also had another important function: it was used as amulets. Apart from a large number of small amulets, the significance of which in some instances can be traced back to the traditions of the ancient Near East (e.g. holed-disc amulets), there is a large group of typically Islamic amulets, the *hidshabs*. These are containers for texts from the Koran, magic squares or blessings, which may be cylindrical, triangular or rectangular, or – more rarely – round or octagonal in shape. Often they were sewn onto the clothing. More frequently, however, several of them are combined (e.g. triangular and cylindrical shapes) and attached to chains to be worn round the neck or across the shoulder.

The most important type of functional jewellery is the belt. The use of belts is much more widespread in Syria than in most other parts of the Islamic world. The characteristic forms of belts are basically derived from the Ottoman tradition. In particular, the very large, almond- or *boteh*-shaped belt clasps are found in Ottoman folk jewellery as far as the European parts of the former Ottoman Empire (Bulgaria, Greece, Albania).

Just as there are difficulties in ascribing particular forms of jewellery to specific regions, it is also difficult to date them. Some individual pieces in the Touma Collection were certainly made in the eighteenth century, but the majority dates from from the late nineteenth and early twentieth centuries. The basic forms, however, are much

159 Temple pendants, silver, fire-gilded, worn by bedouins, Aleppo, nineteenth century.

160 Frontal amulets, silver, fire-gilded with glass stones, called "eyes", Aleppo, nineteenth century, worn by bedouins.

161 Combined temple and plait jewellery in the Central Asian tradition, for bedouin women, Aleppo or Damascus, nineteenth century.

older. They can frequently be traced back to the time of the Fatimids, Ayubids and Mamluks, that is, to Syrian and Egyptian jewellery from the tenth to the fifteenth century.

Because of these difficulties the most practical way of presenting the jewellery in this catalogue seemed to be by classifying it according to the way it was worn. Any attribution to particular ethnic or religious groups, such as the Kurds or the Druzes, is given only when there is firm evidence. Information about specific production sites is based on workshop inscriptions or plausible information obtained on the spot.

Jewellery worn on the top of the head

The jewellery of the region, as in the rest of the Islamic world, has a marked emphasis on the head. This is not only governed by aesthetic criteria but also has to do with averting the evil eye from the face of the wearer.

Head jewellery

These are round discs worn sewn onto a fez or head-cloth. This form of jewellery is found among the Kurds. According to Berliner and Borchardt, round discs were worn on the headdresses of boys and women. For women's headdresses round, chased plates of sheet-metal, coins or almond-shaped pendants with "eyes" were sewn onto the discs with chains. Boys' jewellery of this type has no pendants. The decoration was either chased in poussé-repoussé or it consisted of very coarse filigree wire and glass stones applied in box settings. One fragment, which can be dated with certainty to the eighteenth century, has floral ornaments and a representation of an eagle in an oval medallion. In terms of quality it can stand comparison with the best pieces of chased Ottoman work of the period. The

162 Pair of temple ornaments, silver, fire-gilded, glass stones, Saraqeb, nineteenth century.

163 Pair of earrings, silver gilt, openwork, eighteenth century.

164 Bedouin earrings, above: gold, Aleppo, nineteenth century; below: silver filigree, Deir ez-Zor, twentieth century.

165 Head-disc for Kurdish women, copper silver-plated, Aleppo (?), nineteenth century.

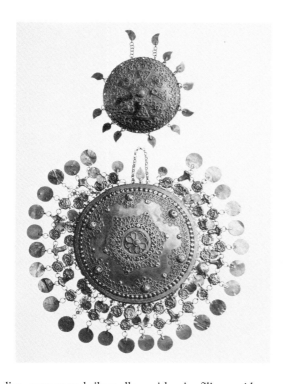

166 Head-disc, copper and silver alloy with wire filigree, Aleppo, nineteenth century.

skullcap-shaped chased metal tops were probably also boys' jewellery and were meant to be sewn onto a fez. They too are noteworthy for their extraordinarily meticulous chasing and should with certainty be dated to the nineteenth century. I know of only one headdress disc with nielloed decoration.

The head-discs of the Druzes are finished with exceptionally fine openwork filigree. They were only worn by women and, as our example shows, were sewn onto their fezes. A row of coins could be attached at the front. On most Druze head-discs one or two rows of glass stones are arranged in circles around a central dome.

The most unusual form of head jewellery is worn by peasant women in the Syrian and Jordanian Hauran, and by bedouin women in the adjoining regions east of Damascus. It consists of heavy articulated chains, which start at the forehead, pass around the whole head and are joined over the head again by another chain. Two further chains are attached to them, hanging down from the temples. At the back a long chain covers the plait. A string of glass beads with silver or gold coins can be attached to the chain around the head. The head chain also has coins, or round metal discs in imitation of coins. The parts along the temples and the pendant on the plait at the back are finished off with larger coins at the end. The coins preferred for this purpose are Maria Theresa dollars. This sort of head jewellery is made in Damascus as bridal jewellery. An example in our collection bears a stamp with the reference Sham (i.e. Damascus) and a workshop stamp of Yosef Abu Adal. As a substitute for this sort of head jewellery poor bedouins sewed gilded copper coins – or imitation coins – onto cotton ribbons.

167 Fragment of a head-disc ornament for Kurds, chased work in poussé-repoussé technique in the Ottoman tradition, eighteenth century.

168 Head-disc ornaments for Druze women, silver filigree, Damascus, nineteenth century.

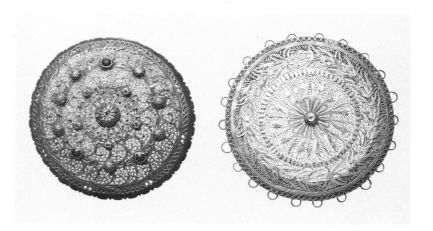

169 Head-disc jewellery for Druzes, chased silver, Aleppo, eighteenth/nineteenth centuries.

170 Necklace for bedouin women, gold with blue glass stones, Hama or Aleppo, c. 1940.

Bedouins and peasants all over Syria wear chains or articulated diadems with one to five rows of chains. These have fringes made of discs, crescents or almond leaves, and are held in triangular ends. They are either attached to the head-cloths by hooks or are sewn onto them. The ends (and the subdividing middle part, if there is one) are set with blue and red glass beads. A combination of blue and red beads is generally preferred for the headdress. Chains and articulated diadems very similar to these are found in the jewellery of the Turcomans, who call them *sunsule*. In Syria they are occasionally referred to as *sinsal*. Most probably they are derived from Turcoman jewellery. Some other very similar types of jewellery should also be noted in this connection, terminating at one end with an acute triangle with a hook, and at the other with a more obtuse triangle with a ring. They were worn in pairs, attached at the temples and joined at the back of the headdress.

A combination of frontal and head jewellery is represented by triangles terminating in hooks and hangings with slender chains and almond-shaped pendants attached about half way up. This type of jewellery is hung on the side of the head-cloth, and the narrow chains are brought to the middle of the forehead.

One very unusual form of combined jewellery is said to originate among the bedouins near Deir ez-Zor. It consists of triangular temple pendants, from which longer plait hangings emerge at the side, and are linked by a chain, creating the effect of a necklace. To my knowledge this type of combined jewellery is only worn elsewhere by the Uzbek Khivas.

Another type of temple pendant consists of triangles attached to chains or cotton ribbons mounted with chased silver appliqué. Older gilded work with filigree and glass stones have pendant chains with coins attached to the triangles in such a way that they end at a slant and so emphasize the outline of the face. The most striking effect, however is created by silver plates from which nine chains consisting of chased elements hang in staggered formation. These are extremely rare. They were probably made in Aleppo and recall temple pendants in Egyptian paintings of the Middle Kingdom.

On the other hand the temple pendants in the shape of a *qubba* (tomb) are clearly in the Islamic tradition. A hexagonal silver fire-gilded plate with a chased decoration of cypresses, most probably is also a temple pendant and not, as its later mount might suggest, the centre of a necklace.

Tear-shaped elements set with glass beads, and round and crescent- shaped pendants with spherical attachments were worn as amulets in the middle of the forehead. They are generally gilded and particularly well- crafted. Some pieces were made of gold with filigree and granulated ornaments. The centre is always marked by a blue turquoise of blue glass paste called the "eye" or "counter-eye". They were associated with the idea of the evil eye.

The concept of the evil eye goes back to ancient times and originated in the Mediterranean region. It is wide-

171 & 172 Woman with combined head and dorsal jewellery and examples of this jewellery. Damascene work. Bridal jewellery for bedouins and peasants in southern Syria.

173 Necklace for a bedouin girl, beadwork with silver amulets, southern Syria.

174 Necklaces for bedouin girls, twentieth century.

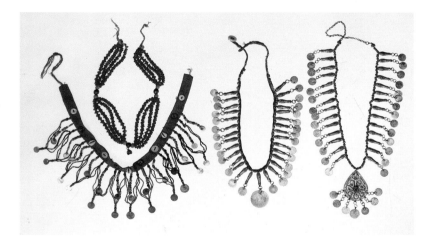

175 Bedouin jewellery; the neck ring made of wire interlace and the pair of copper armlets (right) were collected by Euting in the last century. The jewellery with cowrie shells and shell pendants functions as an amulet.

spread throughout Islamic world. Believers in the evil eye maintain that some people are able to cause sickness, misfortune or damage to property merely by an envious or resentful look. Much of Islamic amulet lore is based on the need to use all possible means to protect oneself against this evil eye.

The dorsal plait pendants worn by Kurds and bedouins have no parallels in Arab jewellery tradition. Like many other elements in Syrian folk jewellery they must have been adopted from central Asia. This is clearest in the case of dorsal plait pendants when they are made up of four chains held in filigree silver semicircles and ending in triangular pendants. The number of these amulet cases matches the number of children (i.e. sons). Today this form of jewellery is no longer in use. Formerly it was worn by peasants and bedouin in the Jezira in eastern Syria.

Earrings and False Earrings

The Touma Collection contains only a few earrings. The stirrup earrings, which are almost circular in shape, with balls and tear-shapes in the lower part, terminating in coin pendants, are part of a general Islamic tradition. Other forms, which are reminiscent of padlocks, go back even further, to Byzantine prototypes. They have a movable clip attached by a cotter to the cast part, and are always gilded and set with blue stones, which are sometimes framed with red stones. On earlier pieces these are turquoises and coral, but in more recent examples glass beads are substituted. Hemispherical, partly gilded earrings with fine filigree are a type found among the Kurds of northern Syria, and are very uniform in style. They generally have almond-shaped pendants and may be set with glass stones or turquoises. A similar craft tradition, although with extremely fine workmanship, is represented by a pair of earrings supposed to have been made at Deir ez-Zor about forty years ago. As Berliner and Borchardt noted, this similarity may be due to the fact that filigree work for the Kurds was made by Jews. The same is said of the silversmiths in Deir ez-Zor. The most unusual form of earring is represented by a pair with slender, raised cups, made of two chased parts joined together, with a very curved clip. In the middle of the cup is a vertical rhombus, which at first sight seems to be filigreed, but in fact is made of sheet metal decorated with chiselled holes. The centre of the rhombus holds a blue stone. This pair should be dated to the nineteenth century, possibly even to the eighteenth.

176 & 177 Frontal and temple bands. Both forms of jewellery were worn by peasant and bedouin women, and are derived from the traditional jewellery of the Turcomans of Central Asia. Aleppo and Damascus, nineteenth/twentieth centuries.

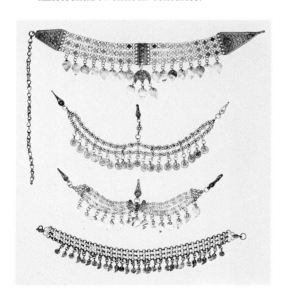

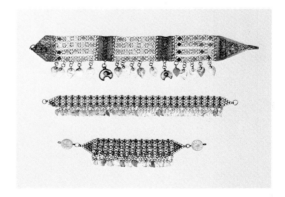

178 Plait hanging made of cast silver beads with coin pendants, Aleppo, nineteenth century.

179 Neck ring in Deir ez-Zor, made for bedouins. Silver with glass beads, *c.* 1940.

180 Neck ring, worn by Assyrians, Christian bedouins from the border area between Syria and Iraq, *c.* 1900.

181 Pectoral jewellery, fire-gilded silver, with blue glass stones. Peasant jewellery from the region around Saraqeb, made in Aleppo, mid-nineteenth century.

182 Neck band, silver filigree, Aleppo, nineteenth century.

183 Necklace, silver gilt with coin pendants, made in Aleppo, mid-nineteenth century, for peasant women and bedouin women.

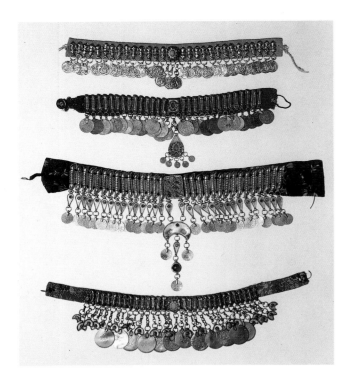

184 Neck bands composed of elements chased in matrices, sewn on to cotton ribbons, mounted. Gold, silver gilt and silver. They were worn by women in the cities and villages as well as by nomads, and differ only in the fineness of their execution. Damascus and Aleppo, nineteenth/twentieth centuries.

Neck and Pectoral Jewellery

Close-fitting, twisted neck-rings with S-hook clasps and five to seven chain pendants with crescents or coins at the ends are common only among the bedouins of the Jezira. They have disappeared from Syrian folk jewellery today. One particularly interesting example with a simple cast cross as the middle pendant, was worn by women of the Chaldaean (Christian) bedouin women, who had migrated to Syria from Iraq in the last century. Closely related to the form of these neck-rings are metal neck bands made of interlaced silver rings with a large clasp plate at the front, held together by a cotter-fastener. They also have chain pendants. The middle chain pendant in our example, which was collected by Euting in Syria in the 1860s, is shaped like a Koran table.

They represent the most common form of Syrian neck jewellery and were worn by city-dwellers, peasants and nomads alike. Individual elements, suggesting the larvae of beetles or butterflies, are chased in matrices. Rings, coins, crescent- or almond-shaped pendants are attached to these elements by means of eyes. The centre is always emphasized. The individual parts were purchased directly from the silversmith by the women, who themselves sewed them onto the velvet or cotton bands. The parts were made in both Damascus and Aleppo. Pieces made for the various population groups mentioned above can be distinguished by the quality of execution or the type of material used.

There are chased parts in gold, silver gilt and silver of various qualities. Since the 1930s close-fitting neck bands of this type for bedouin women have sometimes been replaced by bead embroideries.

Neck jewellery elements consisting of two round discs, each mounted with symmetrically placed crescents and usually gilded with filigree, are derived, I believe, from the Ottoman craft tradition and are influenced by forms of European costume jewellery. They too have chains with coin pendants, or, in simpler versions, with round plates of sheet silver used as imitation coins. Here again there is a striking recurrence of the numbers three and five (and of no others). These silver parts are worn attached to cotton or silk cords around the neck. Close-fitting chains with triangular and rectangular elements with coarse filigree are in the same craft tradition. Their central piece was in the shape of a crescent moon pointing upwards and surmounted by a triangle. Chains with blossom-shaped elements and triangular pendants at the ends hang from these neck bands.

Longer neck chains, which may be worn over the breast, are characterized by a wide variety of different chains. These range from large interlaced rings to chain links suggesting clematis blossom. Pieces of jewellery of this type always have the function of amulets. They end in triangular pendants with blue glass beads or stones. Attached to the sides may be a large number of individual elements, each of which is acquired in a particular situation in life and is supposed to protect the woman wearing it from specific dangers.

Necklaces consisting of three to five rows, articulated with rectangles and terminating in triangles, are in the tradition of European Baroque jewellery. Their only oriental features are details such as the crescents and holed-disc amulets hanging from the bottom row, the preference for blue glass beads or highly stylized hand pendants on the chains. These complex forms of pectoral jewellery are worn by women in the cities as well as in the villages. Among bedouin women necklaces with coins, usually consisting of a single row, predominate. Glass beads may be strung between the coins.

More ambitious craftsmanship than is usually found in Syrian neck jewellery can be seen in articulated chains with fastened cast openwork balls, which are occasionally silvered. They were produced during the last century in Aleppo.

Typical examples of bedouin jewellery are the necklaces with one or two rows strung with glass beads, amber beads or coral. They are also very popular in Jordan. The amber was either imported from the Caspian Sea or found at the Yarmuk, while most of the coral probably comes from the Indian Ocean.

Besides having an ornamental function, neck jewellery in particular always possesses specific properties as an amulet. The significance of colours, shapes and the connection between number symbolism and amulets will be

185—188 Left: rural and urban armlets in a rather Ottoman tradition. The pieces above were produced by Jewish silversmiths in Deir ez-Zor before 1930; those below in Aleppo or Damascus between 1870 and 1930.

189—191 Right: armlets and, in the bottom picture, anklets for nomads; they are similar in style to the nomad jewellery of the Arabian Peninsula. Some of the forms can be traced back to the Mamluk period. The pair at the top right bear the workshop signature of a Christian Damascene silversmith. All were made in Damascus, late nineteenth / early twentieth centuries.

discussed below. Here I shall only mention one particularly striking example of this type of pectoral jewellery amulets. These are pectorals worn by peasant women in Sarakeb in northern Syria, and have three rows and end in triangles. In the middle is a large round disc with chased ornaments. The centre of this disc is formed of an unusually large, luminous blue glass bead, which is surrounded by a garland of small glass beads in the chased bosses.

Arm and Ankle Jewellery

It may seem surprising to deal with jewellery worn on arms and ankles in a single section, but this is justified because those wearing Syrian folk jewellery have never conformed to the systematic approach of ethnologists or jewellery collectors. In principle, anything that can be worn on the arms can also be worn around the ankles. Indications are given by the diameter of the individual pieces. This too is relative, since what fits a strong wrist can also fit a slender ankle.

Strong armlets cast in copper, bronze or silver with integral relief decoration, ranging from bosses (three to five in number) to diagonal fluting, are worn by bedouins all over the region extending from Negev, through Palestine, Jordan and Syria, as far as Iraq. Their shape can be traced back to the Ayubid period. One of the production centres was Damascus. The stamp on a silver armlet in the Touma Collection gives the silver content as 80 per cent and names the place of production as Sham (i.e. Damascus), while the silversmith is identified by his stamp as Fara. The most important consideration for purchasing these armlets was probably capital investment, so their weight and silver content were of greatest importance.

All women wore armlets consisting of two silver rods, either angular or round, twisted together and terminating either in cast polygons (usually with fourteen sides) or forged silver triangles. A blue glass bead is applied at one of the triangular ends, and a red one at the other. The models for this type of armlet, which is called "the twisted" most probably came from the Egyptian jewellery tradition, although the armlets are said to have been made in Damascus. These armlets normally have a very high silver content, and the women usually bought them by weight. The anklets are similar in form. The collection includes hollow bangles with a round cross-section and polygonal ends. Particularly interesting is an example with unusually fine niello work. The basic shape of this type of anklet is found throughout almost all the Arabian Peninsula, among the Muslim population of the East African coast, in the Islamic part of Ethiopia, as well as among the Tuareg of the central Sahara. An interesting variant is a heavy gilded anklet, which looks as if it is twisted but is in fact cast in this shape. A closed anklet with a cotter fastener and a safety chain, is more closely related to Indian jewellery, while a

gilded, anklet cast with snake heads at the ends should be dated to the early Ottoman, if not to the Timurid period.

Narrow, flat armbands with hinges, elaborately concealed cotter fasteners, and niello decoration originate in the Caucasian or East Anatolian jewellery tradition. They were generally made by Armenian or Circassian silversmiths. In the niello decoration simple rinceaux and flower motifs predominate, and occasionally the areas without niello decoration have gilded flowers cut from sheet metal attached with rivets. The cotters may have rings attached to prevent them from being lost. The eye of the cotter often contains a turquoise. One example acquired in Syria has a stamp indicating that it was made in the eastern Anatolian city of Van, but armlets of this type are also supposed to have been made in Aleppo and Damascus, and at Kerak in Jordan. The edges of earlier armlets are formed of silver beading, chased in matrices and soldered to the piece. A very recent variant (probably not produced before the 1950s) consists of very narrow armlets with simple hook fasteners and niello decoration.

Cuffs are also common, following the same principles of production but in a broader version. The earliest examples are still in the classic Ottoman tradition and are characterized by a meticulous filigree application in the centre of rectangular fields. The corners of the fields are then marked by small turquoises. Armlets of this type are supposed to have been made in Damascus. A variant produced in Deir ez-Zor for bedouins has coarser workmanship but follows the same principles of design. At first sight the most striking difference is that the individual fields of ornament are framed by alternating blue and red beads. Nielloed cuffs of the same basic form were made in Deir ez-Zor in recent times. Their decoration is divided in two by a hinge and cotter. The favourite designs are simple blossom motifs or naive representations of mosques flanked by trees. The ridges concealing the cotter fastening bear workshop stamps, such as that of Abdel Jaffer el Muslawi, one of the three silversmiths in Deir ez-Zor still producing nielloed armlets. Another type of cuff crafted at Deir ez-Zor has no hinge, only a cotter fastener, which is passed through interlocking eyes. The decoration of these armlets consists of applied rows of beads and undecorated sheet silver cut in hexagonal or polygonal shapes. This type is supposed to have been produced in Deir ez-Zor between 1880 and 1930 for bedouins of the surrounding countryside.

Armlets with hinge-and-cotter fastenings and a triangular cross-section come from Deir ez-Zor as well. The body of the armlet is wrought into shape. Triangles with three cast hemispheres are applied and the armlet is closed with a clasp plate. The joints are concealed with strips of beaded wire. The rhomboid cover of cotter is subdivided by five glass beads arranged in a cross shape.

More ambitious craftsmanship is evident in armlets of a similar basic shape with hemispheres decorated with either applied filigree or false granulation. In this case the rectangular cotter fastening is embellished with blossoms. This can also be made of false granulation, with only a single turquoise in its centre or blossoms made of turquoises in box settings. Narrow armlets with cotter fastenings and hinges, sometimes only sparsely decorated, seem to be worn by all sections of the population. They have irregular sheet-metal appliqué cut-outs and blossoms, which may be dated with chiselled openwork, or else have simple filigree of gallery wire on a metal ground, or openwork filigree. The form of fastening of the more complex versions, which presumably were worn in cities, follow European models probably adopted from Ottoman Turkey.

Rings can be worn on all fingers of both hands (but not on the thumbs). However, nothing distinguishes them from rings worn in the neighbouring regions. There are examples with glass stones or semi-precious stones, semi-precious stones in rectangular or round box settings, coin rings, cast rings with inscriptions and, since the 1930s, also with niello decoration. They are not discussed here.

Belt Fasteners and Belts

Under Ottoman and Kurdish influence the use of belts became more widespread in Syria than in other parts of the Arab world. The most impressive belt fasteners consist of two parts; large *botehs* or almonds joined together at their blunt ends. The hooks are concealed by a boss. Inside the *boteh* is a smaller *boteh* which has red glass beads in box setting. One example has surface decoration in repoussé technique, the other in false granulation. These fasteners were used for Kurdish men's belts made of leather. In a much smaller form, with chain hangings and crescents or coins at the ends, such *boteh*-shaped fasteners are found on belts worn by peasants, nomads and town-dwellers throughout Syria. Examples from Deir ez-Zor can be recognized by their very plain wire filigree. Damascene and Aleppine works are characterized by a very small-scale, finely worked open filigree. A coloured foil, usually red, is applied to the ground metal. Variants of these urban clasps with fine filigree ornaments are found in various shapes: hour-glasses, trefoils reminiscent of diadems, and extended oblongs. The cover of the fastening hook may be topped by a representation of a bird. Two types of birds occur: one has a shape and pose suggesting a dove, the other also resembles a dove except that it has a crest – it may be intended to be a hoopoe. Doves bring *baraka*, that is, divine blessings, power and luck. Today doves are still released at weddings. In the Islamic tradition the hoopoe is the messenger of love between Solomon and the Queen of Sheba. The fasteners described here form part of women's belts and are mounted on strips of velvet. Other decorations on these belts consist of S-shaped filigree applications, which are held onto the belt with clips. Generally these belts were part of the costume of urban women. Most examples in the collection must have been produced between the first half of the nineteenth century and around

1930. Belts of this type, which were probably always very expensive, were, however, also worn by well-to-do peasant and bedouin women.

Belt fasteners consisting of two round discs linked by a hook, which may be covered with a small boss, also originate in the Kurdish jewellery tradition. Older pieces of this type have integral cast relief decoration with radiating segmentation of the discs and emphasis on the centre. They can certainly be dated to the first half of the nineteenth century. Other discs made of repoussé or poussé-repoussé silver, or occasionally silver-gilt, are stylistically very similar to the Kurdish headdresses described at the beginning of this chapter. They must have been produced from the mid-nineteenth century until the 1920s or 1930s.

Tripartite belt fasteners, with a basic shape recalling diadems, made of fire-gilded silver with openwork decoration, filigreed bosses and coloured glass stones, were produced in Deir ez-Zor during the last century. Although this type of fastener is supposed originally to have been worn by Chaldaean Christians who migrated from Iraq, the bedouins of eastern Syria seem to have adopted it. Its general design is in the tradition of Byzantine jewellery.

Quite often filigreed fasteners are found in connection with belts composed of broad articulated chains of a type for which there is evidence among the Jordanian and southern Syrian bedouins. The coin pendants attached to these belts are another indication that they were worn by the bedouins.

A leather belt with octagonal silver plate in the middle, appliqué chased elements with obtuse angles and glass stones at the ends, all fire-gilded, was probably used by bedouin in eastern Syria as a circumcision belt for boys about twelve years of age.

Belts of very fine woven silver wire with cast fasteners and cast reinforcements around the eyes are derived from the Ottoman jewellery tradition. The relief decoration on the fastener has features typical of the Ottoman period. Belts of this type were only worn in the cities. Our piece can be dated to approximately 1880 and is supposed to have been made in Damascus, where the production of these belts continued until very recent times.

192 Rings, silver with glass stones. Decorated with twisted wire and imitation granulation. The style is similar to the work of Jewish Yemenite silversmiths, nineteenth century.

193 Rings with niello decoration and glass stones, c. 1940. The ring with the little gilded leaves was made for bedouins, nineteenth century.

194 Belts worn by women in the cities and villages, as well as by nomads. Above: chased, gilded silver elements on leather, eastern Syria; centre left: plaited silver belt in the Ottoman style, with workshop mark; centre right: articulated belt for bedouin and peasant women of southern Syria, Damascus, c. 1900; bottom: urban belts, silver filigree elements mounted on velvet, Damascus, nineteenth century.

195 Belt fastenings, silver, Aleppo, nineteenth century.

198 Right: belt fastening, silver, fire-gilded and filigreed, with glass stones. This type was originally worn by Chaldaean Christian immigrants from Iraq. Around the turn of the century it was produced in Deir ez-Zor for the bedouins of eastern Syria.

199 Right: belt fastenings; above: silver granulated, below: chased silver. Made in Aleppo in the nineteenth century for Kurdish men.

196 & 197 Belt fastenings worn by Kurdish men, cast and chased in the Ottoman style, Aleppo, nineteenth century.

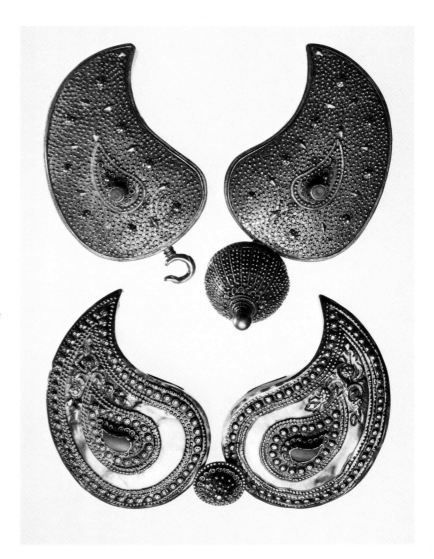

Amulets and Jewellery mainly functioning as Amulets

I define amulets as pieces of jewellery which because of special properties are supposed to protect the people wearing them from misfortune and/or bring him or her magic power and luck. Even today scholars ascribe the use of amulets to superstitious practices and belief. In my opinion such an interpretation is inaccurate. People use amulets to protect themselves from dangers against which they would otherwise have no defence, such as death, lightning, falls, wounds in an ambush etc., as well as from illnesses for which there is no clear cause. In this respect the wearing of amulets is a thoroughly rational attempt to find a way to solve every-day problems. The amulets derive some of their efficacy from the trust placed in them. For example, the course of psychosomatic illnesses nature can be decisively influenced by wearing amulets. A person wearing a love amulet treats the person who is the object of his or her desire more openly and naturally. This certainly makes contact easier. Even from an objective point of view a person wearing an amulet as protection against injury reduces the risk of an accident.

Objections to the use of amulets have always been raised by orthodox Muslim theologians, but they were never able to impose their ideas. This was because the supporters of their use based their arguments on the Koran, particularly the 114th *sura*: 'Men. In the name of God, the Compassionate, the Merciful. 1. Say: I seek refuge in the Lord of men, 2 the King of men, 3 the God of men, 4 from the mischief of the slinking prompter 5 who whispers in the hearts of men; 6 from jinn and men.'

The commonest reasons for wearing amulets are fear of the evil eye and fear of jinns. Jinns are dwarf-like, non-terrestrial beings made of fire or air or a mixture of both, who frighten people at night, and can also cause diseases in domestic animals and human beings, destroy crops. Children are particularly endangered by jinns.

People use amulets to drive away such general fears. A large number of amulets are specific to particular regions or are very precisely tailored to the needs of the particular person wearing them (male or female). As a rule the only way to find out about such needs is through field research, but one should bear in mind that the people wearing amulets themselves often no longer know why they wear them. Even if they do they will not always be willing to give information on this subject, partly because the use of amulets is now often regarded by Muslims themselves as backward and superstitious.

A typical Islamic amulet is normally made of several active components. I can best illustrate this by taking a triangular case containing a written amulet as an example.

The efficacy of an amulet may be derived from its shape. The triangle as a symbol of female fertility is one of the oldest shapes used as an amulet. The idea was already widespread around the Mediterranean in antiquity. Its influence can be found, for example, in the representation of the eye of God set in a triangle.

The material is also important. This case is made of silver, which is regarded as the pure metal subordinate to the moon, and has a beneficial effect on the person wearing it. Blue turquoises or glass stones may be attached to the container as a protection against the evil eye, on the principle that like must drive out like, since the evil eye is believed to be particularly prevalent in blue eyes. As well as blue stones red ones are frequently found. Red is the colour of blood, and the wearing of red glass beads or stones is a protection against sudden haemorrhages, miscarriages or injuries. Pieces of sheet metal or coins hang from the amulet case itself, and usually from the chain as well. The noise they make is supposed to drive away evil spirits.

The number of stones on an amulet holder can also have a magical significance, as can the number of pendant chains and coins. Five pendants, or five stones attached to the container signify the five fingers of the hand that protects and blesses, and also averts evil. The use of the hand as an amulet also goes back to pre-Islamic times. Hands as a sign for warding off evil are found in Palaeolithic cave paintings in Franco-Cantabrian culture. By the time of the rise of the three great monotheistic oriental religions it was too deeply rooted in popular belief to be suppressed, and was therefore integrated into them. Oriental Jews, Christians and Muslims all wore hand amulets. To the Jews they represented the "Hand of God", to the Eastern Christians the "Hand of Mary", while Muslims call them the "Hand of Fatima", after the favourite daughter of the Prophet whose male descendants were the only continuation of the Prophet's line.

Apart from this popular interpretation of the hand – or the number five symbolizing the hand – another interpretation of the number five exists in Islamic theology. According to this the number five symbolizes the five pillars of Islam (i.e. the five religious duties of Muslims): 1. the confession of faith; 2. the duty to pray five times a day; 3. the alms tax; 4. the fast in the month of Ramadan; and 5. the pilgrimage to Mecca.

Other numbers, however, can also be significant in amulets: the number seven for the planets, or the number twelve for the signs of the zodiac, or, in the case of Shi'ite Muslims, the twelve imams.

From this example of a triangular amulet holder we can therefore see that the shape, material, colour of the applied stones, the number of stones are all effective. The most important element, however, is the written amulet kept in the container. There are standard texts for this purpose. One of these is the *fatiha*, the opening *sura* of the Koran: "In the name of God, the compassionate, the merciful.* Praise be to God, the Lord of mankind throughout the world,* the compassionate, the merciful,* who will reign on the Day of Judgement!* We serve you and we ask you for help.* Guide us to the straight path,* the path of those to whom you have shown your favour, not of those who have incurred your wrath and go astray." Another is the Throne Verse: "God. There is no god but Him, the Living, the Eternal One. Neither slumber nor sleep overtakes him. To him belongs what is in heaven and on earth. Who could intercede with Him except by His permission? He knows what is before and behind them. But they know nothing of it – except what he wills. His throne extends far above the heavens and the earth, and the preservation of both does not weary him. He is the exalted and immense one." *sura* 2, 255 (256).

There are printed amulet texts, often containing a mixture of various passages from the Koran, prayers for protection, as well as representations of snakes, scorpions, birds etc. Even today there are still wise men experienced in the lore of amulets. They are usually addressed respectfully as *sheikh*, even though they are not leaders of a religious community. They write special amulet texts to suit the particular needs of the individual seeking their advice. In her study "Untersuchungen zum Schriftamulett und seinem Gebrauch in Jordanien" (1983) Birgit Mershen describes a general characteristic of the amulet writers: "The preparation of texts and amulets is an activity which can only be practised by particular individuals. If one looks at the composition of this group of people one can see that it is not homogeneous. One must distinguish between male and female writers of amulets. Male amulet writers are often clerics who obtained the power to heal or to practise other magic because of their great age or their religious office. Through constant contact with the Koran they have come into possession of *baraka*, the magic power of blessing, which plays a very important role in popular belief throughout the Islamic world." Mershen cites various old sources indicating a widespread conviction that the members of particular ethnic groups, such as the Moroccans and the Egyptians, had particular gifts in the practice of magic.

200 Necklace with triangular amulet, coins, cornelians and glass stones, made in Damascus for bedouins in southern Syria, nineteenth century.

203 Amulets, cornelians and glass stones in silver settings. In the centre an eye to ward off the evil eye. Nineteenth century.

201 Amulet for a townswoman, gold stamped with the Islamic confession of faith, names of Allah, and an allusion to the Throne Verse. Damascus, mid-eighteenth century.

202 Man's amulet with prayer for protection sewn in, eye and hand, Damascus.

204 & 205 Amulet holders, left: for peasants and bedouins; right: urban, silver, chased and filigree, Damascus or Aleppo, nineteenth century.

206 Amulet chains for peasants and bedouins. The form of the case is reduced to a triangle, nineteenth century.

207 Shoulder amulet with triangle and cylindrical cases, Deir ez-Zor, *c.* 1900.

208 & 209 Front and back of chased amulet holders decorated with the Seal of Solomon and the inscription "Mashallah". Damascus, nineteenth century.

210 Rectangular amulet holders, silver filigree on the back, fastener plate inscribed with "Mashallah" in strict kufic.

211–213 Cylindrical amulet holders with coin, crescent, holed-disc or almond-shaped pendants were the most common form. They were worn by women of all social groups. Here the various different forms are illustrated. The filigree-like chain is called a "Jerusalem chain".

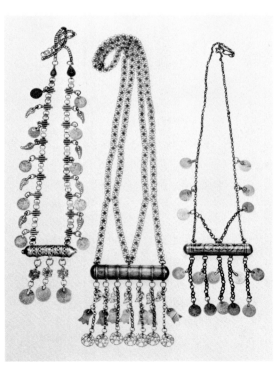

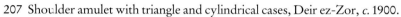

She points out that men were not the only amulet writers. Women too formed a considerable proportion of magicians in the Syria-Palestinian region. "Like her male colleagues, the *sheikha* based her abilities mostly on her possession of *baraka*, with which she was born, or which she had acquired by performing various religious activities, such as the continual recitation of the Koran, pilgrimages or vocational experiences. The possession of magic books, particularly if these were old, played a decisive role in the recognition accorded her as an amulet writers, just as they did for men." Mershen goes on to say that women often referred back to their practical knowledge passed down to them by their mothers and grandmothers. "In particular, magical practices connected with the protection of the family – especially young children – from the evil eye and the jinn are supposed to be part of female knowledge and women's responsibility." In the company of Mrs Mershen I was able to visit a *sheikh* in a village near Irbid. He owned a number old amulet books, from which he selected amulet texts according to the specific needs of the person asking for help.

It is often difficult to decode amulet texts. Besides Koranic texts and prayers for protection they may also contain magic squares. The sum of the digits which results from adding up the figures in the boxes may refer to a particular passage in the Koran.

Although the design of a text amulet holder was based on a wide range of ideas going back far into pre-Islamic time, it is reasonable to call this type, known as a *hidshab*, the most Islamic of all forms of amulet. Apart from triangular amulet holders, rectangular and cylindrical ones can also be found. Frequently large triangular or rectangular cases are attached to chains, together with small cylindrical ones, or the cylindrical holders are combined with a large triangle. It is not uncommon for one of the types of amulet described to act as a substitute for its contents. In this instance the amulet is cast in solid metal. Others may be so small that no text can be inserted. Only a few cases can be opened. Most of them are soldered shut. consequently the person wearing the amulet does not know for certain whether the container does actually contain a text, and, if so, which one. Evidence that the shape of the amulet holder can act as a substitute for its contents is provided by archaeological finds from graves dating from the ninth and tenth centuries. Amulet holders do not have a merely decorative function. Birgit Mershen has pointed out that written amulets, if they are not to lose their effectiveness, need a covering to protect the text from harmful influences. This is also intended to prevent the text from being unfolded and read, since its efficacy would then be lost.

Inscribed Amulets and Amulet Cases Containing Texts

The manner of wearing a written amulet differs depending on who is wearing it and how big the amulet case is. Small amulets are sewn in pairs onto the shoulders of boy's clothes. Boys start wearing these amulets when the first down appears on their chins. Larger amulet cases, usually a combination of triangular and cylindrical shapes are worn by women as a necklace. Very long chains are an indication that the amulets are worn as a shoulder strap. The chain runs across the right shoulder. The amulet case is worn under the left armpit or the left upper arm. Very large cylindrical amulet cases with a triangular amulet attached above them, are usually hung up in the living room.

Amulet texts for men are often simply sewn into a piece of cloth in a triangular shape; this cloth amulet is then worn under the armpit and may have "eye"-amulets and "hand"-amulets attached to it.

Inscribed amulets with engraved or stamped decoration are very closely related to amulet holders containing texts. They are found in the shape of a ragged leaf, triangular, tear-shaped, with a curved rim, or smooth, circular, rectangular, or even in the form of a Koran table. Because of the method of production the texts used here are much more stereotyped than the texts of such amulets handwritten on paper.Most common is the *fatiha*, the Throne Verse, or simply the formula *mashallah* ("as God wills"). Here too the preferred material is silver. In the urban context gold amulets are also found. Their shape is very similar to Iranian amulets of the Kajar period. The apotropaic powers of these amulets can be further enhanced by the application of blue glass beads, or by five pendants with crescents set with glass beads. In examples where the complete montage of chains on these amulets is preserved, it can be seen that even these amulets were usually worn in combination with blue holed-disc amulets, coin pendants and small cylindrical amulet capsules on the chain. A rhomboid pendant with nielloed silver inscription is also certainly an amulet, and at the same time functions as a birth certificate giving the date of birth of the wearer. The inscription says that the young Ridwan, son of Yusuf el-Harif was born on 27 Rabbi I 1386 (i.e. 15 July 1966).

A popular form of children's amulet are animals' teeth, particularly the teeth of hyenas. As a rule two teeth are mounted together to form a crescent, with two or three chains which have coin pendants. The silver mount often has a blue glass bead. These are analogous to the amulets of southern Europe described by Seligmann in *Der böse Blick und Verwandtes*, which are certainly also related to amulets against the evil eye. At the same time the idea of male fertility plays an important role. Teeth are regarded as phallic symbols.

I am grateful to my colleague Birgit Mershen for the information that toad-shaped pendants, which are popular especially in bedouin jewellery, are to be regarded as

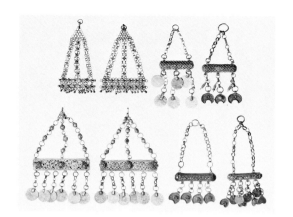

214 Shoulder amulets for boys. They are sewn in pairs on to the shirt. Aleppo and Damascus, nineteenth century.

215 & 216 Amulet chains and inscribed amulet pendants with invocations to Allah, Koranic texts and magic squares, twentieth century.

217 Inscribed amulets in the shape of teardrops and leaves, including the opening *sura* of the Koran and the Throne Verse, nineteenth/twentieth centuries. Below: amulet cast in bronze in the form of a tablet, twelfth century. A nielloed inscription is on the rhombus-shaped silver pendant: a "birth certificate" of a boy born on 18 July 1966.

218 Cross from the Qalamoun Mountains and medallion with a Madonna from Zednaya, blue holed-disc amulet, *c.* 1900.

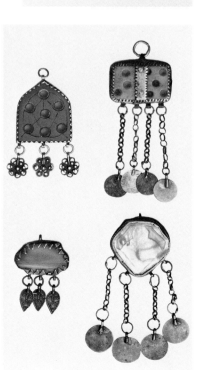

219 Silver-mounted hyena teeth. Boys' amulets intended to bring fertility and protect against the evil eye. Nineteenth/twentieth centuries.

220 Amulet pendants, stone, bone and polished mother-of-pearl in silver mounts, nineteenth/twentieth centuries.

amulets to promote growth in addition to being connected with the idea of female fertility. They are worn on amulet chains or pearl necklaces for girls or young women, although another amulet chain from the Touma Collection suggests that they were probably also used for boys. This may be because toad amulets were also used for teething problems.

Just how various the function of combined amulets can be is demonstrated by a chain (also from the Touma Collection) with a toad pendant hanging from its centre. On each side of the toad is a series of miniature charms: on one side a miniature set of bellows, perhaps an indication that the house of the wearer should never be short of fuel; a sword, showing that the wearer himself should become a bold fighter, or in the case of a female wearer, that she should have brave sons; tongs, like those used to apply the hot coals for hookahs; a sheep, perhaps expressing the wish to have large and healthy herds; a pair of scissors, which I find difficult to interpret; and a copper water jug, showing that the wearer should never run out of water. On the right-hand side are a stirrup, indicating that the wearer or the children of the female wearer should become good horsemen; a battle axe (see the sword above); a pair of paper scissors like those belonging to a calligrapher; a spoon, perhaps an indication that food should never run short; a key, perhaps the key to Paradise, and a weight, possibly expressing the wish that the person wearing it should be successful in business. The simplest forms of amulet are stones in settings or glass in the shape of amulet cases, and also amulets made of Gablonz glass imported from Bohemia, with crescents and star in teardrop shape. A silver eye amulet with a blue glass bead as the pupil, is a very fine example of the fear of the evil eye.

Many of the amulets mentioned so far are certainly worn by Muslims, as well as by Jews and Christians. The use of amulet containers for religious texts and prayers for protection is also common in all these religious groups. Chains with cross-shaped pendants, or chains with chased silver settings for images of saints, can be identified as specifically Christian amulets. Here images of the Virgin Mary are particularly popular.

Despite the variety of jewellery in Syria, as regards the materials used and the ideas of magic associated with wearing it, we have seen that the elements in common predominate. The division between jewellery and amulets made in this chapter may strike some readers as somewhat arbitrary. Many pieces which have been described as jewellery are also of course effective as amulets. However, the pieces described in the section on amulets are those whose importance as amulets clearly predominates over their function as ornament.

221 Combined amulet chain for a girl or young woman. The individual pendants refer to specific wishes of the woman wearing it.

222 A peasant harrowing in the Alawite Mountains.

102

Rural Life and Peasant Culture

Johannes Kalter

Present-day Syria is situated in the centre of the region known as the Fertile Crescent. In antiquity this was the granary of the Roman Empire. Its history, however, and in particular the frequent wars, has meant that the border between nomadic and peasant land was always shifting. The land which has been used agriculturally since antiquity lies west of a line running from Deraa through Damascus to Aleppo. The population density, however, varied at different periods. The climate is Mediterranean with an annual rainfall of more than 400 mm; in the coastal mountains it may be as much as 1200 mm. The rainfall occurs mainly in winter, between November and March. In summer temperatures reach up to 30°C. In winter they fall to around 0°C. East of this line, on a strip between 100 and 200 km wide, numerous agricultural settlements also existed, but because of the instability of this area, they often had to be abandoned. The decline in agriculture was mainly a consequence of the Mongol invasions under Hulagu Khan around 1260 and the devastation caused by the armies of Timur around 1400. After the recovery of agriculture during the golden age of the Mamluk empire, the settlement frontiers receded considerably during the decline of the Mamluks between 1460 and 1517 "as a result of the constant attacks and destruction by bedouins. Especially in the Hauran, in the vicinity of Aleppo and Hama, but also in the Ghouta from Damascus, hundreds of villages were abandoned at that time" (Wirth 1971, p. 159). In the heyday of the Ottomans agriculture recovered again, only to experience a very serious collapse during the years 1750-1830. It was not until the rule of Ibrahim Pasha, between 1831 and 1840, that the trend was reversed. From the middle of the nineteenth century until around 1950 most of the farmland which had been settled in the Roman period was put under the plough again. The dynamics of this process can be best demonstrated by figures published by Wirth (1971): in 1922 the agricultural area in Syria

223 Spring landscape in the southern Alawite Mountains.

(including Lebanon) was about 1 million hectares; in 1938 in Syria alone it was 1.4 million hectares; between 1945 and 1947 it increased to 2.3 million hectares, and in 1960 it was more than 6 million hectares. In other words, between 1939 and 1959 the area used for agriculture had trebled. A further expansion was brought about by the building of the Assad Dam on the Euphrates and the draining of the malaria-infested swamps of the Orontes. At present another big dam is under construction on the middle Khabour. Today about 30 per cent of Syria's total area is used for agriculture: 20 per cent is farmland and the rest for fruit-growing and forestry. In the regions of the plains recently opened up for cultivation, intensive farming with machinery is possible. This meant that in 1975 about half of Syria's working population was active in agriculture. In 1985 this proportion had dropped to less than a third. Nevertheless agriculture still contributes 22 per cent of the Syrian gross national product.

The fact that settlements were established at different times by very different population groups is clearly reflected in the form of the settlements and farms. We have already given some examples of this in the chapter "Landscapes and People – Landscapes and Ways of Life". The most distinctive traditional material culture of peasants, however, is found in the mountain refuges of western Syria, particularly in the Alawite Mountains, and in southern Syria in the Hauran and Jebel Druz. The majority of our peasant household articles are from these regions. However, a large number of peasant costumes in the collection are from Christian refuges, villages on the slopes of the Antilebanon and from the Golan Heights.

Here we shall look at the culture of the Druzes in southern Syria and the Alawites in western Syria in more detail.

The volcanic basalt mountains of southern Syria, where the Druzes now live, is a typical refuge area. In antiquity this was one of the most fertile regions of Syria. It was intensively cultivated. However, when the majority of the present-day Druze population settled in the Jebel Druz, from the early eighteenth century onwards, after conflicts with the Maronite Christians, this area was basically uninhabited. Despite the fertility of its volcanic soil agriculture here is very laborious. The main feature of the landscape are the apparently endless walls built of loose stones. One has the impression that the Druzes have used all their efforts to wrest every square metre of fertile soil from nature. Besides cereal crops, perennial crops, such as olives, vines and fruit trees, also play an important role.

224 One-room house in the Hauran.

225 Reception room of a house belonging to a village elder in the Hauran.

226 Rural house in the Hauran.

227 Living room of a rural house in southern Syria.

230 Farmer's wife in Homs.

231 Baskets woven from wheat straw in coil technique, southern Syria.

228 Peasant woman in front of a farmstead in Chan Sheichun.

As the statistics show in 1987 the Druzes made up between 2 and 3 per cent of the total Syrian population (11 million). But their coherence as a group, and their ability to defend themselves, have meant that their influence in recent Syrian history has been considerably greater than these figures might suggest. Membership of the Druze community is defined entirely by religion, a variant of Ismaelite Islam, characterized by an esoteric teaching dating back to the eleventh century. The word Druze is derived from the name of the founder of their religion, el Darazi. He interpreted this teaching and made it canonical, although in fact it goes back to the Fatimid caliph, el-Hakim (996-1021). Besides Muslim creeds the Druze religion also includes a number of Gnostic elements. The members of the religious community are introduced into the religion by stages, so that only the highest authorities have full knowledge of their religion. The Druze population is therefore divided into two groups: those who religiously initiated, the "knowing" (uqqal) and the religiously uninitiated, the "unknowing" (juhhal). Explained briefly in practical terms, the core of Druze religious beliefs is their emphasis on an inner hidden truth different from and superior to outer visible reality. Man's endeavour should concentrate on this inner truth and knowledge. The esoteric knowledge of this inner truth is conveyed through an initiation undertaken in stages. The difference between the knowing and the unknowing is manifested in different requirements governing their respective ways of life and behaviour.

A number of rules governing the social life of the Druze community distinguish them from their Muslim neighbours. For example, monogamy is stipulated; divorces are rarely permitted and then only on serious grounds. Druze men have an obligation to protect the community with arms. This gives them control over their territory and explains the not inconsiderable military potential which the Druzes had – and still have today in the Lebanon. As a rule Syrian peasants were not armed. They also were not required for military service. They often fled in the face of the attempts by the Ottomans to recruit them. The peasants had to pay what was called "brother money" for the armed protection given them by the nomads. The Druzes, however, could either put up resistance to the demands of the nomads for payment, or deliberately form alliances with them. In every Druze village there is a house for assembly and guests, the madafe. This is where the men meet to discuss the affairs of the community. Here travellers and strangers are entertained, and in the past they also used to spend the night in them. Druze identity is also expressed in their clothing. There are differences between the clothing of the initiated and uninitiated – but the most striking feature was that Druze women were not veiled.

Their ability to defend themselves, their remoteness from other settlements, the cohesiveness created by their religion and the influence of their leading families meant that the Druze culture managed to preserve its independ-

232 A Roman mosaic, now in the Beit ed-Din Museum in the Druze mountains in Lebanon, indicates that in antiquity the Syrian mountains were intensively farmed.

233 Women at a Druze funeral.

ence far into the present century. Even in 1925/26 the French mandatory power had great difficulty in suppressing a Druze uprising. The most important families are the families of Jumblat and Atrash. The Jumblat family is of Kurdish origin and has only lived in Lebanon since the seventeenth century. Before then it played an important role in Aleppo. The Atrash family, according to its own genealogy, is older than the Jumblats, but it did not attain its present position until the last century. After its flight out of Lebanon it supplanted the Druze families which had previously been important in the Hauran. This position was consolidated by Sultan Atrash, who today is a legendary figure. He turned against the Ottomans and was the first Druze leader to enter Damascus in 1918 at the side of the Allied troops. In the eyes of some Druzes this brought upon him the suspicion of collaborating with the colonial powers. However, the fact that his successors fought against the French helped to correct this view. Both families still have considerable political influence in Lebanon and in Syria.

Numerically the Alawites are the second largest religious community in Syria. Their proportion of the total population was given by Wirth in 1971 as 12 per cent and by Franck in 1989 as 7 per cent. Their traditional area of settlement is the mountains of north-western Syria. During the period of the French mandate, between 1920 and 1936, an independent Alawite state was established. Because Hafiz el-Asad, the president of Syria since 1970, is a member of the Alawite community, a considerable part of the Syrian army, and in particular the officer corps, is now composed of Alawites. This means that the members of this religious community have a much greater influence in Syria than is indicated by their proportion of the population. Essentially the religion of the Alawites remains a religion of the mountain peasants of north-western Syria, which is one of the few settled regions in Syria where the members of a religious minority represent the majority of the population.

According to Halm (1988) the religion of the Alawites is a branch of the Shia, and probably originated in Baghdad. It survived on the middle Euphrates, in the Syrian coastal mountains, the Jebel Ansarya (corrupted as Jebel en Nusariye – Alawites are also known as Nuseirians) and in the regions of the Cilician Plain around Adana and Tarsus in present-day Turkey. The Alawites "derive their teaching from the revelation of the eleventh imam, el-Hassan

234 Village wedding in the Alawite Mountains.

235–239 Discs woven from wheat straw in the coil technique with colourful patterns are used as mats for serving food. Unpatterned ones are used as a work surface for household work or for making pottery. Particularly large and decorative examples are used as wall decorations. The centre of the pattern is usually a star or a spiral whorl. Besides geometric and floral motifs, human figures also appear on Druze mats. Syria, twentieth century.

240 Sewing basket made of coloured wheat straw.

241 Cushions with geometric patchwork decoration, Syria, twentieth century.

242 & 243 Square patchwork decorations, usually made in pairs, decorate the walls of peasant houses in southern Syria, twentieth century.

244 Cushions with patchwork decoration and embroidery, Golan region, twentieth century.

245 Woven house amulets with cloth cover, mirrors, cowrie shells and buttons. Southern Syria, twentieth century.

246 Chest used by peasants with coloured sheet metal from tea boxes, southern Syria, twentieth century.

el-Askari to his pupil Ibn Nuseir. The real founder of the sect, however, seems to have been a certain Hasibi, who was first active under the rule of the Buyids at Alkarch, the Shi'ite suburb of Baghdad. He then led an unsettled itinerant life and canvassed for his teaching in Mosul and Aleppo. He died in Aleppo around 957 or 967. Several of his writings, such as his collection of poetry, have been handed down by the sect. His grandson and pupil, et-Tabarani, migrated to Laodicia (which was then Byzantine) on the northern Syrian coast. Through his voluminous writings he completed the formation of the Nussarian or Alawite religion." The Alawites revere the Imam Ali as the embodiment of the divine spirit and teach that he sent Mohammed as the Prophet. Their religion also adopted Gnostic elements, and particularly in their teachings regarding the divinity of Ali and the migration of souls they have moved a long way from orthodox Islam. Because of this they have suffered severe persecutions over many centuries. Consequently it is only in the mountain refuges of north-western Syria that they have been able to survive as a closed society. An outward sign of the constant threat to the Alawites is the fact that many of their old settlements were built within the walls of former crusader castles.

Because of natural and climatic conditions similar to those in the Druze mountains, the cultivation of cereals and trees is similar to that in the Alawite mountains.

Peasant Houses

As in other rural areas in the Orient the peasant houses are usually multi-storey houses with outer walls built of stone or mud, depending on which material is available, and have no windows on the ground floor. Common to all houses is a division into a residential section for the family, a reception area for guests and an working section. Wirth (1971) cites six different types of peasant houses in Syria. On one hand the differences between these types of house are an expression of different ethnic or ethnic-religious traditions and historical experiences, and on the other they depend on the locally available building materials. In the area of Druze settlements, the volcanic regions of southern Syria, traditional peasant houses are built of basalt blocks. The roof construction rests on arches built of close-fitting stones without mortar and has been found in this region since late antiquity. They generally do not have wooden beams.

In the Alawite mountains houses are predominantly built built of rubble stone with a roof of wooden beams, sealed with layers of mud. The houses lean against the hillside and are built to fit the gradient. The flat roof is the favourite workplace for women and fulfils the same function as the open courtyard does in houses on the plains.

Houses of the sort described here are hardly ever built nowadays. Almost everywhere in Syria the standard Mediterranean type of flat-roofed concrete building has taken over. These have steel reinforcements jutting out of the roof and are constructed so that another storey can be added if more room is needed – when the sons get married, for instance.

Nowadays the furnishing of the houses also largely follows Western standards. Traditionally they are very uniform. The reception room had a chest with a carved front. The favourite decorative motifs for these are arches filled with cypress or interlace patterns. The well-to-do could have more richly decorated chests with bone or mother-of-pearl inlay. Chests mounted with sheet-metal taken from tea caddies and similar containers, decorated with oriental motifs, were especially popular in Jordan and the neighbouring regions of Syria.

Fittings and Furnishings

The reception room of a house was also used as the family bedrooms. Along the back wall and the side walls of the room are mattresses resting on straw mats. Today mattresses are usually bought, whereas in the past the women generally made them themselves and filled them with wool from sheep or cotton wool. For the comfort of guests cushions are placed on the mattresses. Most covers used to be hand-embroidered, or, in the Hauran, had patchwork decoration. Other bedding may be piled on a chest in a corner of the room. The side walls have niches for water-pipes, plates and similar household equipment. They can be closed by curtains. One corner of the room is reserved for cooking utensils, which used to be made of copper but are now usually enamel, a fireplace – as a rule this has since been replaced by a paraffin stove – and occasionally a stone hand-mill. Formerly a large earthenware water-container would be placed at the entrance of the room. This is now replaced by a metal canister with a drinking cup. The furnishings are supplemented by a cradle, if it is needed.

The furnishings described so far are found more or less in all peasant living rooms in the region. Local peculiarities are apparent especially in wall decoration. Very often this also serves practical needs at the same time.

Typical of the mountainous regions of Syria and Jordan are round or oval discs woven from straw in a spiral coil technique. The straw is dyed before it is woven, and extraordinarily complex patterns are achieved. Some of these recall Islamic architectural decoration, and others of trees of life or other fertility symbols; Druze examples have representations of humans and animals. Many mats of this kind – especially the very large ones – can only be used as a wall decoration. Others are used as substitutes for tables or as table coverings, on which the large shared bowls are placed. They can also be the bases on which women make ceramic vessels by hand. From the imprints of such spiral-coil mats, on the bottom of excavated ceramic vessels we know that this weaving technique has been practised in

247 Women in the Alawite Mountains baking bread.

248 Young woman preparing *bulghur*, a sort of buckwheat semolina.

249 Wheat measures and sieves made of strips of wood and strung with gut.

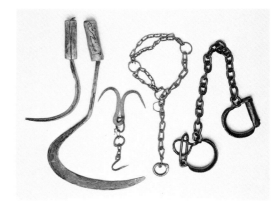

250 Sickles, animal fetters, and hooks. Pieces made by of village smiths, southern Syria.

251 Wooden bowl, funnel and spoon. Products of rural home crafts, southern Syria.

252 Cradle, painted wood. An amulet made of blue glass beads is suspended over the child's head. Southern Syria.

253–258 In times of little agricultural work peasant women in the Hauran and the Ajlun Mountains make robust pottery, which they build up by hand. They produce, for example, cooking pots, ewers and large water pots, as well as (top left) ovens and basins to collect freshly pressed olive oil.

259 Bottom right: Pots turned on a wheel and fired black, with strongly marked grooves, are made in southern Syria by professional potters who have emigrated from Palestine. The amphora-like shape of the large vessel has persisted since antiquity.

260 Farmstead near Ebla with domed huts in a style found in the region since prehistoric times.

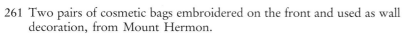
262—265 Inside the farmstead (ill. 260). Above: winter oven and granary. Below: embroidered wall hangings form the most striking feature of the interior decoration.

261 Two pairs of cosmetic bags embroidered on the front and used as wall decoration, from Mount Hermon.

Jordan for several thousand years. The motifs used suggest that these mats could also be a house amulet. At their centre one often finds the eight-pointed star, called "Solomon's Seal", common in Islamic amulets, and adopted from the Jewish cabbalistic tradition.

Also originating in the Hauran are square pieces of cloth with severely geometric patchwork patterns in luminous colour,s creating a highly graphic effect. The structure of the decoration is almost entirely organized on a cross pattern, or else the centre is given emphasis by a cross shape, and the four corners are filled. We have already discussed the significance of the number five in Muslim amulets. These cloths most probably are also used as amulets, besides being decorative. The function of an amulet is clear in the case of round woven or cardboard discs with textile covering and applied cowrie shells, glass beads, buttons and often also mirrors. They generally hang directly opposite the entrance. Other typical examples of peasant wall decoration are decorated utensils. The bags for protecting the flasks containing eye make-up (kohol) play a special part in this. In southern Syria and Jordan since the 1930s the favourite decoration for these has been multi-coloured glass-bead embroidery with geometrical patterns. Pairs of bag-shaped embroideries from the region of Mount Hermon are evidence that such objects can also lose their function and retain only their form. These bags were originally intended to hold kohol flasks, but often only the front of the bags was made and they were then used simply as wall decoration. The favourite motif for the embroideries is the tree of life.

A form of wall decoration found among peasants, as well as among the urban lower class, are glass paintings with popular religious motifs: Noah's Ark, the pilgrim caravan to Mecca, the mythical animal (burak) on which Mohammed rode to heaven, as well as themes from heroic epics and love stories of pre-Islamic times. Particularly popular are representations of the classic Arab pair of lovers, Abla and the hero Antar. Both are shown on horseback.

Today in Damascus only one painter still seems to be producing glass paintings. His name is Abu Subchi Ittinawi, and today his clients are more likely to be tourists than local inhabitants.

Similar themes are found on embroidered wall pictures from villages in the vicinity of Aleppo. Apart from the subjects already mentioned, our collection also includes an embroidered image of the Virgin Mary, and a Shi'ite image of the caliph Ali enthroned between his sons Hasan and Husein.

If there are guest rooms, they are furnished more or less in the same way as those already described. The only difference is that cooking utensils are not used in this room. Kelims or carpets as floor covering are found only among the sedentary Kurds in the north of the country. Also more common in the north are thick, very colourful felt mats which have ornaments similar to Central Asian ones.

Hay and straw are stored in the domestic area of the house, while corn is kept in large containers made of mud mixed with straw. Big oil jars are also kept here, as well as all the agricultural equipment: wood hook ploughs, threshing sledges made of strong wooden planks with stones set in them, forks with wooden prongs which are joined to the handle either by hide or leather wound round them. Where irrigated cultivation is practised there are draw-spades for digging the irrigation channels, large baskets to carry manure to the fields, winnowing fans and sieves which have a wooden frame and – in Jordan at least – are strung with skilfully interwoven gut or leather (in Syria this has long been replaced by fine wire), and grain measures, also made of wood. In Syria it is now almost as hard to find the equipment described here, as it is to find old agricultural equipment in Europe. Everywhere cheaper, but less functional, factory-made tools have replaced the products of home industry and rural craftsmen practising their craft as a secondary occupation, as well as the products of urban artisans. Soon it will no longer be possible to categorize items of peasant equipment by their makers, as Kamail Ismail did in 1975. He describes (pp 104 ff) how the material culture of the Syrian mountain peasants can be divided into five categories:

1. Home-made objects, such as mattresses, straw trays, grain containers made of straw and larger ones made of clay. They were all made by women. Not every woman necessarily made every single article mentioned herself. Those who were more gifted with craft skills often made the objects for many families in the village in return for other work or articles.

2. Products of rural part-time craftsmen, such as the wooden parts of the plough, the yoke, the threshing sledge, harvesting baskets and large baskets for transporting straw and dung. By 1975 the following objects were no longer in use: wooden spoons and wooden bowls, stone hand-mills and mortars made of basalt. These were made by peasants in their spare time, for example, during the period after the harvest when there was little work in the fields. By making wooden parts of ploughs, wooden handles of hoes, sickles etc. they were competing with urban craftsmen.

3. Products of rural craftsmen. The smith had a special status as the maker of ploughshares, hoes and sickle blades (by 1975 shovels were usually obtained from urban tradesmen). Shoemakers too were important: they made sandals, as well as water-sacks from old car tyres.

4. The main products of urban artisans were kitchen equipment made of copper.

5. Factory-made products have now replaced the products of rural and urban artisans. Many artisans continue to do repair work, while others have switched to other, more promising trades. Some, for example, have become car mechanics.

266 Women's pottery from southern Syria, strainer and kneading bowl.

268 Women's pottery from southern Syria, cooking pots, and pots for water and oil.

269 Stamps for marking bread on festivals; in front, stone; centre, ceramic; back, wood. Southern Syria.

267 Water jug with relief decoration, from the Ajlun Mountains.

270 & 271 The king's noble daughter Abla and the bold knight Antar. The classic pair of lovers from a pre-Islamic, Arab epic. Naïve glass-paintings are a popular form of peasant wall decoration.

272 Noah's ark.

273 Fighting heroes.

274 Pilgrim caravan setting off for Mecca.

116

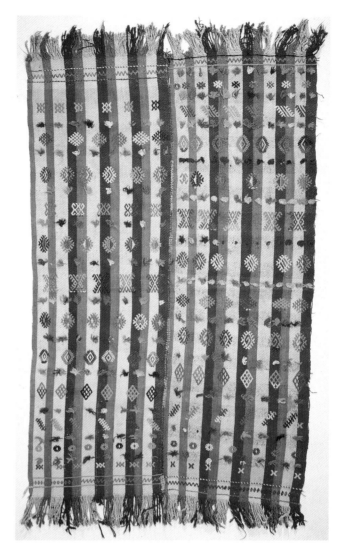

275–277 Embroidered wall decoration used by peasants: an image of the Madonna; the *Buraq*, the mythical beast on which the Prophet Muhammad rode to heaven; and Imam Ali with his sons Hasan and Husein. (The *Buraq* is dated 1960).

278 & 279 The usual floor coverings in peasants' houses are felts or mats. Only the Kurds used flat-weaves (kelims) with simple geometrical patterns in cheerful colours.

117

280 Suchne, before 1900.

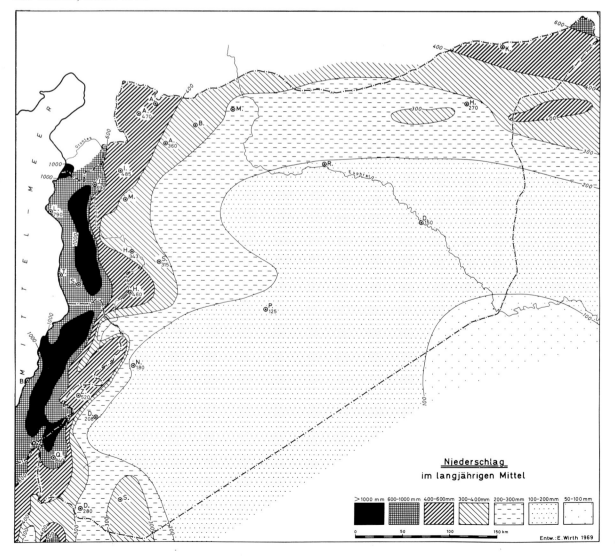

Niederschlag
im langjährigen Mittel

>1000 mm 600-1000 mm 400-600mm 300-400mm 200-300mm 100-200mm 50-100mm

0   50   100   150 km

Entw.: E. Wirth 1969

Average annual rainfall

Wedding in the Oasis of es-Suchne

Peter Behnstedt

(Note: All over the Orient marriage is the most important event in an adult's life. At weddings traditional costumes are still worn, the bride's jewellery and all the trousseau is presented. Peter Behnstedt here describes a wedding in the oasis of es-Suchne, as he experienced it and as it was described to him by the young people.)

The wedding customs which described here by an inhabitant of es-Suchne are typically rural and differ in many respects from those in the towns. It would be unthinkable for young men and young women at a wedding to dance together and hold hands with each other in a city like Aleppo.

For us in es-Suchne marriage has nothing to do with great love, or with the couple "going out" together beforehand. With us it happens quite suddenly. Someone goes and says to his mother "Hey, I want to have so- and-so!" She then goes to the girl's mother and says "Sister, we want to get the trousseau for your daughter!" She replies: "Come back in a few days!"; they have to take counsel. So they call the daughter and tell her. Usually the girls here get married against their will; they are forced into marriage. And then there is something else, which is called the reservation of the bride. This means that a male cousin can reserve his female cousin as a bride for himself. Even if he is five years old and she is seventeen, for example – it can happen that she must wait until her thirtieth birthday, when he is eighteen, to get married.

When the parents of the future couple have given their approval, they call one of our sheikhs, draw up a marriage contract with him and fix the bride price. At present this is set at around 30,000 lira, and the same amount again, which the man has to pay to her in case of a divorce. Then they read the first sura of the Koran together. When they do so the marriage is legally concluded. After about a week they acquire the trousseau for the bride: clothes, perfume, crockery. Then they fix a date for the wedding. If the young man wishes, they arrange a dance a week before the wedding. There boys and girls hold hands and dance in a line (comparable to a *sirtaki*). They also sing songs mocking the members of the respective quarters of the village. Such as:

"Oh we of the Bani Khalaf, we are officers in the academy and you of the Bani Afeiy, twenty of you fit in one cigarette packet!"

One day before the wedding, usually on a Wednesday, the bride's hands and feet are ornamented with henna. She asks all her girl-friends to come and the whole business takes place at night. On the following day she is bathed. For this too her girl-friends gather to wash her, arrange her hair, shave her armpits and pubic hair, and perfume her. Nowadays they remove the hair with depilatory cream. Formerly they used a paste prepared from sugar, terebinth resin, water and antimony. This was applied to the hair and and after a while pulled off, which was very painful. And the same happens to the bridegroom. He too is ornamented with henna and bathed, and his friends gather together for this. When everyone is ready the bride is led to the bridegroom, while they sing songs, such as:

"Oh girl with the beautiful dress
and the shining cheeks
we do not know when death will take us
and if we knew
we would now already be fearful."

Before they now lead her to the bridegroom's bedroom, a few more customs are followed. In front of the bedroom they break a bottle of perfume or a glass of tea. This is supposed to avert misfortune from the couple. Usually they also stick a piece of dough over the door. If it sticks there for a long time, it means that the marriage will last. If does not stick for long, then the marriage will not last long. And some bridegrooms also take a little kitten and wring its neck in front of the bride – to show her who the master of the house is and to frighten her. The day after the marriage is consummated, the friends of the bride come and bring her breakfast. Only the best: cheese, clarified butter, olives, oil and crushed thyme with sesame seeds, yoghurt, and whatever else there is. And what is left she takes to her sister or some other female relatives. On the next day, that is, on the third day, her girl-friends come, congratulate her and give her money as a present, perhaps fifty or a hundred lira, or they give her a pair of stockings or knickers, or sweets. And then animals are slaughtered. That can happen on the day before, on the wedding day itself, or the day after, as they wish. The parents of the bridegroom slaughter at least fifteen sheep, and invite all their relatives and friends. The women, of course, are trilling "lululu-lulu!" all the time, and they sing songs for the bride:

"Oh you who go up the stairs, step by step,
your hair is like gold chains, strand by strand
we have boiled the yellow rice
and scattered it on the floor...!"

281 The oasis of Palmyra.

282—286 Clothing with silk embroidery from Suchne, worn especially on festive occasions, such as weddings. In addition to geometric motifs, stylized date-palms and cypresses are also popular patterns. Only in Suchne are embroidered skirts found, besides dresses, coats and pants. Today embroidery is no longer practised in Suchne.

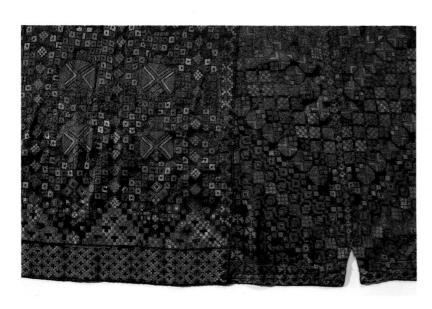

287 Roualla bedouins on migration. In the foreground a camel with a
woman's litter.

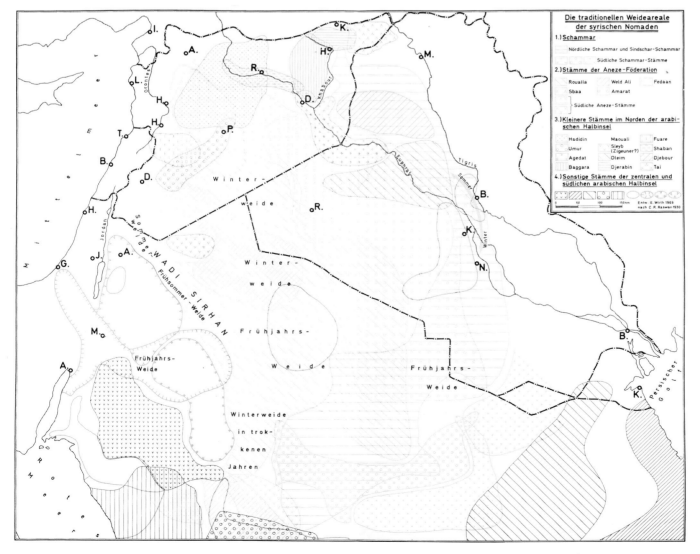

Traditional
grazing areas of
the Syrian nomads.

Die traditionellen Weideareale
der syrischen Nomaden

1.)Schammar

　Nördliche Schammar und Sindschar-Schammar

　Südliche Schammar-Stämme

2.)Stämme der Aneze-Föderation

Roualla　　　Weld Ali　　　Fedaan

Sbaa　　　　Amarat

Südliche Aneze-Stämme

3.)Kleinere Stämme im Norden der arabischen Halbinsel

Hadidin　　　Maouali　　　Fuare

Umur　　　　Sleyb　　　　Shaban
　　　　　　(Zigeuner?)

Agedat　　　Dleim　　　　Djebour

Baggara　　　Djerabin　　　Tai

4.)Sonstige Stämme der zentralen und
südlichen arabischen Halbinsel

Entw. E.Wirth 1969
nach C.R.Raswan 1930

The Culture of the Nomads

Johannes Kalter

For thousands of years the desert steppes of Inner Syria and Mesopotamia have provided almost ideal conditions for pastoral nomadic cultures. From the third millennium BC onwards we have many accounts not only of conflicts between the urban population, peasants and nomads, but also of symbiosis between these groups. The frontier with nomad territory was never firmly fixed. In periods when the state authority was strong and high rainfall was constant over several years, the farmland extended eastwards beyond the 200 mm rainfall frontier; in times when the central power of the state was weaker and rainfall was poor the nomads penetrated deep into peasant land. Despite repeated complaints about their expansion, the nomads in fact played an important role in the complex and finely balanced network of relationships between the urban population, peasants and nomads over the centuries. In the last hundred years the nomad economy has dwindled, as it has everywhere else in the Orient. In Syria it is even threatened with extinction.

At first sight the conditions for nomadic ways of life seem better here than in most other regions of the arid belt of the Old World. Even in the interior of the desert steppe of Syria the average annual rainfall drops below 80 mm in only a few places. "Very few winters pass without at least a few falls of rain causing green shoots to appear. The supply of drinking water also presents comparatively few difficulties. At the edge of the desert steppe there are good karst springs. A number of weaker springs, as well as the rivers Euphrates and Khabour make it possible to provide drinking water throughout the year in some places. After heavy winter rains the *khabras* – the large or small flat depressions – are filled for weeks with good drinking water. Lastly, in the larger, strong deep *wadis*, the underground water can be tapped almost anywhere from a feasible depth. The pasturage of the Syrian desert steppe can be therefore used as camel pasture throughout most of the year and in the winter months sheep can graze there too." (Wirth, pp 254f)

The developments in the various forms of pastoral nomadism do not follow a uniform course. True, the household possessions of both the camel and sheep nomads have changed considerably.Today, however, it seems that under certain circumstances the sheep nomads can adapt to changed economic conditions, whereas it is certain that the camel nomads will become extinct in the next generations. When speaking of Arab nomads, one is usually referring to the camel nomads or bedouins. The Arabic word *badawi* derives from the term *badu* and denotes a dweller of the *badiya*, the steppe or desert. The bedouins generally call themselves Arabs and refer to the sedentary people as *hadar*, a term which includes both the urban population and peasants (Korsching, 1980). In terms of self-estimation as well as in the assessment of the sedentary people, the bedouins were regarded as occupying a preeminent position within the hierarchy of Arab societies. The following is a brief description of some basic aspects of their culture.

The domestication of the single-humped camel (dromedary) took place on the Arabian Peninsula in the second millennium BC. The first written references to warrior camel-riders, called Aribi (=Arabs), are found in Assyrian cuneiform texts of the ninth century BC, which mention approximately one thousand camel nomads in the region of Damascus.

Since that time the economy of the camel nomads has depended on a number of complementary activities, all based on the products derived directly from keeping camels. Camel milk, unlike milk from sheep or goats, is available throughout the year and was therefore the main means of subsistence for the bedouins. When grazing opportunities are good a camel mare can produce up to seven litres of milk. In the dry season the yield drops to one litre or even less. One part of the milk is drunk fresh, while the rest is poured into skins and soured. Some of it is turned into dry cheese. Camel hair is used for weaving kelim rugs, saddle bags, belts, knitting etc. The skin is used for making waterskins, water buckets and sandals; dried camel dung is an important fuel; the urine is used for washing hair and as a disinfectant. The great mobility provided by the camel – riding on a camel one can cover up to a hundred kilometres a day – made it possible to mount swift armed raids against neighbouring bedouin groups and on the villages of the sedentary people. Stolen livestock, as well as food, clothing and other valuables, still provided a useful supplement to the income of camel nomads until well into the present century. Anyone who was able to bring sufficient fodder and water would bring a spare horse on these raids. For the attack they changed from the camels to their Arab horses, which were rested, quicker and more agile. They were the pride of every respectable warrior. The camel nomads kept a modest number of goats or, if possible, fat-rumped sheep for their own use. Like all nomads they ate very little meat. For great feasts camel bulls were slaughtered, and at other times, if guests were to

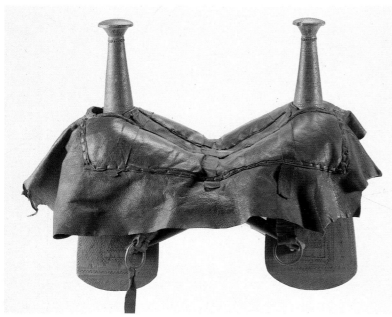

288–290 Camel saddle. Wooden framework with leather binding and brass rings for the girth, decorated with notches and nailhead patterns. The same saddle with cushioning (acquired before 1883 by J. Euting, presumably from the Roualla), and with camel saddlebags.

291 & 292 Camels were lovingly decorated when the bedouins migrated. Left: head ornament with boar's teeth and blue glass beads as an amulet. Right: head ornament and leash mounted with cowries and mirror glass. Southern Syria.

293 Grazing camels in the Inner Syrian desert.

be entertained, goats or sheep. Hunting and gathering also added variety to their diet, especially in spring, when truffles, various roots and wild herbs were gathered. Bedouins received protection money from peasants who settled within their area of influence. Some of them even received it from the local ruler and, in the time of Ottoman rule, from the court in Istanbul. They provided guides and armed escorts for caravans of merchandise or pilgrims, or they themselves acted as caravan merchants. In the second and third centuries AD the city of Palmyra, half way between Damascus and the Euphrates, was the centre of an important state which owed its prosperity to caravan trade on the Silk Road and the Incense Road. The prerequisite for the prosperity of camel nomads was the possibility of undertaking extensive migrations to find pasturage.

The Shammar and the Roualla (who belong to the tribal federation of the Aneze) are the largest and by far the most powerful nomad groups in Syria. "The areas of summer pasture of the Shammar are situated in northern Syria and on the Euphrates, those of the Roualla on the margin of the newly settled land to the west (mountainous lands of central Syria and basalt mountains of southern Syria). The winter pastures of the Syrian bedouin lie far to the south in the regions of south-western Iraq, eastern Jordan and northern Saudi Arabia. The camel nomads cover 600 to 800 kilometres during their annual migration between summer and winter pasture. They also pass through the territory of other states. As long as camels form the major part of the herds such long migrations cannot be avoided, because the camels suffer severely in the winter cold in the desert steppes of northern and inner Syria. The departure southwards from the summer pastures usually takes place as early as September. Usually they do not return until July. The bedouins thus spend only about three months of the year in contact with the sedentary population on the borders of the agricultural areas." (Wirth, 1971, pp 255 f). Thus it becomes apparent that the development of modern nation states with a strong central power has made the decline of camel nomadism an urgent necessity. The formation of a modern police apparatus meant that the flow of protection money from peasants or caravans has virtually ceased. Subsidies from the state have lapsed, and instead the bedouins are forced to pay taxes. Since 1920 dromedaries have increasingly declined in importance as a means of transport. A large freight vehicle can transport the loads carried by about 250 camels. Besides these objective criteria there is also a general anti-bedouin feeling among the officials of these modern states. Their long-distance migrations mean that the bedouin largely escape state control – and what state official can tolerate such a state of affairs? Moreover, their economy is regarded as backward and no longer suited to the demands of a modern state. According to a statistic (cited in Lewis, 1987) the fully nomadic tribes of Syria still had 21,400 tents and 187,500 camels in 1940. The number of members of camel nomad tribes in 1947 was given (in 1971) as 160,000. The crisis was brought about by a change in climate – which is always a risk for the nomads' economy. The years 1958-61 were extremely dry throughout Syria. Lewis gives the total number of camels in Syria in 1958 (including the pack animals of the sheep nomads) as 80,000. In 1961 their numbers had dropped to 11,000. These drastic losses are also explained in part by the fact that the authorities in Syria had little inclination to help the hard pressed nomads. Many nomad families stopped making the effort to built up their livestock again. The men sought employment as migrant workers in the Gulf States, or in Syria as taxi-drivers or policemen, or they even joined the army. Apparently the sedentary way of life in the city was regarded by many of them as less degrading than the switch from camel nomadism to sheep farming, which would have offered a viable alternative. An observation made by Lewis (1987), which we have also come across on several occasions, shows how hard many nomads have found this change. Lewis noticed that some older men and smaller sheikhs have arranged the guest rooms of their houses like the men's area of their old tents, out of nostalgia for old times. The rooms are furnished with mattresses and cushions arranged around a charcoal brazier, which contains four or five copper coffee pots. Yet the rooms are oil-heated, and most of the coffee pots are kept only for show, since the coffee is in fact made on gas rings and served in thermos flasks. With many of the men absent, such rooms are almost like museums, except on the rare occasions when a sheep is slaughtered for guests.

Some of the bedouins, however, especially from the Shammar tribe, have managed the transition to sedentary farming. A reason for this, as Wirth noted, was that some of their summer pastures in north-eastern Syria provided good conditions for productive agriculture as regards the soil quality and water supply. The sheikhs of the Shammar were granted the title of ownership over the arable farms by an order of the French mandatory power in 1940/41. In this way less than 500,000 hectares of arable land in the low-lying area of the Radd to the north of the Jebel Sinjar was allotted to bedouins. In an area divided up geometrically into squares with sides one or two kilometres in length, fully mechanized cultivation of wheat and barley is practised. This decision was made easier for the bedouins of the Shammar tribes because their sheikhs were of high and noble descent and their Western education gave them correspondingly strong influence in such matters. The

extreme devaluation of camels – between 1900 and 1930 prices went down by 80 per cent – threatened to reduce the high standard of living for the sheikhs and bring impoverishment to the whole group. Wirth reports that at first the sheikhs assigned only a limited number of their tribesmen to the cultivation of the fields, while others still kept to their nomadic way of life. At a later stage in this process of becoming sedentary periodic pastoral migrations continued, but only a part of the family participated, and the rest lived in permanent settlements and cultivated the land. In the frequent years of drought the yield of their own fields, which were often no longer worth harvesting fully, was available as a reserve for the herds.

It can be seen from old photographs that nomad encampments with thirty to forty black tents were still not at all unusual in the 1930s. These days such tents are found only occasionally. The traditional bedouin items in our museum collections are just a reminder of their great past.

The fate of the other great nomadic group, the Syrian sheep nomads, has been different. They too lost large numbers of their flocks during the years of drought between 1958 and 1961. The number of sheep in 1960 is given as approximately 3 million; by 1969 their number had risen again to 6 million, and by 1983 to about 9 million. There is a very large market for sheep not only in Syria itself but also in the Gulf States. Just how big this demand is can be seen from information provided by Wirth in 1967: the Syrian army imported about 20,000 sheep a year for its use, in addition to large quantities of sheep meat from Australia. The German commercial attaché at Damascus even made an official inquiry as to whether the Federal Republic of Germany would be able to export several thousand wethers to Syria. Traditionally the annual migration routes of the Syrian sheep nomads were between 50 and 200 kilometres and usually did not cross the Syrian frontier. During the hot, dry summer months the animals graze on the fallow and stubble fields, as well as on mountain farmland. In winter they are taken to those parts of the Syrian desert steppe adjoining the newly settled land of northern central and southern Syria. This means that the sheep nomads use the same pasturage which is used by the bedouins in the summer months. The traditional seasonal migrations have today been replaced by transports of herds by tractor or, over longer distances, by lorry. This makes it possible to reach areas which previously lay outside the pasturage of the sheep nomads. The massive growth in the numbers of livestock and the possibility of using modern means of transport to reach the most attractive areas of pasture have resulted in such an over-grazing of enormous areas that it now seems no longer possible for the pastures to recover. This process is exacerbated by the fact that the herds are no longer dependent on the proximity of springs or natural sources of water since water can also be brought to the herds in tanker lorries from far away. Despite this, however, years of drought still have the same devastating consequences as in earlier times. Many nomads lose whole herds in such crises. Then their only chance of survival is to look for a way of obtaining a share of urban capital. Wirth (1969) wrote on this subject: "In central Syria two types of contract have emerged in order to enable the participation of urban financial backers in accordance with common law. They are observed with surprising scrupulousness by both sides and apparently have proved their worth (A. Naaman, 1951):

a. The town-dweller assembles the herd himself and then entrusts it to a nomad family. In return for this he receives the butter that accrues, and the male young, while the nomads can make use of the wool and surplus milk.

b. The town-dweller gives the nomad as much capital as is needed to purchase a herd. In return he first receives all the complete yield of this herd, such as butter, wool and the male young. The female young are added to the herd. As soon as the value of the products taken by the financial backer reaches the value of the sum of money he handed over, the herd is divided. One half passes to the town-dweller, the other to the nomad. If the food supplies are satisfactory this will happen after two or three years."

If there are repeated losses of herds in years of drought the nomads must again seek the help of urban backers. In this way it is not unusual for independent nomads to become hired shepherds. In 1971 Wirth estimated the number of sheep nomads at around 125,000. A further group of sheep farmers are semi-sedentary, with their pastures and their present villages in north-east Syria and the Syrian Euphrates and Khabour valley. Only a part of the family is away with the herds on their seasonal migration. Even the members of the family who remain in the settlements often prefer to live in tents next to their houses during the hot season.

Transitions between camel nomadism and sheep nomadism, from nomadism to farming, and the migration of nomads to the city, have occurred in Syria at all times. The unusual aspect of the development which has been taking place since the 1930s and 1940s is therefore not what is happening but its speed and extent.

Household Goods of the Nomads

All Arab nomads live in the black tents made of strips of goat's hair cloth, a type which is found in different variants from northern Africa, across the whole Arabian Peninsula, Palestine to the Syrian region, Iraq, Iran, as far as Afghanistan. The tent cloth is woven on a simple horizontal loom and measures approximately 70 cm in width and 7 to 12 metres in length. Five or six such strips are sewn together to form the roof, which is supported by tent poles more than two metres long and terminating at the top with a broad wooden superstructure. Pieces of cloth are sewn to the back and the side walls. The front is left open for most of the year and is only closed in the cold winter. The cloth is held taut by thick goat-hair guy ropes which are sewn to the tent cloth with V- or U-shaped pieces of wood and fastened to the ground with long wrought- iron pegs. The interior of the tent is divided into a larger women's section and a smaller men's section by means of a partition stretched across it. In their craftsmanship and ornaments these tent partitions represent the most ambitious examples of nomadic flat weaving. At the *suq* in Aleppo reed mats are also sold with wool binding in brightly coloured patterns. The technique and ornament recall the partitions in yurts found, for example, among the Pamirkirgizes of Afghanistan. In recent times fabric curtains with patchwork patterns or plastic partitions have appeared. The strips of tent material used to be made by the bedouin women themselves. Today strips of tent cloth and tent ribbons are often made by professional weavers in villages and to nomads in the *suqs* of, for example, Aleppo or Homs.

294 Plan of a bedouin tent.

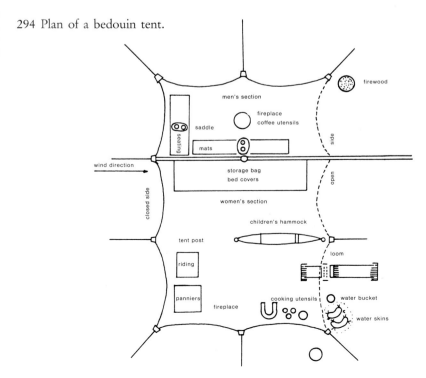

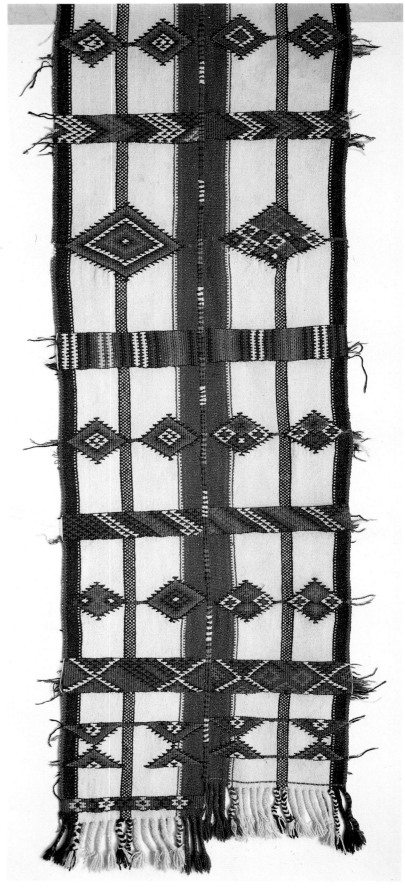

295 & 296 Back walls and partitions form the richest textile decoration in the bedouin tent. They are made in narrow strips on simple horizontal looms and then sewn together.

297 & 298 Camel saddlebags are used to transport the household equipment during migration, and in the tent they are used instead of chests.

299 Horse saddlebag from the oasis of Palmyra.

300 Breast and flank ornament for camels, southern Syria.

The centre of the men's section is a fireplace, usually a portable charcoal brazier with a set of coffee jugs. This serves as the reception room, where the head of the family receives male guests, Along the partition wall at the back of the room – and, if the tent belongs to a man of importance, along the side walls too – kelim rugs with kelim cushions are piled up. Camel saddles may be placed between them to serve as armrests. Hanging on the central tent pole is a leather bag decorated with glass beads, cowries or metal capsules, for the green, unroasted coffee beans, and a smaller bag for the cardamom seeds, which are added to the coffee. In front of the place where only the master of the house is allowed to sit, is a heavy wooden coffee mortar with carved decoration, often with metal mounts, more rarely with extensive camel-bone inlay, and a pestle, which is also carved. Spoons for taking the coffee powder out of the mortar are attached to the mortar by chains. They are cast in metal with decoration in relief or engraved; in exceptional cases they have silver mounts. Next to the brazier is a long cast iron pan for roasting coffee with a turner. The equipment for preparing coffee is completed by wooden dishes in which the roasted coffee is cooled and into which the ground coffee from the mortar is put to be transferred to the coffee pot. The preparation and offering of coffee is fundamental to bedouin hospitality. The quantity and the quality of the craftsmanship of the utensils used show the prosperity of the owner.

After meals the bedouins drink tea, as well as milk and water, but coffee is clearly their favourite drink. It is the first thing to be served to anyone who arrives, no matter whether he is a neighbour from the same camp or a complete stranger. The travellers in the eighteenth and nineteenth centuries described the coffee circle in the tent of the sheikh, and how the order in which coffee was offered to the participants was an indication of their rank. At these coffee circles all the important matters concerning the group were discussed.

301 Bell for the leading camel, cast bronze.

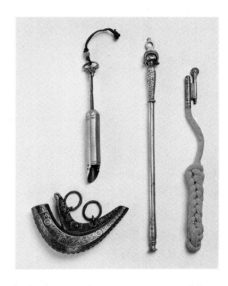

302 Powder horn, powder measure, ramrod for a pistol, and bedouin tinder. Damascus, nineteenth century.

303 Pipe heads, ceramic partly gilded. Damascus, nineteenth century.

304 Powder flask in the Ottoman style to be worn on the belt, cast bronze, Damascus, nineteenth century.

305 Leather power flask.

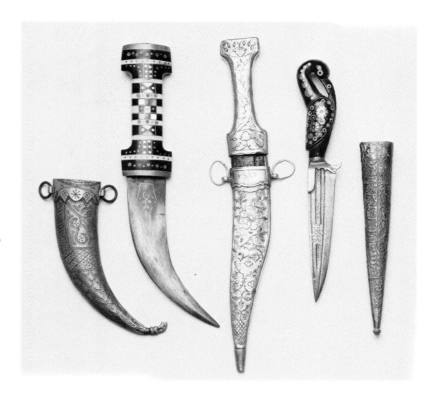

307 Daggers with chased metal mounts and inlaid hilts, nineteenth/twentieth centuries.

308 Coffee mortar with pestle and spoon, roasting pan, cast iron and two trays for cooling the coffee beans after roasting. Wood, (right, with bone inlay), Damascus, nineteenth/twentieth centuries.

306 Spoons for removing the ground coffee from the mortar, cast bronze.

310 Cigarette holders made of amber, bakelite, bone, black coral and coral with silver inlay, silver, and silver filigree. Damascus, nineteenth/twentieth centuries.

309 Prayer beads made of wood, wood with silver inlay, and bone.

312 Sabre scabbard, leather with cloth appliqué, and gun case (acquired by Euting before 1883).

311 Water-pipe mouthpieces, amber with engraved or nielloed silver mounts.

313 Leather container for a water pipe (Euting Collection).

314 Sheep nomad in the men's section of his tent.

315 Small coffee pot with porcelain cups and chased cup-covers made of copper gilt. Pot and cup-covers, Damascus, nineteenth century.

317 Large coffee pot and leather pouches for coffee beans and cardamon.

318 Set of coffee pots, cast bronze. The handles are decorated with leather binding.

316 Copper dish with iron rings, engraved and tin-plated, for bedouin feasts. Damascus, nineteenth/twentieth centuries.

319 A bedouin, now sedentary, in Hama. The reception room of his house is furnished like the men's section of a tent.

The earliest evidence for the use of coffee comes from the Yemen in the fourteenth century. By the sixteenth century the taste for coffee had spread all over the Ottoman Empire. Although this is a relatively recent custom, it has been completely integrated into the everyday life of the bedouin (see Korsching 1980).

As a rule the coffee is prepared by the master of the tent himself. The rhythmical beating of the coffee-mortar – similar to a drum solo – can be heard all over the camp. It also serves as an invitation to come to have coffee.

Water is set to boil in the largest coffee pot. A few spoonfuls of ground coffee are added to the boiling water. The coffee is then brought to the boil several times. The second pot is filled with ground cardamom. When the coffee powder has settled the coffee is poured from the first pot into the second one with the cardamom, boiled again and finally poured at least once more into a third pot. Because it has been boiled up several times the coffee becomes very strong and bitter. Its appearance is almost greenish brown and transparent. A small quantity of the coffee – only about one to one and a half teaspoonfuls – is poured into little coffee cups, which have long been imported from China. Normally coffee is offered three times in a row. If someone wants no more coffee, he returns the cup to the pourer with a slight shake of the wrist. This method of preparing coffee is only customary among the bedouin. Peasants and town-dwellers drink mocca prepared and sweetened in the Turkish manner.

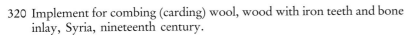

320 Implement for combing (carding) wool, wood with iron teeth and bone inlay, Syria, nineteenth century.

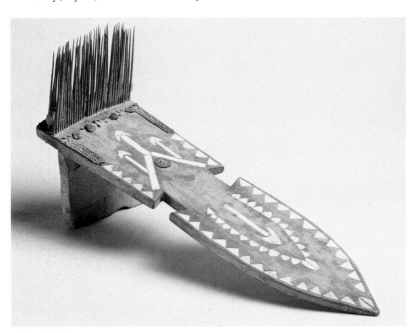

321 South Jordanian bedouin woman spinning.

322 Sheep shears, shuttle and spindles, southern Syria.

323 Simple bedouin cooking equipment with plates, cooking pots, ladles (tin-plated copper), a baking tray (steel), and a small kerosene lamp made of tin plate. Southern Syria.

324 Water pots and vessels with attachments for hanging. The flattened side of the pot on the left it turned to the animal's body when the bedouins are migrating.

325 Bedouin woman grinding corn, Palestine.

326 & 327 Small bags decorated with beads, used by bedouin women for toiletries, southern Syria.

328 Women and children of sheep nomads in the women's section of their tent.

330 Make-up boxes of well-to-do bedouin women, with mirrors; left: with mother-of-pearl inlay (Euting Collection, Damascus, before 1883); right: painted to imitate intarsia; in front, a mirror in a tin-plated copper case.

331 Pans, tin-plated copper. The folding handles of the pans in front are typical of bedouin household equipment.

329 Copper plates and dishes, tin-plated and engraved, Damascus, nineteenth century.

332 Milking bowl, wood with nailhead decoration (Euting Collection, before 1883), leather jug and pouring vessel, wood, Syria, nineteenth century.

333 Leather bags with fringes; left: with metal mounts; right: trimmed with seeds. Syria, nineteenth century.

336 Turned bowl with cover, attachments for hanging and glass rings. Syria, fourteenth century.

334 Water sack made from a goat skin, carefully repaired.

335 Leather bag for making butter (rolled up), and skin for storing butter.

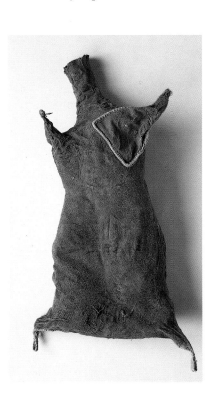

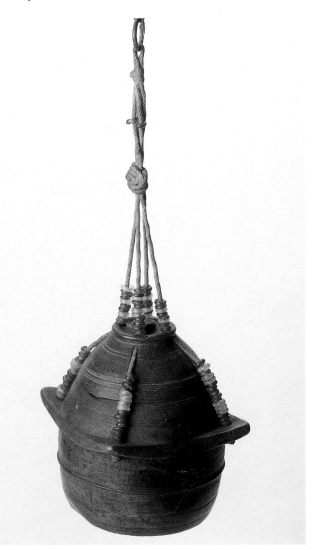

In the women's part of the tent are piles of bed covers and storage sacks, usually heaped against the partition wall, as well as baskets for gathering fuel, cooking pots, flat iron griddles for making bread, a stone mill for grinding corn, carved vessels for milk, large wooden funnels for decanting the milk, and various leather sacks. Fresh milk was poured into goatskins, where it turned sour within a few hours. The soured milk was then transferred to other skins to turn to butter. The goat skin was hung by cords from a simple tripod, and the milk was turned to butter by rocking the skin. The butter and buttermilk were then separated and stored in the shadow of the tent in smaller bags made of lizard skin. Cooking pots, ladles, skimming ladles, bread turners and suchlike were traditionally made of tin-plated copper. Usually these utensils were undecorated and almost identical in form to those found among the bedouins of Palestine, Jordan and Syria as far as the Arabian Peninsula. In the tents of the well-to-do are enormous deep copper plates, which mostly have engraved decoration. On these plates the *mansaf*, the traditional bedouin festive meal was served. One or more whole sheep are cooked in buttermilk, then placed on a plate and covered with piles of rice. The buttermilk, to which wild herbs may be added, is then poured over the rice. I was reliably informed that at a wedding of a bedouin sheikh up to five sheep can be served on a single plate, which is carried by ten or more men.

I know of no differences worth mentioning by which the household equipment of the bedouins could be ascribed to specific tribal groups. Such differences would be most likely to occur in woven products such as tent curtains, cushions and so on. Here particular regions or particular tribes seem to have particular preferences. The Roualla, for example, appear to like flat-weaves with a blue ground and white ornamental stripes. The actual geometric ornaments cannot be attributed to any particular group. They basically consist of lozenges, triangles and stars. If the pieces are not patterned all over, as is usually the case with small pieces, broad strips of ornament are woven across the warp. The background is then formed of strips lengthwise and the women weaving them are very skilled in their use of the different natural colours of the wool, from black to off-white and camel-hair. The adornments of the leading camel is particularly elaborate, and always have the function both of an amulet and of decoration. The fact that it is impossible to ascribe specific style to particular tribes may be the result of the extensive migrations. The Roualla, the largest group, migrate from Jordan, through Syria as far as Saudi Arabia and southern Iraq. Moreover, women marry into other tribes and bring their accustomed patterns with them. It also happens that women from one group are commissioned to do work for women of another group. I have also been told that bedouin women copy the patterns of professional weavers. Clearly anything that pleases is permitted.

Of course, all the other household equipment cannot be attributed to specific groups, since it is acquired from outside. As a rule wooden containers are purchased from villagers, who make them as a part-time activity. The most important centre of production of brass and copper goods was Damascus, which provided them for eastern Jordan, large parts of Syria and also for most of the Arabian Peninsula. In the case of coffee pots there were, however, regional preferences regarding the shape of handles and the ornamentation below the neck. Otherwise this copper and brass ware is also extremely uniform.

Deviations from the standard furnishings described above can always occur. The tents of well-to-do sheikhs still contain magnificent weapons. Even in the past past these were for display rather than for use in battle. Wealthy men always kept swift horses for riding, as well as camels. The saddles and bridles of these highly-prized animals provided another welcome opportunity to show off the wealth of the owner. In the women's part of the tent the equivalent of the splendidly decorated weapons and saddles are the small inlaid boxes with mirrors used to store toiletries and the most valuable jewellery. An unusual example of the de luxe objects for bedouin women is our wool-carding instrument with inlaid camel-bone decoration. In Syria we have not found any of the lavish appliqué work on cloth, some of which has fringes with metal mounts, or leatherwork decorated with seeds, like the examples collected by Euting in the mid-nineteenth century. I cannot say whether they were made for the nomads by specialist urban craftsmen, or whether the nomads themselves carried out this sort of elaborate work on these objects, which are so typical of their culture. In general it is true to say that, depending on the wealth of the owner, all the luxury articles to be found in well-to-do urban households can also be found in the possession of a bedouin.

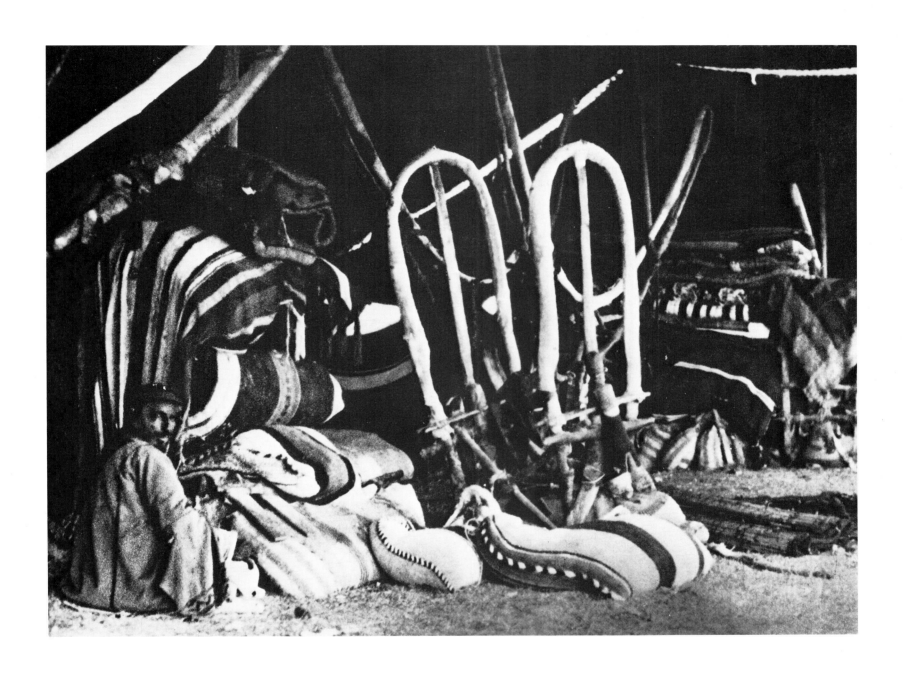

337 Women's section of a Roualla tent with carpets piled up, tent bags, litters
and provisions, before 1934.

338 Bag used by nomads who have become sedentary, in form and decoration on the model of a camel saddlebag. Woven wheat straw with decorative stripes embroidered in wool. Southern Syria, twentieth century.

340 & 341 Horse saddlebags. The decorative stripes on the upper bag are knotted. Southern Syria, nineteenth/twentieth centuries.

339 Camel saddlebag, wool.

342 Horse saddle with saddle-cloth sewn onto it, flat-weave with embroidered ornaments, Roualla bedouin.

343 Saddle, high wooden seat, leather covering, nielloed silver mounts in the Circassian style, with girth, crupper, stirrup leathers and cast stirrups, nineteenth century. It could have been used either by men in the cities or by bedouins.

344 Saddle-cloth with leather reinforcements, made in Aleppo for Kurds, nineteenth century.

345 Mounted lancer in the Syrian desert, *c.* 1934.

Life in the Desert

Margareta Pavaloi

Bedouin tents in the desert, caravans, the free life of the nomads with their warrior tradition, their hospitality, and their talent for telling stories – these images with their mixture of romanticism and adventure have become firmly established in European literature on the Near and Middle East.

Arabic literature, too, idealizes the bedouin – noble, free, proud, armed – and presents a stylized version of bedouin existence as the true lifestyle for an Arab. The yearning for the desert and the desire to prove oneself in the struggle against its hardships are juxtaposed to the fear of its dangers and hardships. At the same time the lifestyle of the bedouin is a constant cause of mistrust for the urban population and the peasants. Idealized and admired, yet at the same time scorned and feared, the noble desert warrior and the uncouth camel-driver are in fact very closely connected.

Only governments were – and still are – united in their aversion to the nomads. As a rule they had – and still have – little sympathy for this uncontrollable section of their population.

For their part, the bedouins themselves also have an ambivalent view of the sedentary population. On one hand the glorification of their own tradition is coupled with contempt for the peasants, who are tied to their land and have to work with their hands; yet on the other there is a longing for the security of settled life in a village or town.

Though we admire the bedouins for their skill as story tellers, their true form of literary expression is poetry. There is scarcely an event, a personal mood or an every-day situation which does not find expression by a poem. (All the following poems are quoted in the English transla-tion in Musil, 1928.) The following poem expresses the desire to live in the village.

A bedouin longs for a settled life:

Oh may I be of the settlers and live on lands cultivated,
In regions where gardens and palms thrive.
To a large well with a round footboard
I would bring tried, fat, sterile she-camels.
Our buckets no one would call small,
And when emptied they would pour forth water in floods.
Thus I say, how sweet it were if many palm trees
with yellow luxuriant twigs would sprout.

If we had a house hospitable, not to be ashamed of,
Sighted from afar by men who have consumed their supplies,
And a mortar with pan for roasting coffee by a heap of red-hot
coals,
And Damascus pots with cups at hand.
My soul would desire a slender-waisted
Mistress who would cut out my heart.
O twig of the gentle banana in the orchard
With its head moistened by the dew and its roots by the creek.
They pleaded: "But she is so small yet,"
O my dear! O twig to whom for its youth respite must be
given!
Her breast is a zbejdi growing in an overflowed vale,
The drops of sweat of the black clouds, pouring forth a rain
shower.

A Slubi wishes to become a bedouin:

O Allah! pray, forgiveness and paradise grant me;
May my fate, as willed by my Lord, be made clear to me.
Greet for me the steed which our kin knows,
I long to stab, for the sake of the eyes of the large milking
camels
And the camels big with young, returning when they hear the
voice of the careful herdsmen.
I long to stab and strike with the spear cunningly,
When fear fills the heart of the hero of the women who are
weary of their husbands.

(All bedouins use a stick to drive their camels. The Sleib are a stationary tribe who are regarded by true bedouins as sedentary. They are renowned for their skill in working gazelle leather, and many bedouins obtain their belts from them. Their territory, situated at the edge of the desert, is considered by the bedouins as barren because it does not provide enough fodder for camels.)

346 Sheep nomads between es-Saura and Raqqa beginning their autumn migration. Tractors (and jeeps) are very popular and practical vehicles in the desert and are highly prized by the nomads.

347 As a result of the government's irrigation projects and the opening up of new areas for agriculture, many nomads are becoming sedentary. East of Aleppo as far as Raqqa, and on the Euphrates, a number of new villages have developed in recent years.

348 Donkey and leading ram are to be seen at the head of every herd. The leading ram has its coat coloured with henna and colourful woollen tassels, a flower and amulets are tied to the coat. Because it is an important animal and looked after with affection, it is protected from danger just like its owner.

349 "Camel thorn" is a typical desert plant. It is the camel's most important food. Sheep are unable to eat it.

350 Meslat Pasha, the senior sheikh of the Jebur, with his family, 1929. The Jebur are a branch of the Zubed, who came from southern Arabia and whose history of migration in Syria (Hauran, Damascus region and Euphrates valley) goes back to the twelfth century. The Jebur first made their home between Deir ez-Zor and Abu Kamal, but then under pressure from the tribes that followed them, migrated to the Khabour; some of them went further, to the Tigris.

A bedouin warns a Slubi not to evade his destiny:

O dweller of the barren desert! thou has laid up sorrow in thy heart.
Do thou no longer ride a horse, O thou maker of leather patches for elbow and knees!
Thy work is in the small tent in the barren desert, so leave it neither it
Nor the dogs inherited from they grandfather, the dogs who always bark.
O thou, whose donkeys have trampled down every fountain where they have drunk,
What is destroyed thou must repair with timber and stone.

In daily life the desert is hardly a romantic place. Its demands on people are severe and unyielding. They can only adapt their lives to the desert, not struggle against it.

Only the intimate knowledge of the desert and the way of life adapted to it, which the nomads learn at an early age, enables them to live in, and make use of, the desert economically. This makes them the "princes of the desert".

The desert can support neither a large population nor large herds. The economy of the nomads is extremely delicately balanced, especially in times of drought: the decimation or loss of the herds means economic ruin.

In times when the pressure of life is extremely high, tribes and families split up. Smaller and weaker groups are forced out of the desert. The latent antagonism amongst themselves, and between them and the sedentary population breaks out into open conflict. The desert is always in motion. A high level of mobility in its broadest sense is the prerequisite of existence.

Nomads are very precise observers of their surroundings. They can read the desert like a book, and can recognize the condition of the soil and vegetation, the presence or lack of watering holes, movements of the sand, the arrival of a storm or the beginning of rain. All this is important for choosing a place to pitch camp, deciding how long to stay, and in what direction to continue one's journey. Nomads find their bearings with the help of the stars, and the nomadic year is divided into five periods based on the rising and setting of the constellations.

The nomadic year begins with the autumn rains. Their arrival is signalled by the rise of Canopus in the first days of October. Canopus reigns for 40 nights, followed by 25 nights of the Pleiades, and 25 of the Gemini. This period of 90 days is the rainy season, and lasts from the beginning of October until January. The second period of the rainy season begins with the rise of the Pleiades.

The "Pleiades rains" are the most important of the rains that fall in this period. They determine the growth of vegetation and hence whether it will be a good or bad year in economic terms.

The third period begins with the ascent of Aucturnus and lasts until mid-April. After this the rule of the stars comes to an end and is followed by the 4-month dry season, the harshest time of the year. By the beginning of October everything is longing for the onset of the rains – a great concern for the nomads.

They observe the sky very carefully and if the 'sun dog' is visible to the right or left of the sun they know that it will rain soon.

If the Roualla see that, despite thunder and lightning, the clouds disperse, they pray:

"O, that he, who sends (angels) to the cloud, may send (an angel) to it on eight riding camels and say to it: 'The gift (of God) shall come down'".

If it only rains a few drops, they lament:

"After this (rain) we have lost what might have brought us gold, (we have lost it) like a vibrating mirage. Truly, we can do nothing without Allah".

Soothsayers are questioned about the duration and quantity of rain to be expected.

It the absence of rain gives rise to serious concern, then, according to Musil (1928), the Roualla hold a procession with the "Mother of Rain". A woman's dress is hung on a wooden cross and carried by a virgin at the head of the procession. she followed by the girls and women. They pass from tent to tent singing:

O mother of the rain! rain upon us;
Wet the mantle of our herdsman.
O mother of the rain! rain upon us;
With pouring rain allay our thirst.
O mother of the rain! rain upon us;
From Allah's measure measure out to us.
O mother of the rain! rain upon us;
A real flood let our share be.

O mother of the rain! rain upon us;
Thy evil is still tormenting us.
O mother of the rain! rain upon us;
Clouds of dust are still blinding us.
O mother of the rain! rain upon us;
The spectre of want speeds towards us.
O mother of the rain! O hungry one!
The chill and severe cold have destroyed us.

Of her who will give us a full sieve,
Oh may (Allah) make the little son grow up a rider.
Of her who will give us a full bolt,
O may (Allah) lead the son to a bride.
Of her who will give us a large handful,
O may the grave open for her enemy.
Of her who will give us a small handful,
Oh may her eyelashes soon grow thicker.

Seat me a upon a weak young camel,
And take away from him who would hold me;
The tears of my eyes are exhausted
Weeping for him from whom they have parted me.

O wolf! O thou who strugglest with the hot south wind!
Drive away the cold breeze of the north wind.
Thou hast surely seen Alja and Abu Zejd,
Who used to dwell in manors high.

(Alja and Abu Zeid are hero figures from peasant tales. It is said that they once lived in the ruins which appear again and again on the horizon of the desert.)

After they have received a gift from each tent the women and girls carry the "Mother of Rain" to a small tent situated off the camp. They divide the gifts among themselves,

351 Nomad woman in Deir ez-Zor. The head-cloth she is wearing was made in Aleppo. Her costume is a mixture of traditional (jacket) and modern (dress) elements, which is characteristic of the region. The child's cap is decorated with amulets to ward off the evil eye, which is said to be rooted in people's envy, and other dangers.

352 Nomads in transit camping in the ruins of Palmyra.

353 The tent of sheep nomads between Palmyra and es-Suchne.

354 Stationary nomads from the vicinity of Qasr el-Heir esh- Sharqi.

355 The desert between Palmyra and es-Suchne.

356 & 357 Wedding dress from es-Suchne made of woven silver brocade. The seams are decorated with silk thread. The woven pattern is made up of small trees of life, symbols of hope suitable for a wedding.

358 *Abaye* made of black wool. The neck is lavishly embroidered in silk. According to Petermann, who acquired it in 1857, it was worn by bedouin notables. (Museum für Völkerkunde, Berlin)

359 Camelhair *abaye*, contemporary Damascene production.

remove the woman's dress from the wooden cross and do not return to their tents until evening.

According to the tales of the Roualla, the Angel Gabriel is the lord of the rain clouds. The Roualla take the view that he is not well disposed either to them or to their territories and therefore only brings sufficient rain to the peasants. He chases the clouds over the desert allowing only a few drops to fall from his wings down to earth.

The nomadic way of life and economy demands the integration of the individual into the extended family, the clan and the tribe. Membership of a family, clan and tribe is regulated by the kinship system. Kinship is defined through the male line (patrilineal). This is expressed by "son of..." and "father of...", which is a part of the name. The organization of clans and tribes is segmentary. All families which can trace their genealogy in the male line back to a common ancestor (real or fictional) belong to the same clan or tribe.

The large tribes of the Aneze or the Shammar each refer, for example, to such a common ancestor, and the names of some of their sub-tribes (Bani Sahr, Aulad Ali) are also an indication of this.

Large tribes are a result of a continuous process of fusion. The reverse, fission, is also a possibility, i.e. the splitting of at tribe into numerous sub-tribes. In principle any family can become the nucleus of a new tribe.

Economic considerations, personal ambitions or conflicts – internal or external – may lead to either fusion or fission.

When the groups split up, the kinship relations between the groups still remain, unless they are deliberately broken off.

The individual derives his identity primarily, if not exclusively, from being a member of a family and tribe. You know who you are because you know to whom you belong. In return you are committed to unconditional solidarity with your family and your wider circle of relatives. Therefore the individual receives protection and security through this social network. You belong to your people and, if at all possible, prefer to live with them.

O my Lord! O thou who returnest!
Lead us back to our kin,
Where we may pitch our tents as is seemly
And encamp on our own grounds.
We shall move away from this region
Forever to disappear from its midst.
Hail to the father of Nawwaf!
Would that he may move and allot to us new camps.

Within the family relations between fathers and sons, and between the sons, are relations of authority and respect, based on relative age. These relations are not free of rivalries and personal ambitions and therefore an underlying tension always exists. Fathers fear losing their power, and sons fear the rivalry of their brothers. The tension

between rivalry and the necessity of solidarity is expressed in a proverb: "I against my brother; my brother and I against our cousins; our cousins, my brother and I against the rest of the world."

By using their prestige, authority and economic power the elders are able to control the rivalry of the younger men and assert their demands on them.

Nomads who have settled in villages or towns maintain their connections with their relatives living out in the desert. Membership of a family or tribe ultimately dominates any local or regional identity over generations. Kinship is an important factor in the structuring and organization of houses and neighbourhoods in the village and city districts. Even in a city quarter people still prefer to live among their own kind. When meeting strangers it is still possible to identify oneself either through genealogical or local links. Within one's social grouping this is hardly possible. Modern life as well as individual wishes and ideas often conflict with the norms and duties of the traditional family. Leaving the family means putting one's social security at risk.

Marriage, the basis of the family and kinship is an important and serious affair. Great store is set by making "right" or "suitable" marriages. These are not left to chance: preference is given to those marriages which conform to the traditional rules. This is not only true of bedouins. They do, however, follow the rules more strictly, since a marriage is not only a matter for two individuals; it is a relationship between two families. The rules prescribe marriage between patrilateral parallel cousins, i.e. the man marries the daughter of his father's brother. He has a prerogative (which is also a duty) to marry her – she is so to speak "reserved" for him. Only if he makes it understood that he has no interest in marrying her is she free to marry another man.

If a traditional marriage goes against the wish of one of the parties involved it can lead to personal and family conflict.

There is none among you who understand me, O hosts!
For my cheeks are wet with sorrow for her.
By Allah! even if I lose my life, I will surely mount my old camel,
Search another country, and flee to the people who encamp there.
I shall steal her with the slender waist, and at night the riding camels will escape with me,
So that I shall be far from my kin in the morning.

There is the possibility of avoiding a traditional marriage by eloping, thus presenting the relatives with a fait accompli, if one dares.

Hail to thee, who ridest the young she-camel captured from the Hazal!
I would fain ride with thee, but my father is angry.

Ah, hail to thee, who ridest the she-camel taller than all others!
I would gladly ride along with thee but am afraid.

A girl can become very angry if her lover does not have the courage to elope, and so deprives her of the possibility of evading a traditional marriage.

Thou with the fine tattooing,
Thou with the fair teeth,
Kiss me and break the neck of the coward
For the next night.

Thou with the fine tattooing,
Thou, who canst not decide,
Kiss me and break the neck of the coward
For the next year.

I wailed as a wolf wails when the dew has past
For the lover who has betrayed me.
After all this suffering I have no courage left
To resist the claims of my kin.

On the man's side there is always the possibility of rejecting a traditional marriage. If this suits the interests of both parties, then there are no further complications. But a rejection can also be a serious insult to both families. The girl's family may regard itself as slighted and its honour injured, while the man's family may feel itself disgraced by his refusal to fulfil his obligations. The pressure from the families can be extremely strong – on the girl and on the man. The advantages of a traditional marriage are obvious. The family background of the future couple is well known. Both parties are familiar with each other's rights and duties, and have the networks available to enforce solidarity if it is

360 The war banner of the Roualla-Aneze, 1899, the emblem of their tribe.

361 Sottam ibn Shaalan, senior sheikh of the Roualla-Aneze, 1899, the Roualla have the reputation of being the noblest of the bedouin tribes in the Syrian desert.

362 & 363 Bedouin jacket, wool, lavishly brocaded with silver threads. Jackets of this sort are still woven to order in Aleppo. The weavers judge them by the form and quantity of the patterns in the dorsal triangle and the stripes on the front. These criteria also determine the price. The lining is made of a printed material.

364 Lightweight summer *abaye*, artificial silk with silver lancé. Contemporary Damascene production.

lacking. A traditional marriage is a safe marriage, whereas an external marriage, although it may be honourable and opportune, is in principle a risky business.

A particularly serious problem arises if the man delays his decision, either because he cannot make up his mind or because he cannot raise the money needed for the "bride price", which is usually high. There is concern that the girl will become too "old" and see her prospects of a marriage elsewhere dwindling. In such a case the girl's family tries to force the man to give up the marriage, a delicate matter since this means offending the man's family. External marriages are approved of, if they can be used to build up or maintain new alliances or good relations with other groups or tribes. Kinship relations and marriages offer a wide range of possibilities of playing politics. This is of great interest to the women too. Bedouin women are very self-assured and strong-willed. They are aware of their status and know their rights. They are as proud of their descent as their menfolk are. To marry a woman of "noble lineage" is the aim of many men, providing they can afford it, as the firm conviction exists that the characteristics considered noble are passed on by the women.

By every means try to beget a thoroughbred son,
For as the fire depends on its foundation
So nobility is in the veins of women
Who are of pure blood descended.

365 & 366 Bedouin jacket in kelim technique, woven in wool and cotton and made in Damascus. Acquired in 1871 for the Museum für Völkerkunde, Berlin. These jackets were, and still are, very rare and are not part of the usual nomad wardrobe. They were reserved for the rich and noble.

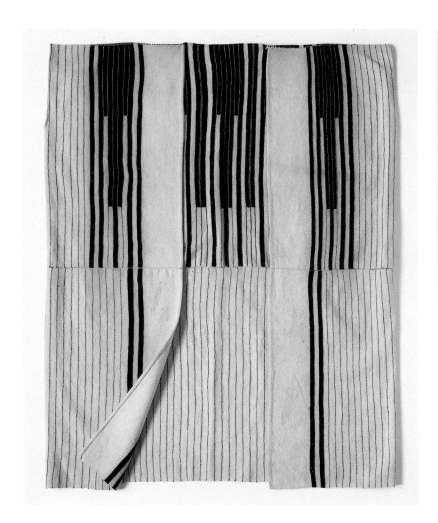

368 *Abaye* made of goat hair and wool with the typical striped pattern, from the Hauran.

367 Traditional nomad jacket, wool, made from two strips of cloth sewn together, with sleeves attached to the straight sides, from the Hauran.

The characteristics most prized include courage, generosity, justness and leadership.

Ah, how beautiful thy arms, O Sita,
With blue tattoo marks!
How beautiful the noise of the attack of her kin
And the sabres blood-dyed as if with henna.
How prettily her camel to its feet is rising
Adorned with purchased ornaments.
A gazelle ran in amongst you
And feared not.

O thou daughter of him who chopped off Heads!
O Sita, our cold-blooded daughter!
Only a rich man could buy her,
While a poor one would, alas, grieve vainly for her.
Sita's kinsmen fall upon the enemy as if on sheep for sacrifice,
Like drunken men, nothing can frighten them;
Careless they are of the most dangerous spots,
And their dishes they constantly fill.

(Sita's mother, Turkiye, was the daughter of the senior sheikh of all the Fedaan. Sita's father was known for pitching his clan's camps where they were exposed to the greatest dangers. In order to marry a woman like Sita a man must have special qualities.)

The girls, naturally ,always want to have a young, bold hero for a husband:

O my Lord! Oh, mayest thou help me
To all that I desire:
I fain would sit on a tall white camel
In a fancy litter,
And with me a young hero who would protect me
At such time when my spittle dries up;
A young hero on a white mare with a long tail,
Of noble breed.

Or the girl asks simply:

O Lord! O my all!
Give me a clear mind,
(Grant) that I may ride a tall white camel
In the midst of my kin.
A husband give me to my taste
And a nose ring of gold.

369 Hajr Abu Wuteid (centre), sheikh of the Feddagha Shammar, 1911. The tribes of the Shammar, long-term rivals of the Aneze, were the second most important nomadic power in Syria.

Children are important and a source of pleasure. The Roualla women do not seek the help of a midwife at the birth. After seven days the child receives a ceremonial bath. On the tenth, twentieth or fortieth day after the birth a festive meal is given, and all the women of the camp are invited. The young mother visits all her relatives with her child, who receives presents. These are its property. It is the mother's privilege to choose the name of the child.

The institution of blood feud, too, cannot be regarded apart from the kinship system. Various obligations, legal norms and concepts of honour are closely linked with this institution. In the case of a violent death all the male relatives are obliged, for justice and honour, to revenge their dead kinsman. The revenge is aimed not only at the person who is guilty of the crime, but also at his male relatives. Depending on the seriousness of the case, negotiations are possible, and the blood feud can be avoided by the payment of a sum of money, providing the relatives of the dead man accept this. The risk for all involved is very high, and great efforts are made to settle the conflict by non-violent means.

In the desert the family and tribe are the guarantors of security and the rights of the individual. The total of unwritten regulations, commandments and prohibitions, which correspond to the norms and values of the particular Bedouin society and regulate the communal life within the group and between the different groups, are called the tribal law.

Anyone who is not integrated into such a social network, who does not place himself under its protection, or who is not affiliated to a group, is a nobody and hence an "outlaw", since nobody is responsible for him. Strangers necessarily fall into this category, just as guests and travellers do, when they are separated from their people and far from places which are safe for them. Their integration is therefore brought about by the institution of hospitality.

370 Ferhan ibn Hudeib, senior sheikh of the Sbaa Aneze, and his son, 1899. Their clothing is that of rich bedouins.

371 Woman from the family of Audeh abu Tayyi, a sheikh of the Huweitat. The man is probably a relative of hers, and, to judge from his costume, he lives in a village or town. She is wearing the traditional dress of northern Arab bedouin women.

373 A nomad woman in Homs. She is wearing a heavy silk head-cloth interwoven with silver thread, as they are made in Homs. Tattooing is customary among the nomads, but it is different for men and women and varies from tribe to tribe.

374 Silk veil (*shambar*). The strips are dyed black, embroidered with silk and decorated with sequins. The two strips are sewn together with a decorative seam, and the silk fringes are added at the ends.
The size (308 x 100 cm) is necessary for veiling the head and chest.

375 Dorsal jewellery made of glass beads with sequins and brightly coloured silk and cotton tassels. It is worn in Harran al-Awamid as wedding jewellery by peasant and sedentary nomad women.

372 Traditional dress (*thob*) of the bedouin women of northern Arabia, with large winged sleeves of black satin with cotton decorated with machine embroidery. The proportions (length: 340 cm, width: 234 cm, length of right arm: 195 cm, length of left arm: 176 cm) seem at first sight to be excessive, but when the dress is worn correctly it is very practical and fulfils all the requirements of a mobile lifestyle. The sleeves – the right one is longer than the left – can be tied behind the back in such a way that they form a bag for carrying shopping and a young child, or can be used as a head covering. The long skirt is drawn through the belt so that it forms two layers and so improves ventilation in the garment. At night the dress can be used as a "sleeping bag" for mother and child. The embroidery indicates that this dress is a festive garment. It is applied so that it shows best when the dress is worn. It is not merely decorative: many elements in the pattern are supposed to act as amulets protecting the woman wearing it. They are embroidered on to the appropriate parts of the dress.

The host is responsible for his guests' lives and possessions. If something happens to the guest as long as he is under his protection, the host is obliged to seek revenge. If the guest's property is stolen, he has to replace it. The importance attached to generous hospitality, and in particular to entertaining guests with coffee is made clear in the following poem.

O Klejb, light the fire, O Klejb, light it!
To light it is thy duty; the fuel will be brought.
To prepare cardamom and coffee beans is my duty,
Thine to have the tarnished pots ready.
Lay upon the fire more fuel, rimt with bark,
And do the roasting as soon as my long-lashed eyes fall asleep.
The mortar's voice will be heard at the night's end,
And a rap on its brim will sound like the howl of a wolf.
Mayest thou, when thou lightest the fire and its flame flares up,
Mayest thou, O Klejb, bring us night pilgrims from far away,
While a coward presses under him a disobedient wife.
Oh, how pleasant is their sticks' tap, tap, on the she-camel's neck!
What is left from yesterday, O Klejb, serve to the common visitors,
For our gain is in them only who do chase the clouds
In a dry, icy wind, O Klejb, that blows piercingly.
With hands folded they sit and urge only with heels
In a pouring rain with a sharp gale,
Or again in a light, moist breeze like snake poison.
To them, O Klejb, speak the language of love,
Even if into my mud hut a proud, stiff-necked man has come.
Tell them what is sweeter than dates on twigs from Gubba
And purer than melted butter bought of Arabs
Oh, how many fat wethers' heads have we thrown away
And besmeared the necks of she-camels from the wound made by the knife.
A pure heart seeks no gossip,
And should those heroes refuse to salute me (I shall salute them).
For both the chief and the herdsman should walk the path of love.
As Allah keeps the account of each being.
A guest is Allah's guest and must not be insulted,
And this one we shall protect against wrong.

(The poet lived in the village of Qnaa and was famous for his generosity and hospitality. Whoever passed by, for instance, on the road to Damascus or to the region of the Shammar, enjoyed his hospitality. The poem refers to a particular event: the night when a group of bedouins came to him after a raiding expedition in pouring rain and entered his house without a greeting. Nevertheless, he wakened his servant Klejb and instructed him to make coffee.)

The Costume of the Nomads

Maria Zerrnickel

In cut as well as in the combination of the garments and the way in which they are worn the costume of the nomads has changed less over the years than that of the peasants and of the urban population. This may be due to the fact that, to a greater extent than the dress of peasants or townspeople, it served practical needs and was adapted to extreme weather conditions. The differences between the individual tribes and clans are expressed in the choice of colour and the way of wearing the headdress and *abaye*, as well as in many details of decoration, while social status is indicated by the quality of the material. The canon of dress has in principle remained the same to the present day. The adoption of the striped silk kaftan, which is today often replaced by the European jacket, is certainly an adaptation of the dress in the towns. Women have probably adopted the veil (*shambar*). Also relatively modern is the wearing of European leather belts, cartridge belts and shoes.

Women's Costumes

Even among wealthy nomads the dress of the women and girls is simpler than that of the men.

The garment of the women (*thob*) is made of dark cotton with triangular "wing sleeves" and is usually sewn by the woman herself, either by hand or by machine. Everyday dress has no decoration. The dress of some groups is huge (up to 3.5 x 2.5m) and has sleeves of different sizes, the right sleeve made in such a shape that it can be used as a bag or rucksack to carry and wrap small children or objects. These dresses are embroidered round the neck, at the chest and the sides. In addition, they may be decorated with a patchwork of materials in various colours, and embroideries. Some of the patterns and colours have a magic function as protection. As the dress is very long it is held together by a belt, which is tablet-woven from red and black wool or cotton. The skirt is folded up and tucked in the belt. A variant on the dresses of the women which has straight sleeves and is made of dark or black sateen is almost always bought. To fold up the hem and create a kind of "pouch" this dress can be girded in two ways: with a European buckled belt or with a narrow, 2m long belt woven of red wool and decorated with a fringe or tassels. The woven belt is wound around the waist several times and is particularly popular with young girls and women, because it enhances the black dress.

Underneath the black dress, which is worn against the skin, some nomad woman, like the men, wrap a long loin belt of rolled leather around the waist. Usually the women own a second dress, which they wear when working. It is of the same cut as the men's garment, apart from the tight half-sleeves and the two slits at the sides of the skirt. This dress is worn by the women when cooking, collecting fuel, milking etc.. In summer it is worn without any other garment, and in winter over all other garments.

The women's coat (*saye*) is made of materials in dark colours, with wide sleeves and side slits. The neckline down to the chest is ornamented with colourful appliqué work. It is worn to all festivities and for going to town. The women turn it up at the back and knot the ends of the hem in front of the chest, thus creating a pouch on the back, in which they can carry their small children or objects (e.g. wool, food, fuel etc.). These coats are bought in the *suq*. The silk kaftan, which in the past was often made of vertically striped satin, is worn by wealthy women over the dress. A cloth jacket usually replaces the winter coat. Women wear this type of jacket more often than the men do.

The short jacket, reaching to the waist, is made of blue woollen cloth and decorated on the inside with coloured appliqué work. The women buy it in the *suq*.

This short cloth jacket with tight sleeves is produced of different qualities of cloth and often decorated with patch-work-patterns. In the pocket the women usually carry a mirror, a pipe, a small container (*makhale*) with eye make-up (*kohol*), incense and perfume.

The *kohol* (antimony) is obtained by the bedouins from Yemen or India; it is mixed with other substances, put in flasks of different shapes and is applied with a pen. The women are convinced that their eye make-up improves their eyesight. The women also dye their palms and nails with henna (on the occasion of their engagement, wedding or childbirth). Until 30 years ago almost all women went barefoot, but wore ankle jewellery. The bedouin women need several kerchiefs for their veiling and headdress.

The large silk head cloth (*margruna*), is wrapped in a particular way and then held in place by a headband consisting of a smaller and thinner scarf that is folded diagonally (width: up to 5 cm). The smaller scarf is called *asbe*, *mindil* or *shitfa*. This scarf is usually made of black silk, has a coloured border and a short fringe. It is folded into a triangle, rolled, tied around the head to hold the veil (*shambar*) and knotted at the back. The Sbaa girls, for example, like the peasant girls, do not wear a veil. They wrap the *margruna*, without rolling it, in several ways around their head.

The veil (*shambar kreshe*) is more than three metres long and 30-40 cm wide, and is made of fine, almost transparent fabrics (silk or cotton crêpe). It is worn in a special way: over the dress, but underneath the coat and jacket; so that the open neckline is covered in front and at the back the veil comes down almost to the ground. The nomad women of the various tribes each prefer different veils, but mostly they are black, more rarely red or yellow. Some of the veils are in two colours. The scarf is made of a red silk fabric about 42 cm wide. Two red strips are sewn together with decorative stitching and dyed black, leaving the edges (6 cm wide). The ends of the scarf are then decorated with fringes and tassels, sometimes also with simple embroidery.

Married women wear the head cloths and *shambars* differently than young girls, who flirt with their hair and headdress. To prevent the front part of the scarf from sliding, the women tie an object to the corner (e.g. key, jewellery etc.).

Only rich women have a second veil of real (red) silk (*shambar ahmar*): the women also dye it black, leaving only the ends red. Often it is embroidered with spangles and glass beads, and decorated with woven fringes and silk tassels. As with all silk fabrics the material is bought by weight.

Men's Costume

The Men's Garment (*thob*)

The men wear a white, shirt-like garment made of cotton with triangular "wing sleeves", which are rolled up and tied at the back when the man is working, fighting or walking. For riding a bedouin wears the sleeves of his white garment down. A festive garment is usually ornamented with blue, red and black embroidery round the neck and at the chest. For "true" bedouins the "wing sleeves" are very important. From the size of the sleeves it is possible to distinguish a bedouin from a semi-nomad, who farms small livestock. Underneath the white shirt some of the nomads wear a loin belt against the skin and very rarely cotton pants.

The loin belt of the Sbaa for instance consists of a narrow strap of plaited gazelle leather (7mm wide and 5 to 6m long), / which is wound around the body several times. This belt is made by the Sbaa themselves or ordered from the Sleib, who specialize in it (cf. Boucheman, 1934).

According to Musil (1928) the Roualla bedouins obtained their loin belts also from the Sleib. The nomads attach great importance to their loin belts. They never voluntarily part with them and "lace" them tightly, when they are hungry. If a man needs freedom of movement while at work, the garment is hitched up through the belt and the hem is tucked in.

The Pants (*shirwal*)

These are made of coloured or undyed cotton and are worn by all sheep nomads as well as by the "nomads" who settle in the oases. Traditionally camel nomads do not wear pants. Pants are almost always bought ready-made in the *suq*. They are worn underneath the shirt.

The Coat

The coat is usually called *saye* and is an important garment for the man. It is always bought ready-made. The *saye* is open at the front, its wide, straight half-sleeves are split so that the "wing sleeves" of the shirt can be pulled through. It usually has two inner pockets and short side slits at the bottom. The coat is worn over the shirt and can be made of various light-weight fabrics. It has no collar and is held together over the chest by two cords. The long wrist-length sleeves are slit, faced with red fabric and are worn turned up. Sleeves, neck opening, inner pockets and front are decorated with cord couching. The fabrics used for bedouin coats, vary from white cotton over black silk-mixture with yellow vertical stripes (warp: silk, weft: cotton) to white silk with coloured vertical stripes or cotton with coloured stripes. The names of the coats vary depending on the material they are made of. The Roualla call their coat *shun*; it is made of striped fabrics. Several of the Sbaa men today wear a vertically striped *saye*, as worn by the semi-nomads and peasants. Garment and coat are girded with a belt of hand-woven wool or made of leather (*mahsam*). Over the *saye* the men wear a leather belt with shoulder straps for the cartridges, which are made in town.

With "true" nomads the sleeves of the *thob* are always different from those of the *saye*. Sometimes a *saye* with "wing sleeves" (i.e. the form of sleeves belong to the *thob*) can be seen among the semi-nomadic groups on the Euphrates. This is regarded as imitation and in bad taste. Everyone knows that the person wearing it is not a "true" bedouin.

The Cloak (*abaye*)

A man's most important garment is the cloak (*abaye*). This cloak can be made of various light-weight fabrics (silk, artificial silk, mixed silk or cotton) or of coarser fabrics: two straight widths are sewn together with their selvedges and holes are left for the sleeves. It is open at the front and can be fastened with two cords; the neck and shoulder seams have narrow embroidery (reinforcement, decoration of the seams) or cord couching. Another type of *abaye* is made of wool with brown and white vertical stripes. A red *abaye* is special and is worn by rich men over of all other garments.

A light-weight *abaye*, made in light colours for the summer is called *bisht*. It is made of coarse undyed sheep's wool, goat or camel hair with white-brown or white-black vertical stripes and has wool embroidery at the neck and seams. Often it is made of mixed fabrics in ribbed weave (warp: wool, weft: cotton).

377 Nomad women in Deir ez-Zor. Their coats are partly embroidered by machine, but have the traditional cut with long slits. Thus the coat can be folded up at the back and the ends can be tied in front of the breast. A kind of pouch is created in which small children can be carried. This function represents a modification of the traditional oversized dress.

378 A nomad couple in the *suq* of Deir ez Zor.

160

The jacket (*damir*) of dark cloth with contrasting cloth lining, split (to accommodate the wing sleeves of the *thob*) and embroidered sleeves with a richly decorated inner pocket, was worn only rarely and only by a few sheikhs in winter or on important occasions, when they would be on

horseback. For some time now it has gained more popularity with many nomads. Sheep nomads like to use it, but for them the lining is cotton, because the cloth jacket is too expensive.

The winter coat (*farwa*) is made of sheep skin (lining) and of dark, mostly black coarse cotton or cloth, and decorated with coloured appliqué work or cord couching. A wealthy Roualla bedouin often also owned a half-length jacket (*nussiyye*) of cloth or a short fur coat (*ubtiyye*) with an additional head cloth.

In winter the man wears all his garments on top of each other, to keep out the cold. The Roualla have a saying: "He who does not wear heavy garments does not even warm up from carrying".

The headdress of the men varies. The "true" Sbaa still prefer a pure white scarf of fine cotton. A second scarf of silk with a long fringe, often with little tassels, is sometimes wrapped around the head by the sheiks and the semi-nomads of the Euphrates. The sheep nomads north of Palmyra prefer a headscarf of brownish yellow wool.

The names of the scarves depend on the material, colour, pattern and size. There are black scarves with red, yellow or pink stripes, red and blue checked ones or pure white scarves with a red or blue border and a short fringe.

A scarf called *mangruna* is woven of silk with silver brocade. Very popular are scarves made of blue or violet silk with red threads worked into it. A kerchief woven of pure white silk used to be worn solely by the sheikhs and only on very special occasions. The habit of wrapping the scarf over a little embroidered cap is borrowed by the settled nomads from the peasants.

The Headrope (*agal*)

This is usually bought, although the sheep nomads often prefer to make them themselves. The *agal* can be worn in very different ways according to social status or personal mood: e.g. a "serious" man wears his headrope straight, a young man however, who is looking for a bride, pulls it forward over his forehead. By wearing headdress and headrope in different ways unspoken messages – expressing love, interest, disregard etc. – are communicated.

Frequently an amulet is fixed to the ends of the cords of the *agal* to ward off the evil eye, and often a little pair of tweezers is added, for removing spines and thorns from the feet.

Wearing Clothes

Margareta Pavaloi

By wearing particular clothing one is making a statement about one's person, about the time and the society in which one lives. One dresses formally or casually, appropriately or unconventionally, depending on one's mood or to suit a particular occasion. Dress can be determined by social expectations (business dress, evening dress) or regulations (uniform). Through one's clothes one can demonstrate that one is a member of a group or deliberately dissociate oneself from it, or one can use clothes to emphasize economic and social status. Although dress regulations hardly exist today, we still have a sense of correct dress, and this makes us experience clothes as either appropriate or inconsistent with the person wearing them or the occasion.

Clothes and fashion have always been not only a reflection of their time, but also of the culture, the prevailing idea of man and the social hierarchies in a society. Dress regulation follows the social order, the style corresponds to prevailing tastes. Cultural norms and values determine "what is suitable" and whether in fact "anything goes". Clothes express an attitude, and to a great extent they determine the behaviour both of the person wearing them and of the person he or she meets. The language of clothes thus forms an essential part of social communication.

Traditional dress is to an even greater degree the expression of cultural and social norms and is largely determined by them. However, it does not suppress the individuality and autonomy of the person, but leaves the individual much scope for the expression of his or her moods and feelings through the form of clothing and the way he or she wears it.

Traditional dress is usually called folk costume, a term which means the ensemble of clothes and jewellery worn by a person. Through his or her costume a person expresses membership of a particular ethnic, social or religious group. One knows "at first sight" whom one is talking to and is able to orientate one's behaviour accordingly. Western observers have always been fascinated by the variety and the colourfulness of the costume, as well as by the fact that dress makes it immediately possible to ascertain a person's identity. Strolling today through Damascus or Aleppo, for instance, one quickly learns to

379 Female statue from Palmyra. The shape of the earrings and necklaces, as well as elements of the costume and the way they are worn, particularly the design of the headdress, have been preserved to the present day.

380 A woman from Homs, probably of Kurdish origin, holding her child as lovingly as the stone lady from Palmyra. Beneath her veil the border of her headband trimmed with gold coins is visible. Her costume is covered by the "street" coat, which is decorated only at the sleeves.

381 A view of the *suq* for fabrics and garments in Deir ez-Zor.

382 A peasant woman from the environs of Homs. The *shambar* is used by women not only as a cover but also as a sash. The use of the veil in such a way is typical of the peasant women from the villages around Homs.

383 A peasant woman from Maarat en-Numan.

384 A peasant woman from a farm near Ebla. The woman wears a dress made of a modern cotton fabric and a flowered scarf, which is, however, combined with the traditional covering for neck and chest. Conspicuous is the covering of the neck opening with the embroidery attached to the veil.

385 Peasant women from the Qalamoun strolling through town in Damascus. Their dresses have a European cut, but they wear the traditional headdress, veil and the trousers typical of their area. The bottom seam of the trousers is shaped in such as way as to cover the heel.

386 & 387 Peasant women from Chan Sheichun. The embroidery on their dresses and their headscarves are typical of the villages between Hama and Maarat en-Numan.

388 bottom right: A peasant in Damascus. He is wearing the traditional wide trousers for men (*shirwal*) and a checkered head cloth, the same as is used by nomads, but no head-rope.

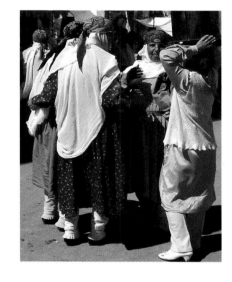

recognize country folk and bedouins by their dress. With the right knowledge it is possible to tell which region or town they come from and which ethnic or religious group they belong to. It is possible to recognize a religious dignitary and the religion he represents. A woman from a traditional quarter of town dresses differently from a modern lady or a young woman consciously following the Islamic tradition. The costume of Kurdish nomad women differs in cut, colour, the way in which it is worn and jewellery from that of their bedouin sisters, and the dress of the Druze peasants differs from that of conservative old men in the town. Traditional dress, most of all that of the women, thus has become an important visual criterion for identifying the person by relating him or her to a particular ethnic and/or religious group, and it plays also an essential part in defining what is strange and exotic to the Western eye. The earliest photographers were already recreating types in their postcards. The sitters were often dressed in the studio with much imagination and according to the photographer's whims, in a way prescribed by European expectations of a "bedouin girl", a "Damascene lady", a "Druze bride" or a "peasant" (Graham-Brown, 1988). Even today we attempt to capture the "right type" with the camera. The reaction to the changes in traditional costume is often a nostalgic regret for the loss of authenticity and naturalness, which tend to be seen as constant and timeless. It is as true to say that traditional costume is the immediate expression of cultural and personal identity, as it is misleading to assume that the norms and values, which determine the latter are unchangeable regulations based on a natural order and immune to all developments of the times. The term tradition is determined not only by constants, but also by many variables with constantly changing characteristics. It is therefore not a static concept, but a very dynamic one: traditional costume expresses change as much as it does cultural constants.

Costume generally played (and still plays) an important role in the cultures of the Middle East. It was (and is) a form of social and political control, and of national identity; in the everyday life of the men and women it is a symbolic expression of personal affiliation and of social roles. So costume has always been involved in conflicts over external and internal changes.

An example of how costume could become a means to exercise political control were the very detailed dress regulations imposed by the Ottoman government. These laid down, for instance, the colour of the turban cloths for the individual religious groups: blue for Christians, black for Jews, white for Muslims, the descendants of Muhammad had the privilege to wear green ones, and the members of various Sufi orders also used their own special colours (Winkelhane, 1987). In the 1830s the Ottoman government ordered civil servants to wear the fez – and this order lead to the fez becoming a generally popular headdress for men. Later, however, civil servants were supposed to adapt to European dress, as a visual statement of the orientation

389 A peasant woman from the area around Damascus (right), a Druze woman from the environs of Damascus (centre), a woman from Damascus (left), 1873.

towards Europe and the progressive attitude of the Ottoman government. On the other hand the Ottoman civil servants, although for different motives, tried to reinforce the traditional regional costumes and the dress codes for women – since changes in that sphere were seen as a threat to the established order. There was for instance an attempt to distinguish "dress" (European) from "costume" (traditional) and to attach different values to them.

A great debate over morals and values developed when women in the towns began to discard their veils. Major changes in clothing began in the 1920s and 1930s in Syria. Dress changed most in towns; increasingly people dressed "à la Franka". The orientation of the urban women towards Paris had probably started earlier, but the new dress was worn indoors; outdoors the "walking-out coat" was worn over it. European influences also appeared in the countryside, the new fabrics, threads and colours also contributed to change, at least in the design of the dress. European embroidery patterns were used, urban dress was imitated, ideas from different regions were adopted. Governments and religious authorities partly regulated the dress, particularly that of the women, because they connected it with ideas of decency in the public sphere and were concerned about safeguarding the honour of women and their families. In the countryside, however, what was seen as "decent" and appropriate was determined rather by tradition and social expectations, and sometimes also by the pressure of religious authority. Discussion about the veil, in particular, was often characterized by the conflict between traditional ideas of decency and ideas of progress – a factor that to this day still dominates this discussion both in the countries themselves and in the West. The Western observer is caught in yet a further contradiction: on one hand the rejection of the veil is to be welcomed as an indication of progress, but on the other hand regretted as the disappearance of traditional dress. Changes in dress thus reflect changes of times and of ideas: in the case of men's dress values such as respect and decency, and in the case of women's acceptance or rejection of such ideas. Women's dress reflects how women see themselves in their historical determinedness and social restrictions. In times of great socio-economic change, the dress of the different classes and regions varies to a particularly large degree, and it cannot be interpreted without this background. Thus the new elite in Syria wore the suit in the 1930s, whereas the old elite deliberately distinguished itself by holding on to traditional costume. Outside the towns questions of status played an important part in determining the way of clothing, and this had many perhaps unexpected consequences: when the veil was discarded by women in the towns, the women in Palmyra began to wear it in the 1930s. Rich women, who did not have to work outside the house, were required to wear a veil. In the Hauran it were the Damascene ladies who were married to Hauranis, as well as the wives of government officials, who initiated the trend for veiling. To link decency with the veiling of women was also a modern idea in the villages. Old women can still remember, how in the past there was no problem about working with sleeves rolled up side by side with the men in the fields; nobody took offence. They explain this by saying that at that time the village was not visited by strangers, who might have looked at them "with different eyes", that everyone knew each other anyway, and that one did not have time for such thoughts. Veiling or its absence is not a reliable indicator for a woman's personal freedom, the way she sees herself or her social status. Social, economic and political factors, which are far more important in that respect, are not always directly observable.

There is also the very personal significance clothes have in the life of the women. Its shape and colour are indicators of the various stages in their life. Girls dress differently from married women, old women choose different colours than young women. A woman has several sets of clothes for various occasions. The most important event in a woman's life and also the most remarkable passage from one stage of life to the next is marriage. Most of her garments are obtained on the occasion of her wedding, and textiles form a large part of the trousseau. Girls embroider the chest and side panels of the dress with their wedding in mind. Feelings, moods and expectations find their way into the embroidery. The trousseau comprises of a complete set of garments, which all play a part in the wedding and are shown in the course of it. At her wedding the bride receives her jewellery, bought by her father with her bride money, and afterwards worn as symbol of her new status together with the veil and a particular headdress. The economic and social status of the bride and her bridegroom is expressed in the quantity of the garments, the quality of the textiles and the embroidery and the quantity of the jewellery. Most of the dresses in our collection are wedding dresses or dresses for festive occasions, and most of them come from rural areas.

Through her clothes a woman also demonstrates that she belongs to a particular village and that she is a member of an ethnic and/or religious group. The local and regional characteristics, grounded in tradition, are reflected in the shape of the costume, its individual elements and the way in which it is worn: which part of the dress is emphasized by embroidery or appliqué work, which colours predominate and which patterns are preferred. The embroidery techniques and the shape of the patterns are also part of tradition. Like the motifs, which are related to ideas of luck, protection and fertility, and which are essential features of a "true" dress, these techniques are learned by the girls from the older women. But there is wide scope for personal taste, variations and new creations in the choice of motif and colour. The realization of the ideas depends on the skill of the embroideress. Women are also inspired by their surroundings, they take up ideas from neighbouring villages and integrate new ideas. The shaping of a dress and its embroidery or appliqué work is thus a complex and

390 A Druze in traditional dress with characteristic headdress. The colours of the costume as well as his headdress indicate that he is somebody who has been initiated in the Druze religion.

391 Members of the family el-Atrash in their traditional Druze family guesthouse (*madafe*) in Suweida. Portraits of their famous ancestors are hanging on the wall.

392 Headscarves and head-ropes which form part of the male headdress throughout Syria. Druzes often combine them with their urban dress.

393 New *abaye* for a man, made to order in Damascus, as was formerly worn by the Druzes.

394 A pair of traditional baggy trousers for men (*shirwal*).

395 A Druze woman's velvet coat. The facing is decorated with appliqué work.

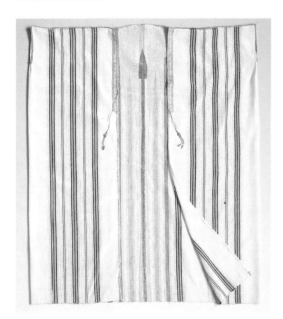

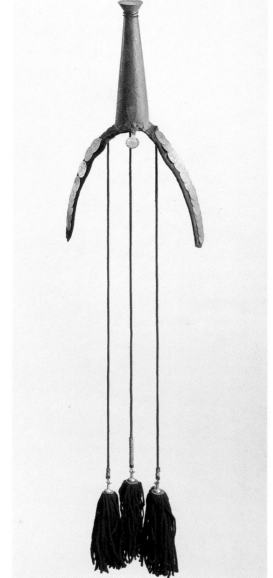

396, 399 & 400 A Druze woman from the environs of Suweida. Her *tarbush* is concealed by a white scarf. Her costume and headdress are in accordance with the traditional canon of Druze dress. It consists of a white veil, the *tarbush*, the dress, which is tacked at the waist, with the typical low-cut neck and an apron (bottom right). On top of this a coat is usually worn, such as the silk coat (bottom left) in damask weave.

397 & 398 Druze women's *tarbush*. The *tarbush* has replaced the so-called Druze hat (top right), which until about a hundred years ago was the most striking feature of the Druze female costume. The high 'Druze hat' (*tantur*) was made of silver or silver-plated copper. It was the sign of a young married woman.

401 A young Druze woman from the Lebanon wearing a *tantur*, 1870—80. When this picture was taken the *tantur* had already become very rare.

very personal expression of a woman, her identity, the way she sees herself and her immediate circumstances.

In addition to this, the traditional dress of the rural regions in particular is a reflection of the interaction between ethnic and religious groups, whose historical movements have shaped the culture of Syria.

The Druzes, because of their religion and their seclusion in the mountains, are a very homogeneous population, and have always aroused the interest of European visitors. Their costume was of course the object of particular attention. To this day the Druzes have very largely retained the characteristics of their costume, but even the Druze canon of dress has been subject to changes, and consequently it reflects in an exemplary way the interaction of traditional and adopted elements over a long period of time.

Bouron (1930), during his stay with the Druzes, compiled the following list of elements of their costume:

Men's Costume
socks (*qalshin*)
baggy breeches (*shintyan*): this type of baggy breeches becomes narrow below the knee and fits closely to the leg from calf to ankle.
short shirt (*qamis*)
bolero waistcoat (*jubbe*)
waistcoat without sleeves (*sidriyye*)
fabric belt (*shale*)
kumbas – coat-like overgarment (*qunbas*)
abaye – wide cloak (*abaye*)
farwa – winter coat with fur lining (*farwa*)
little cap (*taqiyye*)

head cloth (usually cotton) (*kuffiye*)
hatta – silk head cloth (*hatta*)
agal – head-rope (*iqal*) with which the head cloth is held in place
turban (*laffe*), which is wound around a felt cap. (The wearing of this is restricted to the initiated, and there are special forms for the religious leaders.)
leather slippers (red) (*surmaye*)
boots, mainly for riding

A Women's Costume
slippers (*kundara*)
(Women apparently do not wear socks, since they are not mentioned.)
baggy breeches (*shintyan*)
(the *shirwal* baggy breeches are not listed for the women)
long shirt (*qamis*)
kumbas – a coat-like overgarment (*qunbas*)
delicate overgarment (*sabakane*)
fabric belt (*shale*)
apron (*mamluk*)
handkerchief (*marhame*)
bolero waistcoat with wide, split sleeves (*damir*)
(Druze) hat (*tarbush*) of red felt and often trimmed with coins
veil (*futa*)
shoulder scarf for winter (*sharshaf*)
skirt (*tannura*)
jewellery
silver jewellery (worn below the breast – could this refer to the buckle of the belt?) (*qufl*)
silver necklace (*kirdane*)
gold chain on the chest (*shakl*)
fake plaits (*tafar*)
plait ornaments/jewellery (*aqd*)

The so-called Druze hat, today called *tarbush*, is made of felt and trimmed with gold coins, and is similar to the headdress of other peasant women of the surrounding area. Formerly a *tantur* was worn. This was a tall conical tube made of silver or copper, which is known to us from old travel accounts and photographs. It has not been in use for a long time, though some families still keep it. The Pitt Rivers Museum has one such example in its collection; it was acquired by its donor, the Rev. W. Allan, from a Druze woman in the Lebanon, who still wore it herself and had bought it in Beirut in 1882.

In the Lebanon the *tantur* seems to have a long tradition. It used to be worn not only by the Druzes, but also by Maronite women. However, after the wars between the Druzes and the Maronites in 1841 and 1845 the Maronite priests prohibited women to wear the *tantur*. The high tapering headdress of European ladies in the 14th century is adapted from it. A similar shape is found in Central Asia, but more research has to be done to find out where the shape originally came from.

The *tarbush* with the *tantur* were given to the bride, and she continued to wear it as sign of her married status. According to Bourbon (1930) different ways of wearing it indicated membership of different families. In accordance with the dress regulations governing the religious division into initiated and non-initiated, only non-initiated Druze women wear it.

Those initiated into the religion apparently only wear the white headcloth which is held in place with a black head-rope. Only the non- initiated men and women are permitted to wear colours; the initiated wear "non-colours", i.e. black and white. The *laffe*, the typical Druze turban, is restricted to initiated men, who apparently have to wear traditional dress, unlike the non-initiated, who today can be seen in European suits – particularly in town. The wearing of an *abaye* made of white material with black vertical stripes, however, is a privilege of high religious dignitaries, who come from particular families.

The Druzes' turbulent history and the frequent threats to their religion, may be the reason behind one of their principles, which they call *takiyya*. This is the instruction to adapt one's outward appearance to one's environment and to keep religion inside one's heart. It may explain some characteristics of the changes in the Druze canon of dress. Other factors have certainly been the omnipresent influence and regulations of the Ottoman empire, the proximity of the nomads of the Syrian desert, the influence of people of different ethnic origins, who have been integrated in the course of time into the Druze community, as well as intra-Druze affairs. Thus the typical shape of the *qunbaz* for women, with its deep decolletage and tacked-on skirt, seems to be very similar to that of the Ottoman *antari* (Turkish *enteri*), a shape which has been preserved in this remote area for a long time. A velvet coat for women is today called *thob mechmal*, with reference to its material and the fact that it is a fine garment.

If we look at the etymology of the terms in the list of Druze garments, we find in miniature the history both of the region, and of this particular group.

Thus the term for the socks entered Arabic from French via the Turkish language; socks are therefore relatively new. *Shintyan* are the Turkish, *shirwal* the Persian baggy breeches, the waistcoats and short jackets derive from the Ottoman tradition. *Abaye* and *farwe* are typical.

Arab-bedouin garments, as are the head cloth and head-rope of the men and the false plaits and plait jewellery of the women.

The white veil usually worn by the women in Syria seems to be a reminiscence of an event in Druze history. Until 1711 there were two different Druze parties: Qays and Yamani, reflecting the old opposition between the Arabs of the north and the south. The colours red and white were assigned to the rival parties (Qays were red, Yamani white). The Ottomans also differentiated them by the two colours, and this was still done in Volney's time.

The flags of the respective groups were white or red, and so apparently were the veils of the women, too. When a Qays bride went into Yamani territory, she was required to hide her red costume or change to a white veil at the border.

After 1711 this differentiation lost its significance and was substituted by allegiance to whichever leading family was supported at the time, but the white veils of the women were retained.

The variety of shapes and styles of the dresses from the Qalamoun, for instance, reflect the historical dynamics of the rural areas of Syria during the last two centuries. In this area of refuge modified forms of urban dress from the Ottoman period have been preserved, and the technique and style of the embroidery has been influenced by refugees from the Balkans and Crete at the end of the last century. The dresses in the environs of Damascus, the Druze mountains and in the villages of northern Syria show, in pattern and technique, central Asian elements brought there by many groups coming from this area to Syria. In the villages of the third Qalamoun range the "wing sleeves", which are now purely ornamental, tell of the closeness of the desert and the merging of peasant and nomadic ways of life. The cut of the dresses and the motifs of the embroidery of the women in the area between Aleppo and Homs reflect the settlement of the nomadic tribes of the region. Cross-stitch and the embroidery on evenweave fabric as well as the spread of patterns taken from pattern books was likewise adopted in their dress by the women of Syria. The execution of the appliqué work and the decoration of the seams on the dresses of the Hauran show how close the textile techniques and design is to nomadic principles. The continuity of traditional elements and the simultaneous integration of new influences and ideas reveal the creativity of the women in translating not only their own personal history but also contemporary history into their dresses.

402 & 403 Women's dresses from the Hauran. The cut can be found throughout the Near East. The design of the dresses in the Hauran depends primarily on the seam decoration and emphasis on the hem of the skirt by use of patchwork. The dresses are usually made by hand. They are called *shirsh*.

404 A woman's jacket from the Hauran made of wool and cotton. The seams and the border of the jacket have likewise been embroidered and reinforced at the same time with red wool.

405 & 406 A woman's dress from Harran al-Awamid. Cut and elements of design are the same as those found in the Hauran, but for this festive dress particularly delicate decorative seams in different embroidery stitches were used, and a lot of care was taken over the patchwork. The woman certainly has worked all her skill and imagination into the beauty of this dress.

407—412 Jackets from the Hauran for peasant and nomad women. They are made of sturdy cloth and decorated with couching and appliqué work. For the lining materials in contrasting colours are often chosen.

Textile Techniques
Embroidery, Application, Patchwork

Maria Zerrnickel

To adorn the fabrics and clothes men and women give of their best. The male artisans weave patterned materials; the dyers, ikateurs and textile printers decorate the textiles and clothes with colour. In the desert and the village the women are involved with weaving, *plangi*, embroidery, appliqué and patchwork.

Sewing, embroidery, appliqué, crocheting and patchwork are very ancient textile techniques.

Embroidery, together with patchwork, appliqué and *plangi* tie-dyeing, is one of the most important home craft industries of the women living in small towns as well as for peasant women, semi-nomadic women and, to some extent, even for bedouin women. In the Near East the tradition of embroider goes back over hundreds of years. The women guard their skills and knowledge, and pass them on from one generation to the next. Embroidery, with its ornaments and magnificent colours is also an important means of emphasizing the characteristics of dress of particular groups, such as those living in the Qalamoun, Hauran, Harran, in Tell- Mnin, es-Suchne, Saraqeb, Khan Sheichun or other regions of Syria.

Because embroidery is relatively straightforward and easy to learn, and it is possible to buy the necessary threads and fabrics in the *suq*, it has become widespread among women in Syria as well as in other regions of western Asia Minor and the Middle East.

The older embroideries were mainly on cloth woven on hand looms, but since the end of the nineteenth century the embroideries have been increasingly executed on factory-made materials.

The different shades of red which occur quite frequently are a particular favourite of the embroideresses, especially in es-Suchne and Saraqeb. Set against a completely black background their effect is luminous and cheerful, and they create a festive impression. The colour varies from a pale raspberry or pink to dark red, sometimes becoming reddish brown.

The embroideries on the dresses, coats, skirts, pants, cloths and pouches are predominantly executed in red thread on black or dark-coloured cotton and mixed-silk sateen fabrics. This preference for embroidery in red is very deeply rooted, not only due to the relative cheapness of

threads and materials but also to the women's ideas concerning magic and folk religion. They believe that the colour red possesses magic qualities, increasing fertility and protecting from spirits and the evil eye. It is the colour of joy, of wealth, of summer, and of the south, symbolizing the desire for a long life.

However, in the cities European influence, in the choice of colours for embroidery threads, for patterns and fabrics, has become very noticeable, especially in the Damascus Oasis.

The choice of colours is also in part closely connected with ethnic preferences and religious notions. The Druzes, for instance, have developed a special attitude to white and black, the "non-colours", which are reserved for the initiated in religion.

For the Druzes, and also for other people in the Orient, white symbolizes wisdom and purity, while black symbolizes darkness, death, transformation, "non-being". These are qualities linked with reflection and aloofness from ordinary life, as opposed to the spontaneous, uninhibited expression of existence symbolized by bright, strong colours.

When we examine and describe the clothes from Harran al-Awamid and the Hauran, we notice the treatment of the seams on the sleeves, hems, necklines and the narrow upright collar. The seams of the patchwork panels are treated with particular care. They are sewn and embroidered very finely and precisely with red, yellow, white, black and green thread, with the black, blue or red background colour of the fabric skilfully worked into the pattern.

Girls learn how to embroider from their mothers, aunts or grandmothers. Neighbours or school friends also show them how to design beautiful patterns.

Embroidery in Syria and Jordan today is almost entirely the work of women, and is practised within the family. Women and girls work for their own needs and also partly for sale in the *suq*.

The women sew, embroider and attach applications to coats, dresses, pants, cloths, pouches etc. to be stored in chests for the wedding. A bride receives as her dowry several sets of clothes and accessories (pouches, cloths, belts) executed in *plangi*, or with beautiful embroidery and applications.

Usually the embroideress works sitting on the ground with the fabric or dress that is to be embroidered placed on her raised left knee, to which it may be attached by a pin to her dress.

Unlike the other women we questioned, such as the women from As Sfire or es-Suchne, the embroideresses from Saraqeb use neither an embroidery frame nor even-weave (embroidery) fabric, stencils and hooks, and they do not have any pattern drawings, but work entirely by eye (see photograph of woman from Saraqeb, p. 185).

The process of embroidering as practised by the women of Saraqeb is as follows:

First the embroideress uses a light-coloured thread to mark out the pattern on the fabric in long stitches. Then she embroiders the borders of the details within the lines with white thread against the dark background of the garment. The outlines of the patterns thus created are embroidered first with progressively lighter threads: first red-brown, then red, green, purple, orange, pink and yellow, and finally white. This process has the advantage that the lighter areas, particularly the white parts of the embroidered pattern do not become dirty in the course of embroidering, which often takes a very long time. The women have an astonishing sense of balance. Using their experience and taste, they are able to lay out the pattern they have in mind, to execute it, and bring together all the details into a unified, harmonious whole.

The choice of materials for embroidery is based primarily on aesthetic viewpoints regarding the effect aimed at in the embroidery; but the embroideress's notions of magic as well as her social status have an important influence on this. Silk, for instance, is regarded as a noble material and is linked with wealth and social prestige. For the embroidery to function as an amulet, the colour, shape and material are important.

The quantity of embroidered and appliqué work done by a woman depends on whether she is from a poor or rich family. The poorer women were often forced by lack of expensive fabrics and jewellery to decorate many articles required for festive occasions, such as clothing, cloths, cushion covers and bags with beautifully embroidered and appliqué patterns, or to compose many textiles in patchwork from remnants of material combined with embroidery, for the sake of prestige and their aesthetic requirements. The townswomen, on the other hand, treated embroidery more as a pastime.

Over the centuries the women developed a magnificent art of embroidery using partly traditional ornaments, which, although restricted to about 10-15 principal patterns, gave scope for many variations.

The women find models for their embroidery in the woven damasks and brocades, in the flatweaves of the bedouins, in woodcarvings (chests), in felt carpets, in inlay (mosaic), and to a lesser extent in silver jewellery and ceramics. The patterns represent trees of life, palm fronds, cypresses, vases, stylized pomegranates, birds and other animals, mountains, triangles, squares, rhombuses, rosettes, rinceaux and suchlike. These may be traditional patterns, motifs created by individuals, or imitations of models taken from Europe.

The influence of Europe, Asia Minor, the Balkans and Persia on the style, technique and ornaments of northern Arab embroidery can be seen in many embroideries from the last century and increasingly in the present century. Although the Central Asian influences (Turcomans, Uzbeks) on embroidery techniques and pattern-making in appliqué works occurred several centuries ago they are still easily recognizable in Syrian textiles (e.g. on Druze coats, embroidery on women's pants).

Embroidery techniques

The women in Syria, like those throughout the northern regions of the Arabian peninsula, know several techniques of embroidery, both simple and complicated, which they master and use in their work. An embroidery technique is not just connected with the area of its distribution, but also with the type of product it is meant to be used on, and the time required to make it. The embroidery techniques used by the women and the design and arrangement of the patterns is also determined to a considerable extent by the structure of the weave and the cut of the garment. These only allow certain forms of pattern to be used, and this is also the case with weaving, knotting, knitting and crocheting. The quality of the materials (weave, thread, tinsel yarn, beads), the tools (needles, hooks, knitting needles, loom), the skill and imagination of the woman in the end determine the value of the final product.

The embroidery yarns are usually silk, more rarely cotton and occasionally wool. Since the 1930s a very fine cotton thread has been sold in the Near East by the French firm of Dolfus, Mieg & Cie. (DMC).

The most frequently used types of stitch in Syrian embroidery are fine cross stitch, petit-point, running stitch, buttonhole stitch, chain stitch, satin stitch, straight and diagonal hemstitching, couching or onlay, overcast stitching, backstitching, fishbone stitch, featherstitch, open herringbone stitch, square openwork stitch, joining stitch for seams, closed herringbone stitch, hemstitching, eyelet stitch, oversewing stitch, and others.

Cross stitches belong to the two-dimensional types of stitch formed by crossed threads. In embroideries from es-Suchne, Saraqeb, Chan Sheichun, Qalaat Samaan and Dmeir, the diagonal cross stitch, done in one operation, is frequently used. It is always embroidered from right to left. On the reverse it appears as an unbroken horizontal line. This fine cross stitch was embroidered by the women with and without evenweave cloth, on sateen-woven mixed-silk or cotton, as well as on canvas-weave cotton forming

413–419 Women's clothing from Beit Tima (Golan). The dresses are sewn from artificial silk, cotton or velvet. Dresses with tacked waists were identified by their cut as modern (European) dresses and still are differentiated from the traditional ones. The accompanying short jackets made of velvet or cotton are decorated with couching. For the lining materials in strongly contrasting colours are preferred.

414 & 415 The dresses top right and top centre are from the Qalamoun. In their method of production they are similar to those common in the Golan.

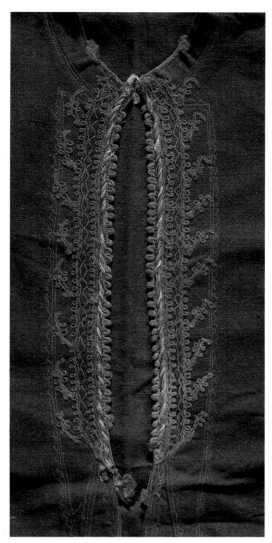

420–424 Women's coats from the Qalamoun (Tell Mnin, above, and Quteife, below). The Qalamoun is characterized by a wide variety of different styles of dress. Although their cut is traditional, these coats are made of different materials and embroidered, using varied techniques, depending on the preferences of the particular villagers.

running borders or as an all-over pattern executed mainly in red thread. Only one coat from es-Suchne is entirely embroidered with wool in different colours. The ornaments most frequently used on coats, skirts, pants and dresses from es-Suchne are stylized palm fronds, cypresses, trees of life, rosettes, foliage and various geometrical forms. The latter sometimes function as amulets.

The clothes from es-Suchne and Khan Sheichun are embroidered at the seams with backstitching, and partly with double-sided closed herringbone stitch. The backstitching forms linear patterns, the herringbone stitch bands, which completely cover the seam. The hems of most dresses from both places are decorated with straight and diagonal hemstitching, and partly with fine running stitches. Hemstitching appears the same on the front and the reverse, and it is embroidered as a strip pattern. The running stitch, a continuous, neat zigzag stitch, appears on the reverse as an unbroken horizontal line and is used for ornamental strips, surface patterns and infill stitches.

Some dresses from Chan Sheichun and Saraqeb are worked with fine, well-executed machine embroidery. The seams are all decorated and reinforced with machine hemstitching.

All the above articles of clothing are embroidered with floral- geometric decoration on the chest-, back- and shoulder-panels, sleeves, side-panels and the hem.

Another group with very varied embroidery techniques are the dresses from the Hauran and Harran al Awamid. The most beautiful of these festive dresses are decorated with cotton bands in various colours (dark red, pale and dark blue) in patchwork technique, with all seams, the small upright collars, neck openings, side-panels and hem embroidered with great care and in bold colours.

The stitches which most frequently appear here are running stitch, petit point, hemstitch, closed herringbone stitch, chain stitch, featherstitch, cross stitch and flat stitch. Petit point is only embroidered over crossed threads; it can form linear patterns, borders and surfaces. Chain stitch, one of the most ancient forms of embroidery, is done with a needle or crochet hook. The needle is stuck into the fabric from below at the desired place, a loop of thread is laid from left to right and stuck in at the point where the needle pierces the cloth so that the work thread lies under the point of the needle; then the thread is drawn through. As this is repeated a chain is formed, showing a continuous line on the reverse. Featherstitch is a sort of half-loop stitch. Both can be used to embroider borders and surface patterns.

Flat satin stitch is often used for free-flowing floral decorations. Couching and overcast stitching are known among many ethnic groups in Syria, as well as in Asia Minor and Central Asia.

Couching and overcast stitching are very similar. To form a pattern from these stitches the embroideress takes the required length of thread (braid) often in a colour contrasting to that of the fabric, or silver and gold thread

425 Embroidery stitches (left to right): chain stitch, couching, satin stitch, drawn work with hemstitching, herringbone stitch, buttonhole stitch, [Maschenstich], cross stitch and half-cross stitch. The embroideresses use all these stitches masterfully to translate their ideas into thread and cloth. The dress with the embroidered winged sleeves, and the details of the patterns, illustrated on the opposite page (426-429) impressively demonstrate the artistic skills of the woman from Quteife who embroidered it.

(lurex) and attaches it with little stitches running across the thread. Coats, jackets and some dresses decorated in this manner come from the Qalamoun and Hauran. The ornamentation on these clothes consists of free-flowing floral patterns on the shoulders, sleeves, neck opening and skirt, forming stylized trees of life, cypresses, vases of flowers, and small geometrical figures. The embroidered patterns in bright silk thread, and gold and silver lamé show up effectively against the dark brown, fiery red or dark green cloth, and against the black cotton material from which coats and jackets are sewn.

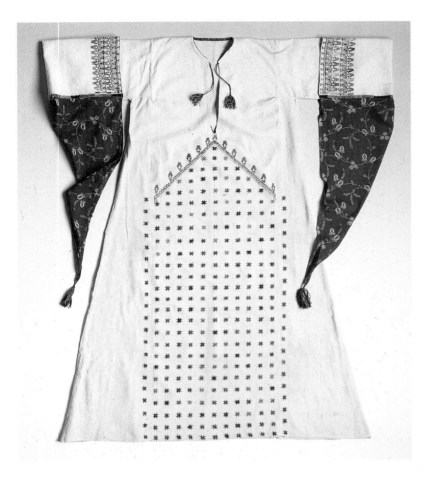

430–435 Festive clothes from the Qalamoun. The technique and patterning
of the embroidery is reminiscent of the forms common in Turkey and
the Balkans, but the motifs chosen – here they are allusions to a prayer
niche and minarets – are Islamic. The winged sleeves on the dresses illustrated here have been attached later to make them into dancing dresses.
This can be seen particularly clearly in the blue dress, although the
sleeves repeat the pattern on the considerably older middle part. It is
common to re-use embroidered parts from an older and damaged dress
when making a new one.

179

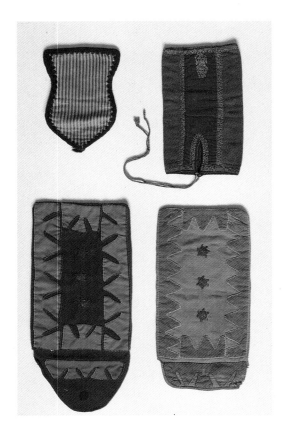

436—438 Money purses decorated with meticulous embroidery, and mirror bags.

439 & 440 The motif of birds facing each other goes back to Persian prototypes.

441 A woman's coat decorated with couching and appliqué, from Tell Mnin.

180

442—444 Women's waistcoats from the Qalamoun. The older one is decorated with couching, while on the more recent examples cross-stitching is mainly used. They worn not only with dresses, but also with trousers.

A group of the women's dresses with wing sleeves from Qutayfeh, Dmeir, and Tell-Mnin have rich embroidery executed very finely and precisely on the wing sleeves, coat tails and seams.

The ornamentation and style of embroidery are reminiscent of Anatolian, Greek, Balkan and European embroideries, and only the types of patterns used, such as "prayer niches", "minarets", vases and trees of life, connect them with the Islamic Orient. The cut and design of the appliqué work seen in Druze coats suggest a link between the Druzes and those ethnic groups living in Syria, who originally came from Central Asia, such as the Turcomans and Uzbeks.

We found a rare type of ornamentation on women's coats from Kafar Tacharim in north-west Syria. Both tails of the coat are decorated with large triangular patterns on the outside and inside. On the outside the ornament is embroidered with buttonhole stitch in brightly coloured silk, while on the reverse the stitches simultaneously attach a pattern of appliqué work to the inside. Thus the embroidered and appliqué triangles and squares are the mirror-image each other, arranged in quadruple repetition of symmetrically placed patterns resembling rams' horns.

445—447 Men's waistcoats. Waistcoats of this sort were formerly worn both in the town and in the country. Waistcoats with panels made of Aleppine Kashmir copies were very popular. The pattern on the panel of the waistcoat, bottom right, is in the Balkan tradition.

181

448–452 Festive dresses from es-Suchne, made of black silk satin, embroidered with red silk thread. The dense cross-stitch pattern, in which stylized palms and cypresses predominate, seems to be an immediate reflection of the natural surroundings of the women in the oasis of es-Suchne. This tradition of embroidery with its very individual symbolism is practised today by the women in Sfire (using evenweave embroidery fabric). There are links by marriage between es- Suchne and Sfire.

The woman works the red, yellow, pink, green, orange and blue patterns of the embroidery and of the appliqué material onto the black sateen cotton of the coat to create a striking effect. The black cloth forming the background colour is integrated harmoniously into the composition. The two other coats in the Linden-Museum collection are decorated in a similar manner. On one of them the ornaments show the same pattern as above executed in a fine backstitching of brightly coloured silk. On the third coat the embroidery shows a very rare sort of couching, in which the special, very fine embroidery runs in branches over the onlaid thread and gives the whole pattern a shimmering surface. A striking motif of this embroidery are the swastikas, which are presumably meant to bring good luck and protection.

The turned-up cuffs of the sleeves of the coats described above are made of fine materials such as silk atlas brocade, silk atlas and ribbed- weave silk mixture, and are embroidered in brightly coloured silk with fine cross stitches, fishbone stitch, buttonhole stitch.

The women's scarves from Baalbek (Lebanon) represent something very unusual in textile decoration. They are made of tulle in natural colours or black, and are decorated in silver tinsel yarn with geometrically arranged, floral-zoomorphic patterns. The tinsel yarn is beaten into the honeycomb and diamond-shaped tulle cells with a little hammer to form the pattern. A short piece of tinsel yarn (6-9 mm) is pressed in between two cells diagonally across the corner, crossed over and fastened. To create the pattern all the subsequent pieces of silver tinsel yarn are beaten in horizontally, vertically or diagonally over one, two or more tulle cells. This is presumably man's work.

453—455 On these coats the motifs characteristic of es-Suchne can be clearly seen: palms, cypresses, trees of life and amulet triangles. In the desert plants are signs of life, and the women seem to have created gardens of their own with needle and thread. And the preservation of life was a matter of equally great concern – provided we can interpret their embroidered amulets in such a way.

456—459 Another type of embroidery is represented by the dresses from Saraqeb, Chan Sheichun and Maaret en-Numan. The dresses from Saraqeb are characterized by their large surfaces of red embroidery on dark cotton, and their finely worked seams. The motifs are geometrical and resemble the forms of bedouin jewellery. This woman in Saraqeb embroiders without using fine canvas and creates the pattern she has in mind for the dress with great confidence. She embroiders not only to supply her own needs but also for sales.

460—464 The dress from Maaret en-Numan (top left) and the other dresses from Chan Sheichun are similar in design to those from Saraqeb, especially chest, shoulders and side panels. They differ, however, in the choice of colours and in the embroidery of the back of the dress, both being typical of the two towns. Such differences can express a local identity within a wider regional context.

465–466 Details of a dress from Chan Sheichun. The cross-stitch embroidery of the chest and shoulders is usually padded. Here the strict geometrical is loosened by the presence of a human figure and a little dog. Embroidered onto the shoulder is an amulet triangle with pendants, elongated into a stylized tree of life running down the sleeve.

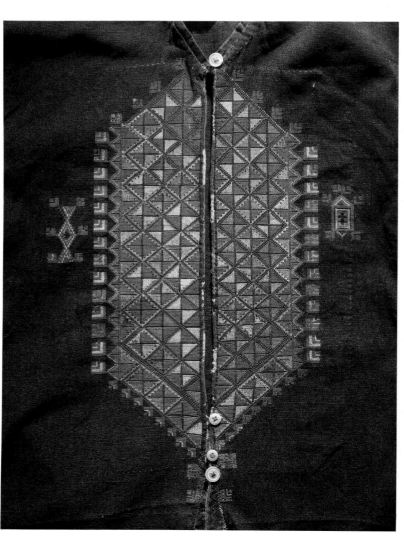

467—469 A woman's coat from Qalaat Samaan. Here the women emphasize the chest and to a lesser extent the sleeves, and they decorate the seams. The coats are fastened with cords or buttons. The embroidery appears discreet against the dark background. Sometimes the inner facing is decorated with appliqué work in contrasting atlas silks – a coquettish feature, which draws attention to the gait of the woman wearing it.

470—472 Women's coats from Qalaat Samaan. Apart from the embroidery on the front and sleeves, the coat is decorated with colourful appliqué work on the facing. The silk satin used for the appliqué is woven in Aleppo. The details are stylized tree motifs, cypresses and conifers. Like their sisters in es-Suchne, the women of Qalaat Samaan find their inspiration for patterns from their surroundings.

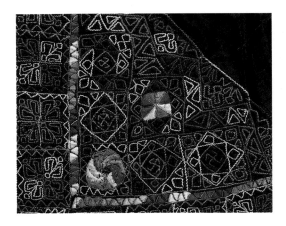

473-475 Women's coats from the environs of Kafr Tacharim. These coats differ in cut from the preceding ones, since the skirt is considerably wider. The decoration of the coats is concentrated on the upper opening and the facings. The whole surface of the triangular patterned areas of the two facings is covered with embroidery. The artistic skill is evident in the coat, top left, on which the embroidered pattern on the outside corresponds to the appliqué work inside.

Making Arab Clothes

Maria Zerrnickel

476—478 Women's coats from Mhardah. Here other principles of design for a coat are used: the right side panel is emphasized and the inside of the left facing. The seams are richly embroidered and emphasize the cut of the garment. The ends of the sleeves have an openwork pattern executed in hem stitch – a peculiarity of these coats.

In conclusion we must mention the "modern" dresses of the young women and girls from the Golan. These dresses made of brightly coloured artificial silk atlas with damask patterns, of viscose, black sateen cotton and purple velvet are decorated with appliqué patches in contrasting colours, factory lace and braids, sewn to them by machine.

An Arab sets great store by his clothes and his appearance. Clothing is a sign of his social and political position in society, it underlines his membership of a particular extended family, a tribe or clan. It satisfies his ambition and his need for prestige.

This is demonstrated by the following Arab proverbs:

"You may eat according to your own ideas and needs – but you must dress according to the ideas of society"

and

"For every occasion the correct garment."

The complete traditional dress of an inhabitant of Syria, whether bedouin, peasant or inhabitant of a small town, is often strikingly simple, except in the case of the high income groups in the cities.

Today urban clothing has almost completely lost its traditional variety, splendour and colour. This is because of the strong European influence. The European way of dress has replaced the traditional urban clothing, reducing it to a few individual articles such as head coverings for men, and the veil and headdress for women.

The rural people generally possess only a few articles of clothing. Work clothes and clothes for going out and for festive occasions are worn almost without exception in summer and winter alike. For this reason, Arabs attach much importance to the quality of material, workmanship and decoration in the finish and design in their choice of clothes.

The traditional set of clothes of the nomads and semi-nomads and, with slight deviations in shape, the peasants, consists of a long shirt, worn with or without a belt, a coat, a cloak (*abaye*), pants for peasants (bedouins rarely wear pants), a head cloth with head-rope and (recently) shoes.

The head scarf is a particularly important part of the Arab national costume and is mainly made by men. Head cloths of all sorts for men and women, head-ropes, fezes, sometimes also the shawls for veiling women, winter coats and jackets are made by male artisans. (Spinners, twisters, ikateurs, weavers, dyers, printers, and furriers are involved in the production of the items mentioned above.)

The traditional oriental cut of clothes has hardly changed over the centuries.

The ancient costume of the Medes, as we know it from existing representations and descriptions, consisted of long, wide-cut garments. These survived almost unaltered over the centuries in the Near East and became more wide-spread during the Islamic period. Their main characteristics are "wing sleeves" and a straight cut.

Most of the articles of clothing in the Syrian collection of the Linden-Museum have retained the traditional oriental cut. The urban wedding dresses, on the other hand, the dress of the Druze women and the "modern" clothes for young women and girls from the Golan are of a European style in cut and sewing.

The basic differences between the oriental cut and the European are the following:

1. The strip of cloth measures double the length of the dress; it is folded and has the neck opening cut in the front part (for coats the cloth for the front part is cut open to the full length).

2. No armholes are cut; the sleeves are sewn on directly to the selvedge of the piece of cloth at the shoulder. To avoid tension and tears, triangular, square or pentagonal armpit gussets are inserted.

3. To give the dress the width necessary for walking, side-panels of various cuts are inserted, which begin at the armpit gussets.

4. The clothes do not have Chinese collars – or only narrow ones. The sleeves are without cuffs, but often have a shorter or longer slit at the front so they can be turned back. The side panels of the coats usually have either short slits for walking or (in the case of bedouin women's coats) very high slits. The front tail parts of the coats are often widened in the lower part with wedges of cloth.

Women of all ethnic groups in Syria play a considerable part in making traditional clothing for everyday and festive wear. They receive the fabrics usually made in the cities (Aleppo, Damascus, Hama, Homs) by the male artisans, or else imported (silk, mixed silk, artificial silk, cotton), and work on them in their houses or tents to turn them into clothing. They cut the clothes, sew them together (often still without the help of a sewing machine), skilfully adorn the seams with decorative stitches, and embellish them using embroidery, appliqué work, tie-dyeing (*plangi*), patchwork and other techniques.

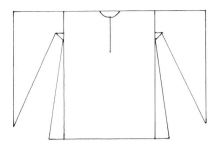

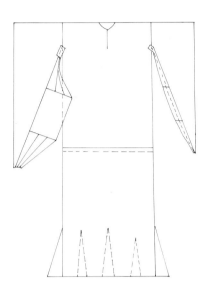

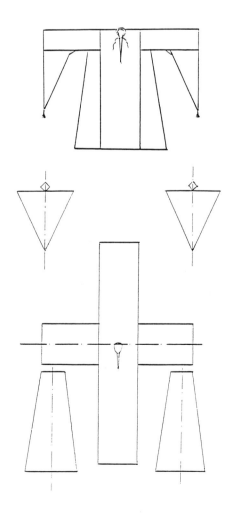

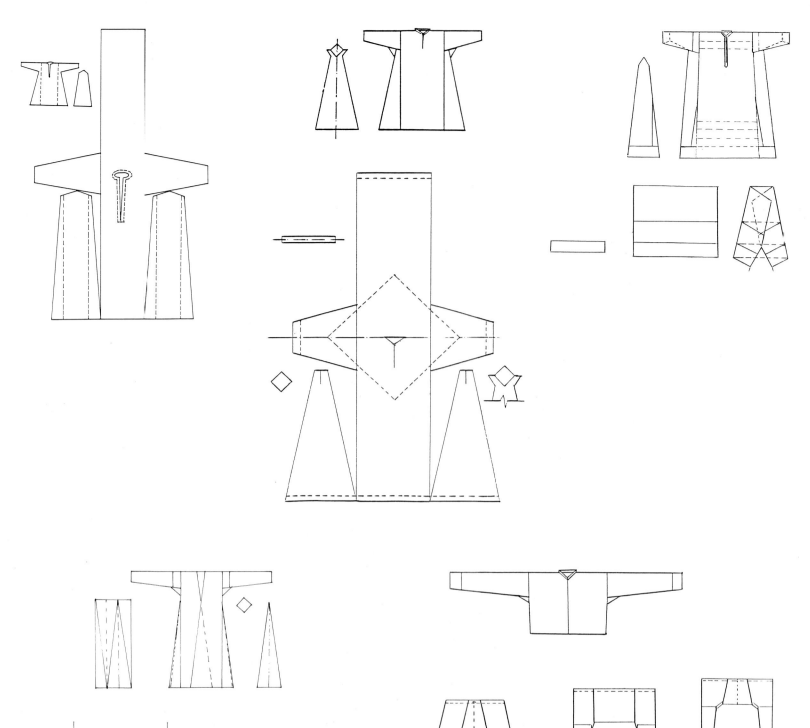

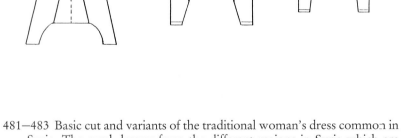

481—483 Basic cut and variants of the traditional woman's dress common in Syria. The rural dresses from the different regions in Syria which are presented in this catalogue are made according to the cuts discussed here.

484 Basic cut and variant of the traditional coat. Women's and men's coats differ only in the width of the side panels and the height of the side slits, and in the shape of the neck-line.

485 The cut of the jacket is basically that of a shortened coat. The traditional wide pants, for men as for women, are sewn from one of these three cuts.

479 Cuts of bedouin clothing. Above: the men's garments, below: the large (northern Arabian) women's dresses. In the men's and women's garments the winged sleeves are particularly pronounced and begin directly at the shoulder.

480 Cut of dresses with winged sleeves attached. Here the winged sleeves are purely decorative.

Dyeing and Resist-Dyeing

The Syrian cities of Aleppo, Damascus, Hama and Homs were once famous for their ikats and printed cloths (batik, lime resist-dyeing, stencil printing, *plangi*), as they were also for their dyers.

At Aleppo there was a particularly large number of dyeing workshops and these functioned well. The various artisans practised indigo dyeing, multicoloured dyeing, the dyeing of ikat threads, calico printing (batik) and other processes.

The indigo dyers made up the largest proportion. In Aleppo before the First World War there were 60 workshops of this sort (G. Dalman, vol. V, 1937), of which only two or three are still in operation. Today the dyers (*assabbâg*) are all old men, and there is no new blood to carry on this craft.

In the past they used natural dyes to colour yarn in large quantities in skeins and various cloths by the metre. Today, however, only garments already sewn are dyed, such as pants worn by by peasants (*sirwal*), veils (*shambar*), dresses (*taub'abla*), which the women tied up with *plangi* patterns. They are commissioned by peasants and semi-nomads from the surrounding villages. As well as the indigo dyers in Aleppo and Hama there are also still a few black-dyers (Aleppo, Homs, Damascus), who nowadays rarely work with natural dyes, preferring the cheaper aniline dyes, which are easier to handle.

The calico printers (Batik – wax resist-dying) are hardly to be found nowadays, since they have been replaced by factories producing printed fabrics. The dyers have adapted to the new situation better and can still be found in many workshops.

Of the various kinds of resist-dyeing using multi-coloured dyes we could still find the following techniques in use in the cities of Syria in 1990:
1.) lime resist-dyeing
2.) ikat
3.) *plangi*
4.) screen or stencil printing

Tie-dyeing (*plangi*)

The women's dresses and veils with *plangi* patterns in our collection come from Hama, Homs or Damascus (Tell Mnin). All were acquired after 1970. Most of them have been hardly worn or not at all. In two of the dresses the necklines have not even been cut open, which means that they were made by the women to be stored for a trousseau or for sale.

Kerchiefs and dresses are sewn by hand from narrow (30-60 cm) hand-woven fabrics, except for three dresses which are of factory-made cotton. Usually the raw silk and cotton fabrics are woven from hand-spun, knoppy silk floss or cotton yarn in loose plain weave.

Tie-dying, with or without inserts, is done by women. In October 1990 in Hama were able to observe this technique:

The woman tied individual parts of the cloth to a design she has devised herself, forming small bunches raised completely or partly from the surface, so that they stand out like pellets (see photograph). She began tying the hem of a yellow festive dress with wing sleeves of nubbly floss silk. The woman held the part to be tied in her teeth and deftly wrapped a cotton thread round it. In the next moment she had tied the second and then the third pellet. Tying in this way is usually done without inserts. During the subsequent dyeing (in red, for example) these areas are protected from the dye and may also appear in the pattern as small folds.

The form and method of wrapping the tied parts do not have much variety, but the women can do them in various sizes and use them to create complicated decorations.

There is evidence that tie-dyed patterns were already in use in Syria and possibly also in other Near Eastern areas by the fifth and sixth centuries, perhaps even earlier.

The *plangi* technique allows the women to create monochrome as well as multicoloured patterns. For the latter the tying has to be repeated several times or has to be executed in a particular way with a corresponding number of dyeings (three to five).

A number of different methods can be used to create a pattern by *plangi*. One method is to fold the fabrics lengthwise (the sleeves, the front and back and the side-panels of the dress) and then tie the layers together. (It is rare for the cloth to be folded more than once, since this only works for large patterns.) Patterns tied with two layers of cloth are symmetrical, with the same pattern – as well as the same mistakes in tying or dyeing – repeated left and right. When the tying thread is removed, one side shows small raised pellets, while the other has small depressions.

In the other method the parts of the fabric or dress are not folded before tying, since the dress is already sewn when the women start to do the *plangi*. But a certain symmetry can be achieved (if desired) by repeating the same elements of the pattern in the same sequence along a central axis.

The sequence of tying and dyeing can be executed in two ways:

One is to do all the tying (for white, yellow and red) at once, before the first dyeing, if the dress, cloth or fabric is left white or in its natural colour. First the tying for white, then for yellow, and then for red over the other two. The whole piece is dyed indigo. Then the areas to be red are untied and dyed red. The areas to be yellow are then untied and dyed and finally the areas for the white pattern are untied. The process creates a bright multicoloured pattern on a dark background.

The second method follows a different sequence. First the areas which are to remain undyed are tied up, then the cloth is dyed red (the lightest colour). What is to remain red is then covered, the cloth is dyed dark and finally all the ties are removed.

The ornamentation consists of geometrical forms (rhombuses, triangles, circles), and sometimes stylized blossoms, lozenges and trees of life.

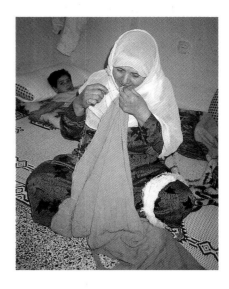

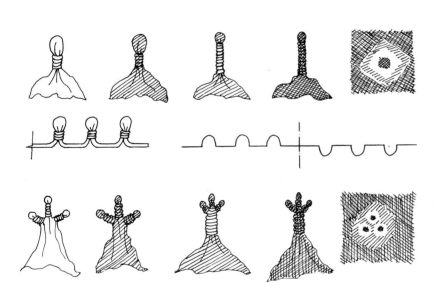

486–487 A woman from Hama demonstrates the technique for making *plangi* patterns.

488–491 Sketch of the processes for the three variants of *plangi* which appear in our examples. The result of the process illustrated in the centre is shown, for example, by the detail, bottom right.

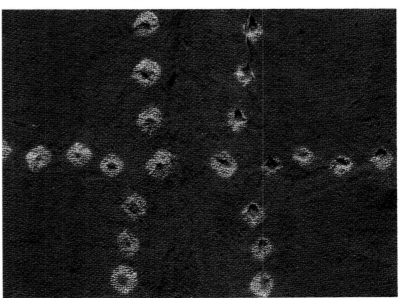

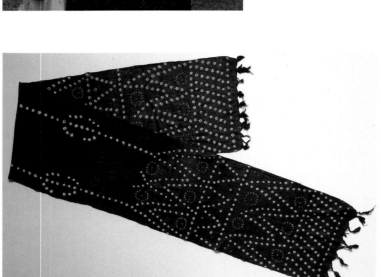

492 A young woman from Hama. She is wearing a festive *plangi* dress with brocade embroidery along the neck-line.

493—500 Dresses and veils from Hama. The patterns are executed in various *plangi* techniques. The patterns are very geometrical; they follow the forms of bedouin jewellery and the ornamentation on peasant ceramics.

196

197

In many cases the colour and shape of the pattern are not applied purely for decorative reasons, they also bestow magical protection on the person, as, for example, the red colour of the *plangi* on black or dark veils; the yellow spots are supposed to protect the young woman from the evil eye and "spirits".

Plangi dresses and scarfs are still sold in the Syrian markets, though not in large quantities.

The patterns are usually made up of circles a few millimetres wide with a tiny dot in the centre.

In Syria the *plangi* technique nowadays seems to be used especially by the bedouins and nomads who have become sedentary. It is practised by women. As one of the women we interviewed in Hama told us in 1990, the quantity of dresses made by the women depends on the personal demand and the number of orders received.

The modern *plangi* dresses are decorated additionally at the neck opening and on the chest panels with brocade embroidery (lurex). They are used as wedding dresses, for the trousseaux and are worn on festive occasions.

The shape of the sleeves of *plangi* dress is the same as those usually found in other dresses: either long, narrow sleeves with continuous patterns, or else the patterns are on the cuffs or on the lower edge of the "wing sleeves".

Lime resist-dyeing on aniline black in Aleppo

In the dyeing and printing workshops – in the Suq asabun, for example – loose-weave silk and artificial silk cloths are printed. These are used as headscarves of bedouin women, peasant women and women from the small towns. Most of the production goes for export to Jordan, Iraq and Saudi Arabia.

The square cloths (from 1 x 1 m to 1.35 x 1.35 m) of real silk with printed decoration are still produced only in Aleppo.

The dyeing, printing and some of the drying of the scarves take place in one and the same room.

The aliline black solution is in a large pot or tub, in which the cloths treated with lime are placed. A small pot contains the solution of lime slaked in water and a binder prepared from starch.

A wooden or padded stamp cushion covered with cloth is inserted into the smaller container. The cushion is then used to moisten the stamp (*qalib*) with the solution during the printing.

The *qalib* with which the lime resist is applied is made of wood in the shape of the pattern outlines which are later to be treated in colour. For greater absorbency of the stamp its underside is covered with cloth.

The *qalib* is made by the printer (*tabba*) himself.

There are no limits to the choice of printed motifs. The *tabba* either uses old traditional patterns or creates new ones. He matches the taste of his clients and adapts to suit demand.

The printer works sitting on the ground with a low table in front of him padded with blankets. The piece of cloth is spread out on this table and the lime resist is printed on it. After printing, the pieces are placed in the pot with the black aniline dye, then taken out one by one and hung up to dry. After the dye is fixed, which takes several hours, the cloths have to be washed out thoroughly because aniline dye harms the material. The rinsing of the cloths under running water is often done by women. Some of the lime resist is also removed in this way.

After drying once again the cloths go back to the printer in the workshop, where the stopped out areas on the cloths are now printed in colour using unpadded stamps. Several colours can be used depending on what is required. For each colour a particular stamp is used, corresponding to the part of the pattern. This work is mostly done by children or the mentally handicapped, who earn very low wages.

In autumn 1990 in Aleppo we were able to observe three different ways of applying the patterns to the pieces of cloth:

In one instance the headscarves were decorated only along the borders, while the inner parts were dyed black.

In another the whole surface of the cloth was patterned in colour and the stopped-out areas were left white. The stamps for this are much bigger and cover exactly a quarter of the cloth, which is printed all over by using the stamp four times.

In the third instance mainly geometrical patterns in the required colour were stamped on natural-coloured or artificial silk. Stamping is done four times. Since the patterns here do not overlap, this creates a four-part division on the cloth similar to cloths from the Persian area.

As well as lime resist-dyeing, screen printing is used for a large number of cloths printed in Aleppo (see photograph).

Screen printing is a process in which areas of a fine woven screen are covered so as to be impervious to dye. These correspond to the areas of the pattern which are to remain uncoloured. To print the pattern on the fabric the dye is transferred onto the cloth through the uncovered areas of the screen by means of a knife-like instrument (*rakel*). In the modern process it is sprayed on by means of an atomizer. The sieve may be made of silk, bronze, polyamide or polyester gauze.

501—507 Workshop in Aleppo, where silks are stamped by hand (lime resist) or printed by silk-screen.

Ikat (*tarbit*) and ikateurs (*ar-rabbât*)

Resist-dyeing by partially covering the bundled strands of thread with a fixed pattern before dyeing and weaving is known as ikat. Ikat is an Indonesian word; in the Turkish and Persian speaking areas it is called *abr*, and in Arabic *tarbit*.

Individual sections of the thread are protected before dyeing by a wrapping or some other covering.

If a particular patterning of the material is desired, the yarn must be arranged already during the resist-dyeing process in the pattern that is to show in the finished weave.

One can speak of warp ikat or weft ikat or double ikat, depending on whether the warp or weft or both are patterned. Materials which have ornaments over the whole surface are called full ikat. If the patterns are restricted to strips running along or across, the material is called strip ikat. If no attention is paid to the pattern planned for the material, the ikat process is very simple. The yarn is wrapped or tied in knots at random places before dyeing, and the result is a speckled pattern.

On the finished cloth one can recognize true ikat patterns from the way the colours run in the direction of the patterned threads or merge into each other.

The range of patterns possible while making an ikat is limited by the directions of the warp and the woof, but nevertheless allows for a surprising variety. As in all resist-dyeing processes it is possible in ikat to produce monochrome (including the natural colour of the material) or multicoloured patterns.

For this it is necessary to use repeated tyings, or combine them in a particular way with the same number of dyeings as there are colours required.

In the collection of Syrian textiles at the Linden-Museum there are three types of warp ikat represented by five coats (made of *qutni*), three bath cloths (*mi'zar alhammâm*) and three wrapping cloths (*baqgê*).

In Aleppo ikat material and cloths are are still made at the house of the Zâhir brothers (Ilias and Gorgi), who learned the craft of the ikateur (*rabbât*) from their father. The *rabbât* craft was passed down from grandfather to father and from father to sons in the Zâhir family. Until the 1950s their ikat business flourished, but sales fell at the time of the Palestine crisis. Since the 1960s the brothers – their father has retired – have divided their work: Ilias (helped by his son) is the ikateur, while Gorgi is concerned with buying and selling.

Their principal product is the bath cloth (*mi'zar alhammâm*), made of full ikat, which is worn wrapped around the loins in the public bath (*hammâm*). It is woven as an individual piece in various sizes. The bath cloth is made of silk or artificial silk, more rarely of cotton. Warp and weft are always of the same material and are woven in plain weave. A typical pattern is the "shuttle" (*makkuk*). Other ornaments such as block patterns or double arrowheads appear only at the edges of the cloth.

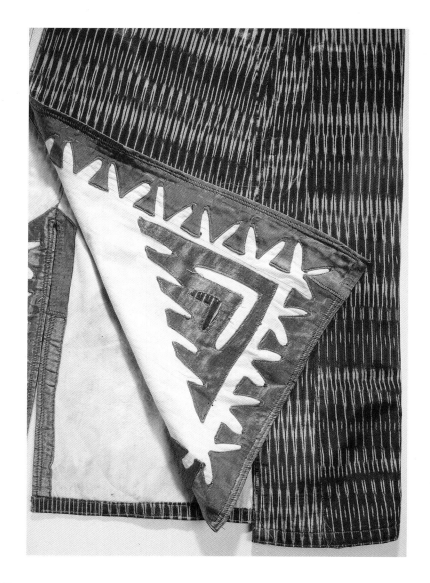

508 & 509 Examples of ikat from Aleppo: a bath cloth (above) and a coat (below).

The Zâhir family also makes part-ikat cloths and sometimes *qutni* by the metre, but for these the range of patterns are fewer. This is not because of the lack of skill of the *rabbât*, but because of the limited demand for full ikat fabrics, since the work needed to make them means they are too expensive.

The bath cloths are sold in Syria, Turkey and Iraq, and sometimes also in Iran and Afghanistan. The cloths are woven in red, claret and black. Iraqi customers prefer red, and the Turkish claret and red, while the black cloths are bought by Assyrians and the more conservative customers among the Syrian urban population.

Ikat fabrics, with silk or artificial silk warp, but cotton weft, are now generally known as *qutni* ("the cotton ones") (silk mixture, atlas or satin silk, rib-woven silk). The *qutni* fabrics are woven in Aleppo, Hama and Damascus.

These fabrics are used in the towns as bolsters for chairs, cushion covers, for coats and clothing materials (among the Alawites), and generally as lining and appliqué for clothing.

The satin or atlas weave is the rule for the fabrics known as *gutni*. It is characterized by widely separated intersections. In this type of weave long bare sections of thread are left visible. When these have been given ikat treatment they form a smooth, shiny surface which brings out the pattern particularly clearly. The pattern is formed of narrow seven-stepped rhombuses, which appear to be stretched lengthwise along the horizontal axis. In Aleppo these patterns are called "sparrows' tongues".

Apart from satin-weave there are also *qutni* fabrics in ribbed-weave (warp-weave). In warp-weave the cotton weft threads completely disappear and the ikat patterns and the whole appearance of the material is thus given a quite remarkable splendour.

The third type, *baqgé*, was woven as a cloth for wrapping washing utensils and was often square in shape. In the past these wrapping cloths were made of real silk, today they are of artificial silk and always woven in plain weave. They are only made to order (for trousseaux).

As well as full-ikat fabrics, part-ikat cloths were produced in Aleppo and formerly also in Hama. In the latter the ikat patterns appear as decorative strips. The older cloths have "arrow-head" patterns, the more recent ones block patterns.

Narrow or medium-width atlas or rib-woven fabrics (30-50 cm) with fine ikat motifs arranged in strips to form a vertical pattern are characteristic of Yemen, Syria and Asia Minor.

In all three places this is continuous patterned material woven by the metre.

The coat of pale yellow material in atlas weave, with vertical stripes, has a very clear "arrow-head" motif in white-red and white-blue with narrow warp-weave stripes (black-yellow) framed by plain red stripes.

The "arrow-head" pattern may well function as an amulet.

The origins of the ikat process, particularly of the warp ikat, are to be located in East and Central Asia, and possibly also in India.

The technique and design of patterns in the ikat process are very complicated and time-consuming. The thread must be fixed in specific lengths, groups and arrangements while creating the ikat patterns, to make their use in the weaving process easier.

To produce an ikat requires the efforts of several specialists:
1. *al fattâl*, twister
2. *almusaddi*, warp-layer
3. *arrabbât*, ikateur
4. *assabbâg*, dyer
5. *almulqi*, leash-threader
6. *annassag, annawwâl, alhâ'ik*, weavers

(The Arabic terms are taken from R.J. Moser, "Die Ikat-technik in Aleppo", *Baseler Beiträge zur Ethnologie* 15, 1974.)

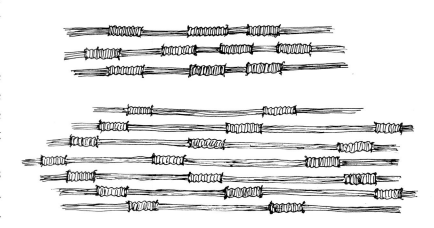

510 Ikat dyeing: examples showing the creation of patterns which appear on the ikat coats in this collection. Above: the motif known as "bird tongues", below: "arrow heads".

Obtaining and Processing the Raw Materials

Maria Zerrnickel

The camels kept by the bedouin, and the goats and sheep kept by the semi-nomads and peasants, together with agriculture and silkworm breeding, were and still are the basis for obtaining important raw materials such as wool, cotton and raw silk.

The processing of the wool to make yarn, felt, tent strips and coarse woollen materials has a long tradition among all bedouin tribes and semi- nomads. The cultivation of cotton in Syria was concentrated mainly in the Orontes valley and the Euphrates region. Cotton (the annual *herbaceum*) was brought in the sixth century BC from India to Persia and thence to northern Arabia, where it was cultivated. The arboraceous perennial cotton plant from India was already known in the Assyrian Empire as an exotic plant, but it is not suitable for cultivation. Today the intensive cultivation of cotton is practised predominantly by Syrian peasants in the Orontes valley and nomads who have settled on the Euphrates to farm the newly irrigated and drained fields.

The knowledge of how to breed silkworms, and obtain and refine the silk, came around the fifth century AD along the trade routes first from Khotan to the oases of Central Asia, whence it gradually spread through Persia to Byzantium and the coastal region of northern Arabia. In Syria some mulberry trees were planted on the foothills of the Alawite Mountains and the Antilebanon, and some along the Euphrates. Sericulture has long been practised, mostly in these regions inhabited by Christian peasants.

Today the obtaining of raw silk is predominantly in the hands of Christian and Alawite peasant women.

The processing of wool and cotton, and particularly the care of silkworms, the obtaining and reeling of silk, and the weaving at the archaic horizontal loom of the bedouin – all these activities were exclusively women's work.

The prerequisites for the production of textiles are a knowledge of the implements needed for spinning, reeling, twisting and weaving – such as the various types of looms (vertical standing weighted loom, horizontal and shaft loom, hybrid and draw loom, Jacquard loom etc.) – and knowledge of recipes for dyes. Damascus, Aleppo, Homs and Hama have long been famous for these crafts – above all for the skills of the silk and cotton weavers (brocade, damask).

This knowledge is, however, also the best evidence of the quite remarkable ability of the artisans in the towns and of the bedouin women in the desert. They bear witness to their patience, industry, commercial interest and healthy ambition.

Silk (*harir*)

Silk is without doubt the raw material best suited to weaving. Silk was first used for making textiles in China, where the discovery and domestication of the silkworm dates from at least the third millennium BC.

For a long time China held the monopoly in silkworm breeding and thereby for the production of silk yarn in large quantities. In other parts of Asia only the cocoons of the wild silkworm were used more or less haphazardly.

Chinese silks were much in demand as an import because of their long tradition and outstanding quality.

Assyrians, ancient Syrians, Babylonians, Persians, and later the Greeks, Romans, Byzantines and Arabs – all delighted in the magic of the lightly shimmering sheen, soft grip and comfortable feel against the skin, of silk textiles, which were warm and yet pleasantly cool, and hung in wonderful folds. Fine silks were always been – and still are – much sought after as a trading commodity and luxury article.

The export of *grège* (raw silk) along the the Silk Roads was very profitable for China and led to the spread and establishment of silk- weaving in regions further west.

Knowledge of silkworm breeding, of the cultivation of the white and black mulberry trees (*tut*) and of the processing of the silk remained for centuries a secret kept from the Near East and northern Arabia, until the fifth century AD.

The know-how for large-scale silk production came to the region from Persia in the Sassanian period (third to sixth century AD), and historical sources tell how the *Bombyx mori* (silkworm) was brought to Byzantium during the reign of Justinian (second half of the sixth century).

The breeding of silkworms, the cultivation of mulberry trees and the production of silk in northern Arabia suffered several setbacks over the centuries – and sometimes was even brought to a halt – by wars, epidemics of the silkworms or trees, poor climatic conditions, or social and political crises. Nevertheless the silk-making process was passed down to be renewed and developed over the generations.

In present-day Syria and Lebanon silkworm breeding and *tut* tree cultivation is practised in the eastern coastal regions, to the west of the Orontes and in the foothills of the Alawite mountains and the Antilebanon.

In October 1991 we visited a silkworm-breeding family in Syria living in Al Rasafa, a village in the south-eastern Alawite Mountains. We were allowed to examine their mulberry tree plantations and make an assessment of their work (see photograph). The plantation consisted of 41 old trees (around 30 to 50 years old), and several newly planted trees, indicating that silkworm breeding was set to continue.

Mrs Lmia explained to us the life cycle of the silkworm which lasts about 55 days from the egg-egg-"seed" to the emerging from its cocoon of the Bombyx mori moth, its "courtship dance" and the laying of eggs.

The "seed" is stored in a cool constant temperature for about ten months. Mrs Lmia showed us the eggs from her refrigerator, a round hand made bowl made of cow dung, a handful of white cocoons (*kazi*), a broom (*chih*), and gave a very lively, enthusiastic and detailed account of her strenuous work for the care of the silkworms.

The incubation period of the "seed" (*bourour*) begins in March as soon as the first leaves appear on the *tut* trees. For seven days and nights she carries the "mother of the worms" (moths' eggs wrapped in soft paper and and cloth padded with cotton wool) below the breast, since a constant body temperature is necessary to obtain strong, healthy worms, who will all pupate at the same time. This method of incubation was already in use in ancient China.

On the seventh or eighth day the eggs turn greyish white and begin to move. With great effort the tiny (2-3 mm long) black, spiny worms bite an opening in the egg shell and emerge. First they attach themselves by several silk mooring threads to save themselves from falling from their original incubation place. In nature this would usually be the branch of a mulberry tree, whose leaves provide the grub with its food. Mrs Kadaur places the pupating worms in the warm bowl, and they attach themselves to its base. The newborn creatures immediately reveal their voracious appetites: they have to be fed 48 times every 24 hours with young, tender, fresh mulberry leaves, finely and carefully chopped. They must be free of dew. During the whole of the silkworms' development (about 33 days) the foliage must not be wet, otherwise the worms will die or later there will be water instead of silk. But neither should the leaves be too dry, or else the silk will be brittle. The room in which the worms are kept must be clean, dry, bright, airy but with no draughts, and the temperature must be constant.

In the first five or six days until the first shedding of the skin, the spiny worms form little clumps and have to be separated with goose feathers or little sticks so that their spines do not become to firmly hooked together. After the shedding of the first skin (the shedding of the first three skins takes a day in each instance) the worms are bigger and now require 30 meals every 24 hours, more in the daytime than at night, when they eat more slowly. The worms still have to be watched and cared for round the clock. After they have shed their skins twice more (on the 9th or 10th, and 15th or 16th days) they are then fed only three or four times, though with larger quantities. They

also need ever more room (they are already up to seven centimetres long) and special frames are built for them. Before each shedding of a skin the worms go rigid and fall into a deep sleep with their heads and upper part of their body turned stiffly upwards. The fourth and last shedding of the skin lasts two days (on the 23rd day).

After eight or nine days (on the 33rd or 34th day), shortly before they reach the spinning stage, the worms take on an almost transparent amber colour. Mrs Kadaur lays out the dried osier branches. The worms (*doidi*), now up to nine centimetres long, move slowly and climb onto the *khih*, where they lie and begin to spin silk threads round themselves in figure-of-eight spiral movements. It usually takes seven days to spin a cocoon (*khamaka*). After fifteen or sixteen days – if the cocoons have not been taken to the state reeling factory at Dreykish, where the pupae are killed by heating – the moths emerge and damage the cocoons, which are then of a lower quality. The ripe cocoons are sorted and the larger ones, which seem to be better quality, are separated for further breeding.

Genuine, fine natural silk consists of the delicate, strong fibres secreted by the mulberry silkworm (*Bombyx mori*) as it pupates. They consist of 75 per cent fibroin (protein body) and 25 per cent sericin (silk-glue).

A growing silkworm eats about 30 grams of mulberry leaves in all; on the first day it weighs approximately 0.47 milligrams, on the thirty-third day approximately 3.65 grams.

The white mulberry tree provides the best fodder for the *Bombyx mori* grubs.

The cocoons are treated with hot water or steam to kill the pupae. Then, after the outer tangled fibres have been removed, the silk of three to eight or ten cocoons is reeled off, to give between 300 and 800 metres of reeled silk (*grège*). The outer layers (floss) of the cocoon, which cannot be reeled, are processed to make schappe, floret or bourette silk.

Raw silk cloth made of high quality waste (floss-silk), which has hardly been de-gummed and cannot be reeled is called knopped-weave. Knopped-weave silk has a distinctive appearance because of the irregular structure of the knopped yarn, from which the fabric is woven mostly by hand (cloths with and without *plangi* in Hama).

The clothes in this collection that are made by hand or machine from knopped silk, are red, yellow, indigo, dark brown and black in colour. With one exception, they are all decorated with *plangi* patterns.

The reeled-off silk is de-gummed, twisted and dyed in the manner required, or else left in its natural colour. It is then distributed by the state via agents to weavers in Damascus, Aleppo, Hama and Homs.

The 30-50 grams of silk yarn allotted is usually insufficient, so many weavers sell their share to wholesalers, or supplement it with silk yarn from the Lebanon.

This fine silk is used to make ikat, damask and brocade fabrics with various patterns on shaft looms and Jacquard looms with punched cards, as well as simpler taffeta silks for head cloths which have patterns printed by the silk-screen method and are very popular with bedouin women in the *suq* of Aleppo.

Silk and silk mixtures (silk warp, cotton weft) as well as artificial silk, mainly in sateen weave with ikat patterns, are used for making festive coats for women and men. Black silk, silk mixture and artificial silk in atlas weave are used for making women's dresses, skirts, coats and pants; these are richly decorated with embroidery in red silk thread. In Homs large silk scarfs are woven with brocaded and lancé patterns for women and men.

In Syria silkworm breeding is concentrates in the western part of the country, along the Mediterranean coast with its mild climate.

The conditions necessary to breed silkworms success-fully are, at particular times of year, the right temperature, moist air, and fluctuations in temperature between day and night. But most important of all is the thriving of the mulberry trees needed to feed the silkworms.

The cultivation of large areas with mulberry leaves as plantations for breeding silkworms is more or less restricted to the Mediterranean coast, in the region between Satifa, Masyaf, Margab, Dreykish, north of Latakia around Sahyun, smaller areas on the western slopes of the Alawite Mountains up to approximately 600 metres above sea level. Around the town of Hama, near Maaloula and west of Damascus, and in Lebanon, we saw individual mulberry trees as well as plan-tations.

The constant removal of the leaves and the severe cutting of the shoots for silkworm breeding are important factors in the development of new varieties of trees. Among the different varieties bred for their very high leaf yield are *Morus alba Monetti* and *Morus alba Rosa di Lombardia*.

In Syria, west of Hama, at Rasafa, which is situated in a gorge, we were able to have a closer look at a plantation consisting of various sorts of mulberry trees, which varied in age and in the manner in which they were used. As can be seen from ill. 513, this is a plantation grafted on to tall trees which are planted five metres apart and are very heavily used. From the statistical analysis of measurements taken here, we calculated that this plantation produces up to a thousand kilograms of leaves per hectare for silkworm breeding. A detailed and comprehensive analysis would only be possible, however, with additional data collected in the spring.

From the small number of new plantations we concluded that silkworm breeding in Syria is in decline, and not just because of diseases of the silkworms and the mulberry trees. Although there still is a world demand for real silk, for which even the best artificial fibres are no substitute, since 1930 Syrian silk has not been able to offer serious competition to Far Eastern silk as the world market, since the overall yields are too low.

Wool

In northern Arabia the bedouin and peasant women process some of their wool themselves at home, while the rest of the wool, unspun but cleaned, is sold in the *suq* and processed in factories. It is later bought again by the bedouins and peasants in the form of yarn. The men shear the sheep, goats and camels and bring the uncleaned wool to the women to be further processed and used in the tent or house. The women clean this wool of dung, thorns and stalks, beat it with bundles of canes or a bow to loosen it, then comb the wool with a comb, or tease it deftly with their fingers.

The bedouin women of northern Arabia spin and twist the wool using the traditional spindle (*maghzal*). After-wards the spun wool is wound into skeins as needed, and dyed or left undyed. The the wool is woven in plain weave or ribbed weave on the traditional horizontal loom (*nati*), or on a hybrid shaft loom with two pedals made of rope, or else on a pit loom.

The woven cloth is only 20-50 cm wide. The wool from the humps and necks of young camels, which is particu-larly fine, soft, supple and silky, with its warm natural colours (dark brown, light beige to white) is very highly prized by the bedouins. This camel wool is spun into a fine tight thread and then woven. Camel-wool fabrics are used to make the most most expensive of the festive cloaks (*abaye*) and are worn by rich bedouins, as well as by peas-ants and men in the towns, both as a national costume and as everyday dress. The winter jackets and cloaks (*abaye*) are made of coarse woollen materials, wool mixtures (wool warp, cotton weft) in dark and light natural wool colours (ribbed weave); some are embroidered with woollen thread.

Goat and sheep wool is used to weave tent strips, kelims, partitions, bags, bands, belts, girths and suchlike. They are decorated with plaited cords, with or without tassels, and embroidered in woollen thread.

Spinning, twisting, weaving

Spinning, twisting and weaving are very ancient tech-niques. Ethnologists and prehistorians assume that they developed when man became sedentary and began to prac-tise agriculture and animal husbandry.

In the Ancient Orient climatic and political conditions meant that the transition from nomadic to sedentary life (and vice versa) was always fluid – and this is still the case today. It can therefore be assumed that spinning, twisting and weaving were techniques originally passed from the sedentary people to the nomads.

Since around 4000 BC the free-hanging spindle has been used. It consists of a shaft, which is usually of wood, and a whorl, which may be made of pottery, bone, stone, ceramic or wood.

In the course of time the simple spinning wheel was developed; the spindle is fitted horizontally into a frame and driven by hand by means of a belt drive. Wool, flax, cotton, silk and other fibres are spun, reeled off and twisted. Spinning, reeling and twisting was a secondary activity carried out by women at home.

Weaving

Weaving means the crossing or interlacing of two different systems of threads: the parallel warp threads running lengthwise, and the weft threads, which are passed across them. All early looms are geared to the same weaving process: setting the position of the warp threads (the shed and countershed), inserting the weft thread and beating it in. The archaic horizontal loom constructed of wooden parts with a narrow warp rod is called a *nôl* or *nol arabi* by the Arabs. It is very simple and consists of only a few elements:

1. Warp rod, for keeping the warp taut and (in some cases) for rolling up the fabric.
2. Shed stick and heddle rod with leashes for holding the warp threads.
3. Sword beater for forming the shed and beating in the weft.
4. Stick spool or shuttle with the weft thread.

The warp threads may be finite or endless. In our drawing they are finite. The loom can be quickly set up by two women outside the tent, in the tent, or in the house or courtyard, and can be as quickly dismantled. It is therefore ideal for bedouins and for semi-nomads.

The most complicated work is the preparation of the warp threads for weaving. The threads of the part of the warp below the shed stick have each to be passed through loops or leashes, which are secured by a rod running across the warp. With this equipment the weaver can form the shed with the help of the shed stick, insert the weft, and then form the countershed across the whole warp, fix it, and so on.

To insert the weft thread into the warp (make a pick) she needs a shuttle with a spool of thread, or a stick spool with the weft thread wound round it. To form the shed and countershed, and to beat in each new weft thread, she uses the sword (*minshaz*). The weaving process begins with the thrusting of the sword into the shed formed by the position of the shed stick. The sword is then turned upright and the weft thread inserted. Then the shed stick is pushed away from the weaving, and the heddle rod with the warp threads attached to it is raised. This forms the countershed. The weaver now thrusts her sword in again, turns it upright, inserts the weft, and so the process continues. Since the *nôl* usually only has a narrow warp beam and heddle rod, the fabric or strip of kelim is only 24-50 cm wide (very rarely, using modernized looms, the width may be up to 60-70 cm).

The weaving technique most used by bedouin women and the women weavers of the semi-nomads is known as *kelim* (carpet) in the Turkish-speaking world. Kelim is a flatweave in which the special form of plain weave means that either the warp or weft is invisible. A distinction is made between warp-faced and weft-faced fabrics. Most of the kelims we have looked at are weft-faced.

Historical records indicate that this technique came to the northern regions of the Arabian Peninsula originally from China or Central Asia. The Jordanian and Syrian flat-weaves in the Linden Museum demonstrate a variety of processes, but basically two techniques are used. The kelims, bags, bands and belts are woven or worked or made by different variations of the two. Weft weave is formed when the weft threads are beaten closely together with the beater (sword). The warp threads, which are usually of undyed wool or cotton, though they may also be coloured, are thus hidden. If individual weft threads in particular colours (e.g. red and blue) form the pattern and these threads meet parallel lengthwise on the warp, each weft thread is wrapped around the warp thread and drawn back. Consequently slits occur a the edge of the pattern whenever there is a change of colour.

This is called slit-kelim technique. The patterns formed in this way follow straight lines, but if the weaver moves drawn-back weft threads one warp thread along each time the weft thread is inserted, then there are no slits, and triangles, rhombuses and diagonal lines can be formed.

In the weaving process described above there are other possibilities for creating various sorts of patterns not only in colour but also in shape. For example, at the point where the weft threads meet an additional woollen thread in a contrasting colour can be worked in over two or three warp threads, or the weft threads can be looped together where they meet. In both cases there are no slits and new patterns are created, and in the second instance the loops are are only visible on the reverse. A similar technique can be seen in other fabrics. Here the weft threads are not looped but linked together, thus creating a new and original type of pattern.

In the techniques discussed so far the weft threads forming the pattern run parallel to each other and form only geometrical ornaments. Round shapes (infill patterns) can be created by using a weaving process in which the weft threads run in an arc to each other with an additional brightly coloured thread. In this way – again without slits – floral and figural images can be created. The technique is similar to European tapestry weaving.

Another method, based on basket weave or kelim weaving, is the *cicim* technique. Here an additional thread, often garishly coloured, is run over two, three, four or up to seven warp threads parallel to the weft creating an apparently raised pattern, like embroidery. On the reverse of a fabric woven by this method continuous or cut-off cross-threads can be seen.

The technique known as *zili* differs only very slightly from the one just described. Here the additional thread that forms the pattern is again drawn over a maximum of four warp threads, but is interrupted by a warp thread and tied. The fabric resembles flat-stitch embroidery.

The last and most complicated kelim technique is called *sumakh* and is also represented in our collection. In this method weft and warp are both completely hidden under the coarse added threads that form the pattern. The patterned surface is formed by looping (knitting) the threads of the basic fabric from the reverse over two or four warp threads. This technique allows a wide diversity of ornaments to be created, whereby the whole surface of the fabric is covered with a raised pattern, as in knotted carpets.

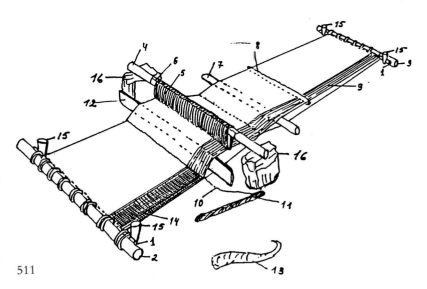

511

Loom (*nôl*)

Horizontal loom in northern Arabia, still used by bedouin women today. (The Arabic names are taken from S. Weir, 1976.)

The loom consists of:
1. two warp rods (*mutrag*)
2. breast beam for securing the warp rod (*ga'al-nati*)
3. warp beam for securing the warp rod at the far end (*ras al-nati*)
4. heddle rod (*minyar*)
5. leashes (*nireh*)
6. the upper part of the string from which the leashes are knotted (*gattar*)
7. shed stick used to separate the warp threads (shed and countershed) (*haf, mahafah*)
8. string running (with or without stick) a round the upper warp threads to prevent the warp threads from becoming tangled
9. warp threads (*sita*)
10. weft thread (*lahmeh*)
11. stick spool (*maysha'*)
12. sword beater, for beating in the weft thread (*minshaz*)
13. beating hook (gazelle horn), a particularly important tool for bedouin women, used for beating in the weft thread when making patterns in the flatweave fabric (*mishga, mihta*)
14. woven fabric
15. four wooden or metal posts set in the ground to keep the warp threads taut.
16. two stones (or blocks, or boxes) of the same height for supporting the heddle rod (*huda* – pl. *hawadi*)

Some parts of the loom (4, 7, 8, 11, 12, 13 and 16) are moved during the weaving process, the others are fixed until the weaving is completed. The whole *nôl* can be quickly dismantled as required and rolled up for transport.

206

512 Harvesting cotton. A lot of cotton is grown along the Euphrates, on the land newly gained by the irrigation programme.

513 Mulberry trees near Masyaf. The cultivation of silkworms is still practised in the region between Safita and Masyaf.

514 A plyer in Homs twisting the skeins of thread which will then be taken to be dyed.

515 A woman weaving es-Suchne at a shaft loom with foot pedals.

516 A weaver in Aleppo at a pit loom.

Tablet weaving in Damascus: Master Abdyl Wahabaita

Tablet weaving has been practised all over the world for thousands of years, as can be seen from archaeological finds and historical descriptions. Bands and belts are still produced by this method by many peoples today.

In Damascus we looked over the shoulder of a master tablet weaver at work and he wrote down for us the Arabic names of the tools he used.

The master said that the only absolutely essential part of the tablet weavers equipment was the tablet (*shapar*). Tablets measure five centimetres square and are made of leather or card, with a hole at each corner.

A warp thread (*madhe*) is passed through each of these holes. If the tablet is twisted a cord is formed. The number of tablets corresponds to the number of cords. In our case there were twenty tablets threaded with black-and-white, green-and-red and green-and-brown threads. When all the warp threads had been threaded they were drawn through a ring at the left-hand end and knotted. The ring is fixed in the wall, only 5-8 cm from the ground. A warp measuring 320 cm could be drawn taut in his workshop. At the right-hand end the warp threads were drawn through the holes in the wooden weaving comb, over a small roller and tied with white cotton thread to a post set in the ground. The rest of the warp thread remained coiled by the post.

The craftsman laid all the tablets horizontally on their ends, thus forming the shed of the weft thread (*hashe*). The weft thread is wrapped round a wooden spool (*makok*) 17 cm long and 2 cm wide, with two notches at the ends. To beat in the weft the master uses a traditional weaving sword 38 cm long with a handle (*sife*) made of wood, bone or ivory. About 15-20 cm from the left-hand end two shed sticks (*nails*) are inserted. The weft thread interweaves with the twisted cord to form a patterned band or belt. Tablet weaving is thus a combination of plaiting and weaving.

Master Abdyl-Wahabaita learned the craft from his father, who had received a certificate of excellence from the French. During the summer holidays his youngest son is learning from him.

517 A tablet weaver in Damascus.

518 Tablet-woven belts. These are worn mainly by nomad women in the Hauran.

519 The belt of this "milking apron" is made using the tablet weaving technique. One end is decorated with a snake.

208

The production of fabrics

The twister

The making of a fabric generally begins with the spinning (wool, cotton) or reeling (fine silk) of the fibre. In the cities the processing today starts with the twister (al-fattâl). Because of the large supplies of factory-made yarns, the twister in Syria today has hardly any commissions, so he is forced to take on a second skill, that of a warp- layer (al-musaddi), as well.

The work of a *fattâl* was particularly important for the twisting of fine silks to produce the traditional silk weaves, such as ikat, *qutni*, damask and brocade.

For twisting and warp-laying a *fattâl-musaddi* needs a drive wheel (*dulab*) and spools. Today these are modern factory spools, with and without yarn. Nowadays the traditional *kufiya* used in the past is hardly ever used, since the yarn arrives in the workshop already on a handy spool. The *kufiya* used to be an indispensable piece of the twister's equipment in the time when the yarn did not come from the factory but in skeins directly from the spinners. The skeins could easily be placed over the *kufiya*, unwound, twisted and wound up again.

After the twisting the laying of the warp begins.

The warp-layer (al-musaddi)

The work of a *musaddi* includes the dividing up of the warp threads into the heddle warps and shed stick warps, the making of the crossing between these, the counting of the warp threads and the measuring of the length of warp desired (e.g. 260 metres).

For these tasks the warp-layer uses two pieces of equipment.

As soon as the *musaddi* has finished his work the hanks of yarn are sent to the ikateur (*rabbât*), the dyer (*sabbag*) or straight to the leash- threader (*mulgi*), depending on the what they are to be used for.

The ikateur (arrabbât)

If the thread is to be used for ikat fabrics the *rabbât* begins by tying it to form the particular patterns. A number of skeins, which are not intended for ikat, are dyed beforehand. For ikat patterns the undyed skeins of thread are stretched out (along a garden wall, for example) and then tied at particular places. When all the skeins have been bound the are sent to the dyer. They are dyed as many times as there are colours required for the ikat pattern (e.g. red, yellow, blue). When the tying and dyeing are finished the skeins are dipped in starch and then stretched out to dry. The skeins are lined up, for the sets to be counted the damaged fibres to be bound and repaired. When the skeins are finally repaired and dried, they are wound up according to the patterns (centre or side panels of the fabric to be woven) metre by metre into skeins and taken to the workshop of the leash-threader (*mulqi*).

The leash-threader (al-mulqi)

The *mulqi*'s task is to thread the individual warp threads through the leashes of the loom shafts and the reed holes of the comb. He does this not only for ikat weavers but for all other fabrics made on hand-looms of all constructions. His work demands a very special sensitivity, especially where ikat fabrics are concerned. As soon as he has the formation of the pattern clearly in his mind he spreads the skeins with the ikat patterns out on the ground and arranges them in the order of the pattern to appear on the finished cloth. The number of shafts varies from four to twelve, depending on the weave and the pattern of the fabric. To draw the warp threads through the leashes the *mulqi* requires one assistant.

They sit opposite each other with the suspended heddle rods (four for plain weave) fixed between them and the warp threads ready in separate sets. The *mulqi* opens the leashes and takes the thread held out to him by his assistant. He runs the thread through for about 20 cm and then lets go of the two leashes. He repeats this procedure until all the warps are threaded through the leashes. (For a bath cloth approximately 1.16 metres wide, 2800 warp threads are needed.) When the warp threads have been drawn through the shafts, the same method is used to run the threads through the reed holes of the metal comb. The comb takes the place of the shafts and is secured. To pass the threads through the reed holes of the comb the leash-threader now uses a notched knife. The assistant takes the first thread and places it on the notch of the knife which the *mulqi* then puts it through the reed hole. In this way all the warp threads are threaded through the comb in the correct order, and the leash-threader's task is done.

After the removal of the leash shafts from the comb, the whole ensemble (hanks of warp thread, threaded heddle rods and comb) is taken to the weaver.

The weaver (an-nawwâl, an-nassâg, al-hâ'îk)

In Syria today various sorts of hand looms are still in use. For weaving ikat fabrics in silk and artificial silk the shaft loom (without punched cards) is used. Wool and cotton are often woven on a pit loom.

Many old Syrian shaft looms have been improved by the addition of modern equipment, particularly in Damascus, but to a lesser extent in Aleppo, Homs and Hama, on which silk and artificial silk are woven into damasks and brocades or other fabrics. They have been fitted with Jacquard machines and fast-shuttle device.

The basic framework for all sorts of looms (shaft loom, pit loom, hybrid loom, draw loom or Jacquard loom) is always in principle the same, apart from some deviations and modernizations.

It consists of four upright posts joined together. At the back is the warp beam on which the warp threads are wound. From here they run through leashes which are attached to two pieces of wood and form a shaft. After this they pass through the weaving comb and are tied to the cloth beam at the front. The weaver sits on a bench or a board in front and, by working the pedals which are connected with the shafts, forms the shed he requires, passes the shuttle through and beats in the weft thread firmly into the woven fabric with the weaving comb which hangs in a sley in the basic framework.

The shaft loom

After the hank of warp threads, with the shafts and comb, has been taken from the *mulqi* (leash threader) to the weaver (*annawwâl*), the first thing he does is to insert the comb into the swing drawer and stretch out the warp threads attached to the breast beam. When the sley and breast beam are ready for use, the shafts with pedals attached are suspended from the frame. It takes five or six hours for the *nawwâl* to do this. The more complicated the pattern, the more shafts with pedals are included.

To do the weaving the weaver sits on a board placed so that when his legs are almost extended they reach the pedals. This raised position gives him a good view of the whole loom.

Today the shaft loom is often equipped with a fast-shuttle device. The shuttle (*makkuk*) with the weft thread is hastened on its course back and forth by pulling on a handle.

As he weaves the *nawwâl* operates first one pedal so that the shaft to which it is joined is lowered and the other shafts are raised and form a shed. By pulling the handle he shoots the weft thread across and then beats it into the woven fabric with the sley. If the weaver wants to weave in a smaller pattern or his name, he uses a smaller shuttle with a different coloured thread and draws the weft through the newly formed shed only as far as the width of the the pattern or script. The cross- patterning is only possible with plain weave; there is no point in doing it with atlas weave since the weft threads are completely concealed by the warp threads.

Pit loom

This works on exactly the same principle as the shaft loom, except that the warp is not stretched out so far and runs horizontal only for a short distance before turning backwards and upwards 120 degrees. This means that it takes up less room. Breast beam, sley, framework and pedals are constructed in a similar way to the shaft loom, but are smaller. The warp threads run from the breast beam almost horizontally to the first roller. Passing beneath this they then turn diagonally backwards and upwards for two or three metres and round another roller. They are weighted down so that they hang vertically behind the back of the weaver.

The weaver at the pit loom sits on a board at ground level in front of the breast beam. The space for the pedals is a pit.

This loom is used especially to weave carpets (flat weave), small fancy kerchiefs made of wool, cotton or mixtures, but larger cloths made of silk or artificial silk can also be woven on it. Nowadays the pit loom, too, often has a fast-shuttle attachment, though this is not used for particularly small patterns and partial patterns, where frequent changing of the weft thread is necessary, in which case a number of small hand shuttles are used.

From draw loom to Jacquard machine

The draw loom was widely used for weaving complicated patterns (damask, brocade) until the invention of the Jacquard machine (by J.M. Jacquard, 1752-1834) in the nineteenth century.

The weaver formed the shed for the fabric base with pedals and shafts, while an assistant placed in the "figure or drawing area" high above on the loom created the sheds for the motifs in the pattern by pulling up groups of cords with the corresponding warp threads suspended from them. (This process is now accomplished in many looms by means of punched cards). Moreover the warp threads were not threaded on shafts but in individual leashes each with a little rod weight below, threaded through a horizontal board with holes carefully made in it and carried up to the drawing arrangement above.

The Jacquard machine was devised to control the warp threads drawn through the leashes, each leash having a *platine* (weight) attached. The size of the patterned surface depends on the number of *platines* (there can be more than 800). The *platines* are controlled by means of series of cards attached together, which are punched with holes corresponding to the pattern, or else by "endless" bands made of paper or plastic.

Damasks and brocades are produced on looms equipped in this way. A genuine damask (usually silk) has an even alternation of warp and weft atlas, which gives the fabric its characteristic shiny quality.

Brocade is a patterned, damask-like fabric made of natural or artificial silk with metal threads woven in. There are also brocades made entirely from gold or silver threads. Brocade threads usually have a cotton or linen core round which metal threads (lamé) are spun. Today special threads, such as lurex, which do not oxidize, are mainly used.

Textile Stories

Margareta Pavaloi

Brocade, atlas and damask – these costly fabrics have been directly related to Syria's textile luxury. The wealth and reputation of Syrian cities and their *suqs* were based on them, and their variety and fine quality have aroused admiration and enthusiasm in visitors of all periods.

Besides textiles made in Syria itself, fabrics fabrics from a great variety of countries were also imported, enriching the selection available. The cities were located at major intersections and their existence was based on their role as centres for long-distance trade between India, the Far East and the Mediterranean. Until the beginning of the nineteenth century trade relations with Europe were of equal importance to those with Mesopotamia, the Arabian Peninsula, Persia, Egypt and the more far-reaching links with Africa, India, Central Asia and the Far East.

Volney, who stayed in Syria at the end of the eighteenth century, describes Aleppo as the most important entrepôt for trade with Armenia and Turkey. Caravans were sent from Aleppo to Baghdad and Persia. The connection with India was via Basra and the Persian Gulf, and with Egypt and Mecca via Damascus. Aleppine trade with Europe went through the ports of Alexandretta and Latakia. Among the most important trading goods mentioned by Volney are textiles of wool or other native yarns, coarser fabrics, which were woven in the countryside, fine silk cloths made in Aleppo, cotton from India, muslin from Iraq and scarves from Kashmir. Other travellers in their turn praise the brocades from Damascus.

Textile production, with all the supply industries connected with it, was always the most important economic sector not only in the Syrian cities but also in many other cities throughout the Islamic world. The great demand for textiles of all sorts arose from the special importance that textiles had and still have in the material and social context in the Islamic world. Considering the range of fabrics and the manner in which they were used, it is tempting to speak of a "textile culture". There was an enormous demand for fabrics not only from the court and the palaces, but also from the urban population, especially the upper class. This was not only for clothing but also for interior decoration, which mainly consisted of textiles. When Browne visited Damascus at the end of the eighteenth century he described houses with "divans and large sofas of the richest silk ornamented with beads" (Browne, 1800: 568-69).

This demand for textiles was matched by the demand for labour. A large part of the urban population earned their living by working in the textile sector. Browne remarks of Damascus: "Damascus is the seat of a considerable trade and its manufactures feed a large number of Mohammedans and Christians. They produce silk and cotton goods..." (Browne, 1800: 552)

The history of textile production in Syria goes back a long way. It was determined essentially by two factors. One was Syria's geographical position as a bridgehead between the Mediterranean world and the Near and Middle East, which determined its historical and political destiny. This meant that, except for a few periods, it was always part of the great empires or a bone of contention between them. Until the Arab Conquest and the establishment of the Umayyad Caliphate in the seventh and eighth centuries textile production in Syria was dominated by Hellenistic, and later Byzantine and Sassanian traditions: heavy Persian and Byzantine fabrics, silks from Antioch, purple textiles from Tyre and fine Alexandrian fabrics were much in demand. Trade in textiles between Byzantium and the Sassanians was, however, under strict supervision, and the export of embroideries from Susa, for example, or of Byzantine purple fabrics was restricted. The Arab Conquest, the spread of Islam and the establishment of the Caliphate meant the disappearance of frontiers, restrictions and controls. An open market in culture and trade extended from the Mediterranean to India and Central Asia. Within it craftsmen, goods, techniques and styles could circulate freely and influence each other. Textile production was determined by new markets and new requirements. Islamic textiles brought together the legacies of Byzantium and the Sassanians, and absorbed influences from India and Central Asia, as well as from China. At the same time they developed their own very individual style. With the Arab Conquest Syria became an important centre for the production of textiles in the Islamic world.

The second determining factor for textile production in Syria was (and is) the access to raw materials. Two of these, linen and wool, had been available since time immemorial. Linen was mostly imported from Egypt, and wool was supplied by the nomads of the Syrian steppes and deserts. Silk and cotton, on the other hand, were raw materials new to the Mediterranean world and for a long time they had to be imported. The control of raw materials and the trade routes along which they were conveyed was a major political concern. Silk, especially, and the luxurious fabrics made from it, was not only a necessary accessory for the

520 & 521 Bath wrap for going to the bath before the wedding, in very high quality brocade embroidery. The patterns of this Damascene work follow European models. Early twentieth century.

522 & 523 Collar and cuffs decorated with beaten silver tinsel yarn. The inscription incorporated into the decoration wished health to the woman wearing it.

524 Two-piece wedding dress of a lady from Damascus around the turn of the century with rich brocade embroidery and beadwork decoration. The patterns are reminiscent of art nouveau ornament.

525 & 526 Bath wrap from Damascus, late nineteenth century. The style of the brocade embroidery is in the Persian tradition.

527–529 Damascene wedding dress made of velvet with brocade embroidery, early twentieth century. The treatment of traditional motifs such as the little vase and the rinceau border is inspired by art nouveau.

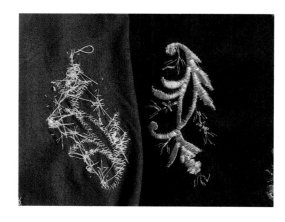

whims and lifestyle of a particular social class, it was also of decisive economic and political importance.

Syria's geography was favourable for the introduction of silk at the beginning of the sixth century in the northern regions and the Orontes plain, as well as the cultivation of cotton, particularly in the region between Hama and Aleppo and on the upper Euphrates. A typical product of Syria was, therefore, a mixed weave of cotton and silk, often an atlas fabric with stripes running lengthwise, such as alepin, which is still produced today.

Just as important as the raw materials for the textiles were dyes. Before the age of chemistry the procuring of natural materials for the production of dyes was time-consuming and expensive. Dyeing was part of the enhancement of textiles and recipes and dyeing techniques were guarded as jealously as the secret of silkworm cultivation. The emergence of the Islamic world changed and improved things considerably regarding access to raw materials. The expansion of trade in the Islamic world and the opportunities it opened up are illustrated by an anecdote told by Saadi when he describes his meeting with a rich merchant on the island of Kish (quoted in Lombard 1978: 162). The merchant confided to Saadi: "I would like to take Persian saffron to China, where I have heard one can obtain a good price for it, and then Chinese porcelain to Byzantium, Byzantine brocade to India, Indian steel to Aleppo, Aleppine glass to the Yemen and striped Yemeni textiles to Persia."

Silk: Wealth and Power

In antiquity silk was still a rarity. For a long time people did not even know exactly what silk was, since China kept silkworm breeding and the production and processing of silk a strictly guarded secret. It is not surprising that people made concentrated efforts to discover this secret, or at least to control the trade routes along which the silk came. Two important trade routes, branches of the Silk Road, ended in Syria: one of the overland routes ran from Central Asia via Persia and Iraq to Aleppo and on to Antioch. The other was a sea-route from India across the Indian Ocean and the Persian Gulf to Basra from where a land route could be taken either via Baghdad and Mosul to Aleppo, or through the Syrian desert to Palmyra and thence to Damascus and Tyre. From Syria the silk trade was continued into the Mediterranean and Europe.

Rome imported its silk from Syria and the Lebanon. The silk-dealers, or *sericarii* had their own quarter in Rome. To wear silk garments caused a sensation, and the response was not always enthusiastic. For a time it was forbidden to wear silk garments in the Senate, since they were regarded as feminine and therefore restricted to women. The Christians in Rome were even more unambiguous, declaring that a true Christian does not wear silk. But the seductive character of the material was too great for these puritanical attitudes to prevail. The wearing of silk garments soon became habitual, for the rich and powerful. When the Syrian potentate Heliogabalus from Homs visited Rome at the beginning of the third century he is supposed to have been the first man to wear clothes made entirely of silk.

For Rome the silk trade became an important source of revenue, but it remained dependent on Persia. When Diocletian made peace with Persia in 297, the border and customs post at Nisibis became the hub of the silk trade between the two empires. In 301 Diocletian fixed taxes and prices for silk.

Palmyra, too, owed its rise to the silk trade. Situated in the middle of the Syrian desert, it was the most important entrepôt for the caravan trade between the Euphrates and the Mediterranean. During the energetic rule of the legendary Queen Zenobia, in particular, this desert kingdom ruled from Palmyra achieved wealth and political importance. There was trade not only in silk fabrics made in China, but raw silk was also imported to be spun, woven, dyed – and, of course, worn. Evidence of this is provided by fragments of textiles, including silk damask, found at Palmyra. The style of clothing (above all the women's costumes) and jewellery seen in statues have in part persisted to the present day. But with the shift of trade routes due to wars and the resulting insecurity of the routes, Palmyra's heyday came to an end, and like so many places in Syria it became a "dead city"; bedouins now rest in the shade of its majestic ruins.

There are many stories about how silk was smuggled out of China. One of them tells how a Chinese princess, when she married a prince from Khotan, took silk cocoons across the border in her bridal coiffure to give them to her future husband as a present.

Byzantium's most important suppliers of silk were Central Asia and Persia. Duties and taxes made silk an expensive raw material that was difficult to obtain. In order to cater for the demand of the Byzantine court, Justinian established a monopoly of silk processing, which was practised exclusively in the state *gynaecea* (textile factories). Private silk weavers were forced onto the black market. When in 540 the war with Persia cut off the supply of silk, many Syrian and Lebanese silk-weavers emigrated immediately to Persia. After their victory over Byzantium the Persians finally gained control of the silk supply, which led to a crisis in textile production in the *gynaecea*.

The secret of silk production was brought to Byzantium by two Nestorian priests around 553. After a visit to their co-religionists in Central Asia they returned across the border with the eggs of the silkworm moth concealed in their walking sticks.

The leaves of the white mulberry tree, which grows in the Syrian and Lebanese mountains, are the staple food of the silkworms. Silk-spinning factories sprang up in Beirut, Homs and Hama. Since this period the production and processing of silk has been one of the most important factors in the economy of the Syrian and Lebanese region.

When the Muslim armies under Khalid b. al-Walid conquered Damascus, he seized three hundred camel-loads of silk. The tribute paid to him amounted to 10,000 gold pieces and 200 silk garments. Like the early Christians in Rome the first Muslims regarded the use of silk as a luxury that was detrimental to true religion, but in fact silk now became indispensable for the Umayyad court, just as it had been for the Roman emperors. This was often disapproved of: a Bedouin princess from the Euphrates region is said to have told her husband, Muawiya, that wearing a Bedouin cloak in the midst of her relatives would make her happier than all the silk at the court of Damascus.

The conquest of Persia not only made the Islamic world a serious rival to China in silk production, it also meant that it controlled the most important routes of the Silk Road, giving it the monopoly of the silk trade. Like the Byzantines before them, the caliphs and later Muslim rulers established state workshops for their own requirements, but without closing down the private workshops. The general name given to the textiles made in these workshops is *tiraz*. Fatimid Egypt was famous for them. Textiles played an important role in the politics of gift-giving of the Muslim rulers. Honorific garments were bestowed and precious cloths were horded. Garments and valuable cloths were passed down from generation to generation together with the stories of how they were acquired. The detailed knowledge about the variety and provenance of textiles as well as the need for luxury textiles is very marked: "May God cover me with striped cloaks from the Yemen, with linen cloths from Egypt, brocades from Byzantium, with silk from Susa and China, Persian garments and capes from Isfahan, with atlas silk from Baghdad and turban cloths from Ubull, ... with Armenian breeches ... and with velvet from Merv. May God load me with carpets, with large carpets from Qaliqala and Maisan, with mats from Baghdad." Such was the desire of a well-to-do Muslim in the eleventh century (quoted in Lombard, 1987: 180).

The terms used for the cloths and garments made from them give an idea of the wide range of textile production. The names refer to the places where the textiles were made, or to the materials, their weave, embroidery, and much more. This information can be used to trace the place of origin of particular cloths and techniques as well as their distribution (and imitation). Talented artisans with the necessary knowledge were very much in demand and were requested to work for the courts. Their skill was often their undoing. After wars the victors very often took them by force to their courts. This explains the sudden appearance or disappearance of particular fabrics and techniques in various regions of the Islamic world. For example, Chinese silk-weavers were brought to Kufa by the Abbasids (Chéhab, 1967). After his campaign in 1401 Timur "confiscated" the Damascene silk-weavers and other artisans and took them back with him to Central Asia (Lombard, 1987).

Much care was expended on the production of the raw material and the control of the finished product. In sources from the end of the twelfth century we find instructions on the cultivation of cotton and flax, silkworm breeding, dye making, etc. Manuals for market overseers contain detailed information of procedures in the case of falsification of fabrics and dyes. Kremer noted in the mid-nineteenth century that "silk is weighed under judicial supervision" (1855:8).

Sources describing the specific contexts in which textiles were used show why textiles play such an outstanding role in Islamic culture. It is in the nature of the sources that they concentrate particularly on the courts and the urban upper class. They tell us about the fashions and practices at the courts, the requirements of the urban population, the circulation of textiles in social contexts, such as weddings or on special occasions, and the distribution of textiles as a sign of recognition or expression of benevolence from the powerful to their subordinates (Scarce, 1989; Lombard, 1987). Certain fabrics, patterns and dyes were reserved for the Muslim rulers; the court and dignitaries, particular social groups and religious minorities had their own turban cloths and were governed by precise dress regulations. Particularly in the urban milieu clothes regulations were a concrete expression of social relationships, a reflection of traditional norms and values, as well as of the fashions of the time. The issuing of such regulations was a political instrument whose power should not be underestimated. All this demonstrates the value Islamic culture attached to textiles, both materially and spiritually. But not only was the use of particular textiles integrated into a cultural pattern of life, this was also true of their production. The organization of work was determined by the old crafts. This resulted in the interdependence of the various individual craftsmen involved in the making of a textile, and thus in the emergence of close, social and work relationships, and in a necessary sense of solidarity. The economic life of the craftsmen and hence of a whole social fabric is thus dependent on the continuity of a whole cultural pattern in which the textiles have their place and which gives these objects their social and cultural character. It is only against this background that the scale of the changes which set in at the end of the nineteenth century can be gauged.

The integration of Syria into the expanding European markets in the second third of the nineteenth century, marked the beginning of far-reaching socioeconomic changes which were to have repercussions particularly on the textile industry. Syria was discovered as a new market for European industrial fabrics, and the treaties concluded after 1838 between several European states and the Ottoman Empire ensured very favourable export conditions for their goods. The European consuls had the right to observe the market situation on the spot, defend the interests of their governments and grant a number of special privileges to the local Christians in order to secure and deepen business contacts. At the same time Syria became an important supplier of silk as a raw material, especially for the French silk industry in Lyon. The region that is now Lebanon was the principal supplier for the French market, and silk was the staple commodity in the port of Beirut, whence it was shipped to Marseille. Silk once again became a political issue. In Syria the number of newly planted mulberry trees increased rapidly, and in regions which had been regarded as secondary silk-producing areas, such as the district around Safita, production was intensified. At favourable altitudes many peasants began to plant mulberry instead of their olive or fruit trees. But after 1930, when the demand for Syrian (Lebanese) silk collapsed and the silk industry in Lyon went into decline, many peasants who had switched to sericulture faced financial ruin. The reeling of the silk, in so far as it was done in Syria at all, was mechanized. Many Armenian women worked in the silk spinning workshops. Much French capital was invested in these enterprises and the machinery needed was imported from France. A number of Syrian businessmen who were in close contact with Lyon founded factories or mechanized their textile production. Some of the factories still use machines from this period. The flooding of the market with cheap British fabrics, as well as the shortage and increased price of raw materials for the traditional sector led to a drastic decline in Syrian textile production: in Damascus, between 1830 and 1850, it was reduced by almost a half, and the production of traditional articles fell by almost three quarters. Kremer (1854:21) lamented (somewhat inaccurately): "The diwans which were formerly covered with brocade, which, however, became famous under the name of damask, are now covered with English calico." In the towns people began to wear European dress.

Nevertheless, the Syrian textile industry still managed to defend as share in the market. It was able to do so by increased concentration on the local markets, by supplying them with customary fabrics, by introducing cheaper imitations of traditional cloths, by making structural changes, such as processing industrial raw materials (e.g., yarns) imported from Europe, and by establishing specialized centres of production in the cities. Aleppo, for example, switched to the production of cheaper varieties of traditional striped materials, to processing more cotton, and it remained the centre of dyeing in Syria. Damascus specialized on the making of expensive textiles such as gold brocade and silks, and concentrated on wool, some of which was used for making Bedouin cloaks. In Homs, on the other hand, the typical heavy silk cloths with patterns in gold and silver threads were still woven for the peasant and nomad clientele.

The second serious setback for the traditional textile sector in Syria was a consequence of the Second World War and, more generally, of the modern development and industrialization of Syria which came with independence.

530 The classics of Aleppine ikat: silk bath cloths.

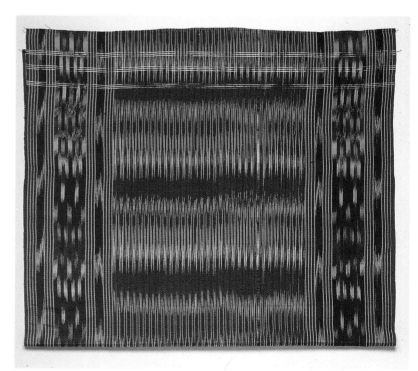

532—535 Men's and Women's coats made of ikat fabrics woven in Aleppo. The ikat pattern of the woman's coat, bottom left, is also said to have been woven at Homs until the 1950s. The detail, bottom right, shows the pattern of the coat's damask lining.

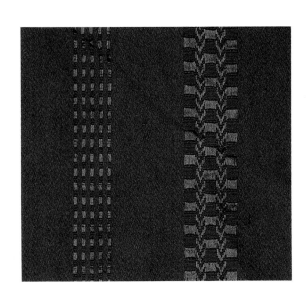

Aleppine Fabrics, Aleppine Weavers

Situated close to the cotton-growing regions of north-eastern Syria and the silk-producing areas around Antioch and the Alawite and Lebanon mountains, Aleppo was already one of the great centres of textile production during the Ottoman Empire. People spoke with justice of the "great Aleppine trade", and its *suqs*, *hans* and *qaysaries* still bear witness to this tradition.

Apart from periodic fluctuations caused by external and internal political factors, Aleppo was able to maintain its position as a centre of textile production until the beginning of the nineteenth century. Schubert (1839:295) could still write: "It is said that more than 40,000 workers are employed just in the manufacture of atlas and striped or floral silks, often worked with gold." From the middle of the nineteenth century, with the economic and political decline of the Ottoman Empire and the strengthened European presence and competition, the situation worsened. The Aleppine textile business was in a very difficult position faced with goods that were factory made and were not subject to enormous duties and taxes. The number of hand looms was drastically reduced: of 10,000 operating in 1820 only 5850 were still working in 1890.

After the collapse of the Ottoman Empire Aleppo was to some extent relegated by the new frontiers to a marginal position. Technological innovations such as mechanized looms (by 1901 there were already 50 Jacquard looms in operation in Aleppo), new raw materials such as artificial silk, and electrification in 1929, led to a reorganization of the textile sector towards new methods of production and a new range of goods orientated towards Europe. In 1939, ten of the eighteen Aleppine spinning and weaving workshops were restructured.

After the First World War, the Second World War made the economic situation worse. The textile producers found themselves cut off from their old markets and from the supply of ready-made products on which the textile sector was dependent.

After independence, the "cotton boom" of the 1950s brought a short- lived prosperity for weavers. The repercussions of the changes that had taken place before did not really begin to be felt until 1955. Up to then there were still between 4500 and 7000 hand looms in operation. The new state programmes for industrialization and especially the controlled distribution of silk to private weavers forced the old Aleppine textile production into a marginal position from 1968 onwards.

However, textile production in Aleppo remained very important, although it was now concentrated in the modern state factories. In 1972, 54 per cent of the workforce was working in this sector, nationwide the figure was 47 per cent (Cornand, 1986). The marginalization of the traditional textile sector can again be seen in the large reduction in the number of hand looms. In 1973, there were still 3,500 traditional weavers, but today only around 200 are working in the traditional way. In addition there is also an unknown number of looms operated in home industry. The attitude of modern industry towards traditional weaving is shown by the comment of an industrialist from Aleppo, who told J. Cornand in 1982 that 100 to 150 hand weavers were all that were needed to supply the demand from a stubborn clientele.

It is all the more surprising to find the diversity and fine quality of fabrics still made by hand, using very specialized processes organized in the traditional way. The fabrics, scarves and cloths woven today are a nostalgic echo of a once flourishing industry, and a visit to the weavers in their workshops is a saddening experience. Most of the weavers now are old, weaving metre after metre with incredible patience. They have usually learned their trade from their fathers, but their own sons rarely follow them because the pay is too low. When these weavers go, it will mean not only the end of a tradition but also the loss of the knowledge which, in earlier times, had ensured the fame of Syrian textiles. The closing down of the weavers' workshops is changing the character and identity of whole districts of the city, a process that has been going on in Aleppo since the end of the nineteenth century.

Most of the workshops still active today are concentrated in the northern quarter outside the city walls, i.e. outside the Old Town. The removal of workshops to this district began as early as the sixteenth century and intensified in the seventeenth, when the restricted space within the city walls in the *suqs* and *hans* was no longer sufficient for the rising demand for space for craftsmen. At that time the weavers were still working in *qaysaries*. Many of the buildings still bear the marks of the 1822 earthquake, when in many houses the second storey was damaged, but was never repaired.

The *hans* and *qaysaries* of the Mdine also house the offices and warehouses of the merchants, who are also employers and patrons. They award the commissions to the weavers in the northern district, they provide them with the necessary raw materials, they make the contracts with the suppliers and specialists. This is where the daily production is delivered, where the agents and middlemen come and go, where the textiles intended for export are packed and dispatched, and from where the shops in the *suq* are supplied. There is a close relationship between the patrons and their workers. The patron is still the first person a worker turns to with his problems, including his personal ones, but the patron is also the one who pays what are sometimes miserable wages. Many of the weavers are paid by the piece.

The merchant-employers and patrons have at their disposal the capital and the networks needed for selling the products; the craftsmen have no access to these. The dependence of the patrons on their craftsmen is due to the specialized technological knowledge of the craftsmen. Since patrons, as a rule, are quite ignorant in this respect, it constitutes, as it were, the craftsmen's capital. Often this knowledge concerns only individual work processes which are parts of the total production process of a textile; there exists a certain hierarchy among the various specialists.

Special markets, special goods

The textiles that the Aleppine weavers are still making today are by their own admission only a faint reflection of the range they once produced. Often they point with a gesture of resignation at the dusty cards for their Jacquard looms, which are no longer used, either because there is no longer a demand, or because production is too expensive, or simply because the silk needed for them is no longer available.

Probably one needs to have known the old times to comprehend this, for the supply of hand-woven textiles is still very high. Generally, lengths of cloth are woven. One length (*saye*) is sufficient for making an upper garment or a coat (*kumbas*). The word *saye* has become a general term and synonym for the clothes made from the cloth. Men's and women's clothes are made from the same material, but they differ in cut. The long coat for men has been shortened under the influence of European fashion to jacket-length. Men's garment, waistcoat and coat are often made of the same cloth. The men's costume is completed by a fez. Today these traditional garments are mostly worn by old men. The cloth is usually striped lengthwise and is most often atlas weave or ribbed weave. The Turkish word for the much sought-after atlas silk on cotton fabric is *alaja*, in Arabic it is called *qutni*. Its imitation in cotton is called *dima*. The lengthwise stripes vary in their sequence of colours and in pattern woven into them. The warp threads are mounted corresponding to the colours of the stripes, and the punched cards for the desired patterns are installed. Formerly the warp threads were silk, but today in many instances they are replaced by viscose. The weft is cotton and is hidden by the satin weave so that it can only be seen on the reverse. The names of the fabrics refer either to the number of coloured lengthwise stripes (e.g. "Seven Kings" for seven stripes of different colours before the first colour is repeated) or to the patterns woven into these ("Water-wheels", "Chain", etc.). The textile dealers and producers have developed their own complex specialized vocabulary. Often a single word contains technical data as well as information about the material, colours and pattern of a fabric. These textiles are woven on Jacquard looms, or "French looms", unlike other cloths which are woven on "Arab looms", of which there are various sorts. The great demand for these traditional fabrics means that there was, and still is, a close relationship between the craftsmen and their clientele, since whatever is made from them is used in a cultural context and is governed by a firmly rooted preference for certain forms and colours. In 1844, a French observer noted that the stable "Arab" market ensured the existence of Aleppine textile production.

In 1850, the French consul complained that, despite their "superiority", French silk textiles had no prospects of sales in Aleppo because the population preferred the striped cotton and silk fabrics, or silk fabrics worked with gold thread, which were made all over Syria and from which the citizens of Aleppo made large profits. Much is still produced for export. Certain striped textiles are very popular with Palestinians, many fabrics and silk-embroidered cloths are much in demand in the Gulf States, striped rib-woven fabrics are exported to Yemen, and Sudan imports checked cloths of a particular type edged with patterned stripes. The purchasers, who use these striped fabrics for traditional clothing, come from the countryside or are nomads. The customer can buy or order the fabric at the shops in the *suq*. When ordering he can specify the material, type of weave and pattern. Wholesalers have a sort of pattern book consisting simply of a large collection of pieces of cloth from which the customer can choose the one he wants. In towns in Syria, and in the Gulf States, the lengths of cloth are used as upholstery material. The customers for this include the top hotels trying to create a traditional ambience. They are also bought by tourists.

Lengths of ikat fabric for making clothes are not often woven any more. They are made to match the striped fabrics in their appearance. The ikat pattern is carried on the warp threads. The pattern known as "Birds' Tongues" is very ancient, and also popular is a motif reminiscent of a spearhead. The art of the ikat master consists of binding the warp threads in the correct sequence for producing the patterns, and of supervising the dyeing and mounting warp threads on the loom. He does not use a model for his work, but knows exactly how many threads must be bound at which intervals, and the sequence in which they must be dyed. He can reproduce this without making a mistake. The resulting polychrome textiles are very beautiful with sequences of colours running into each other. A classic among ikat cloths is the bath cloth (*mezar hammam*) and cloth for wrapping the bathing utensils (*baqje*). Formerly these cloths were often lavishly embroidered or brocaded with silk, gold and silver threads. The bathing equipment of the bride for her obligatory visit to the bath before her wedding consisted of particularly beautiful towels and bath cloths. The finest bath cloths were prestige objects made of silk, and the patterns were in accordance with an established canon. But because of the changed living habits of the upper class the production of silk ikat bath cloths has ceased, and the old examples have become collectors' pieces. The bath cloths made today are bought by the less wealthy classes, by people from the more traditional districts of the city and from rural environs, for whom the visit to the baths is still an established part of their life, not only as a pleasant necessity but also as a social occasion. The bath cloths are still ikat-woven but the material is artificial silk or viscose, the patterns are still the traditional ones, but they are much coarser and are woven with much use of lurex thread. In Aleppo they can be bought in the *suq* (in

536 Dyer's workshop in a courtyard of a Qaysarie in Aleppo.

537 & 538 Aleppine weavers.

the soap *suq* and elsewhere). A *mezar* measures 2.10 x 0.99 metres and requires 3000 warp threads made of artificial silk, or 6000 of real silk. The centre panel and the borders have different patterns. The central motif may be one or more rhombuses, or the middle and borders may be distinguished from each other by ikat stripes of different widths. The centre panel may also be left blank. Typical of old bath cloths is the use of cypress motifs on the two borders. This motif is derived from Persian influence, and is found on cloths like those produced at Kashan or Yazd. The full name of the bath cloths is "Persian cloths" (*mezar ajami*, *futa ajamiye*). Some of the traditional patterns have very ancient forerunners. They are known from the cotton ikat fabrics which were made in the tenth century in the *tiraz* workshops in Yemen, which also have parallels with the textiles depicted in Indian wall paintings of the sixth and seventh centuries. In the eleventh century bath cloths of this type were produced in Persia (at Rayy), presumably after Yemeni craftsmen had settled there. The appearance of the cypress motif on the bath cloths can also be traced back to this period.

Another speciality of Aleppine textile production are cloths used by men and women as head coverings. This market too survives because of conservative urban and rural clientele, who maintain the old cultural norms and the traditional way of dress. The merchants and weavers know the requirements of their customers and seek to satisfy them. The head covering is a very important component of traditional dress, since it carries information about various aspects of the person wearing it, such as his or her particular ethnic-religious group, locality or region, and social status. The head cloths vary in pattern and colouring from village to village, from group to group -those of the women often more so than those of the men. Married women prefer different colours to young girls or old women. Each cloth is usually made in a variety of qualities, depending on the price. For the men in some districts of Aleppo natural white cloths are woven, one sort in patterned silk (*semniyye*) and another in cotton (*mendil mbakkara*). The cloths called *baghdadiye* are cotton and silk fabrics decorated with silk embroidery. Most of them are exported.

Kerchiefs made of dark silk (dark red or brown) with one central motif (e.g. fish or banners) in the first third (which also serves as a trademark) are sought after in Deir ez-Zor, Abu Kemal, in Kuwait and Iraq. The general term *dirhemiye* includes all cloths which are bought by weight (1 dirham = 3202 grams in Aleppo). (As a rule silk is bought by weight.) Depending on their method of manufacture they are called *kasrawaniyye* or *homsiyye*. The cloths are square and vary in size from 1.10 to 2.40 metres. They are woven from heavy silk and their distinguishing feature consists of patterns woven in silver or gold threads. The cloths end in long knotted fringes. Most of the silk circulating in the private market, especially Syrian silk, is used for making these kerchiefs. The individual types are differentiated by their background colours and the woven

539 & 540 Weaver in Aleppo weaving a striped silk atlas with the pattern known as "waterwheels". Such a fabric was used to make the woman's coat on the left.

541–543 Display window of a textile dealer in the *suq* of Aleppo showing a selection of classic stripped silk atlases. The jacket and pants are made in a cotton imitation of striped atlas silk.

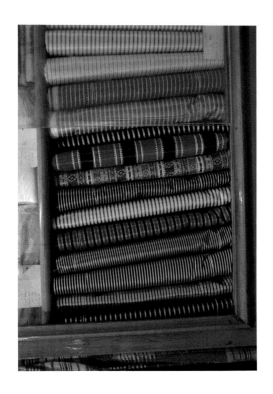

544 Sheikh Munther and his bride, Lebanon 1895. His half- European, half-traditional costume is typical of the period of change at the end of the nineteenth century, when the bourgeoisie (especially the Christian bourgeoisie) began to dress "à la Franka". The well-to-do lady of the city now turned to Paris for her fashions.

patterns. Each type has a name. For example, the Kurds (in Turkey, too) prefer the lilac and green colours and the cloths of the *stanbuli* type, the peasants of the villages north of Damascus prefer the *homsiyye* and the women from Palmyra, Raqqa and Resafe wear the *mghammaa*. These cloths mostly have dark background colours, often black or various shades of red. As far as we know, white cloths of this type are no longer made, and the old specimens that still exist are rare. The most expensive cloths are the heavy silk cloths with woven patterns made of silver or gold threads. The specimens made of cotton or artificial silk with lurex thread are cheaper. Another factor governing the price is the size and type and number of the patterns, since these determine the amount of silver thread used. The technical skill required is the same whether the weaver weaves the complicated patterns with silver or lurex. The weaving technique for the pattern is called *ghall*, meaning lancé work and brocading. Only certain weavers master this complicated and expensive technique. The weaver works without a model, since he knows the pattern by heart. In the making of lengths of cloth the work of the *muzayyik* and the *mulqi* (that is, the dividing, checking and stretching of the warp threads and the threading of them through the leashes) are of crucial importance – but in this case the final result depends entirely on the skill of the weaver himself. This explains the hierarchy between the individual weavers. Many of these cloths are signed, either with a cartouche (e.g. the "Two Lions" mark) or with the name of the master. In the case of other cloths we know from the pattern who wove them. While it is true that cloths of this sort are made in Aleppo, the real centre of their production is – as the name suggests – Homs.

Another component of traditional clothing is the sash, preferably made of silk (*mahzam harir*). The average size is 0.80 x 2 metres. Three or four strips are sewn together with a decorative seam to make the required width. The sashes end in knotted fringes. They are made individually and sold by weight. The cheaper pieces are made of cotton or artificial silk. A widespread type (extending beyond Syria) is the "Tripoli" sash, so called because it was originally made in Tripoli. It consists of three strips of differently striped silk fabric in green and orange, or red, black and

222

545 A bride in Damascus, 1870.

546 A Syrian lady, 1880.

white. Running across the longitudinal stripes are weaker transverse stripes, thus creating a checked effect. The range of variations reflects the differing preferences of the customers.

The sashes woven in Kashmir wool which once formed part of the traditional men's dress of the urban upper class are no longer made. Even in the past the best and most highly prized pieces were imports from Persia and Kashmir, which were preferred to the locally produced articles.

The term *kamar ajami*, *shawl ajami* ("Persian girdle", "Persian scarf") indicate this. *Kashmir* used to be the name given to the sashes with a paisley pattern, but today it is generally used term for belts of this type. The care taken in choosing the sequence of colours and the number of stripes, the harmony of the intended effect, the fineness of the stripes in the woven pattern – these are all criteria used in assessing and valuing the cloths, which are priced accordingly. These sashes were always prestige objects of a wealthy and respected social class. Though they are no longer worn today, they are still kept in families as a status symbol and passed down from father to son. People also make efforts to acquire them; in the Gulf States they have become much sought-after collectors' pieces. Because of the spread of the European belt the production of traditional girdles for men has been much more sharply reduced than of girdles for women. A number of types of lavishly woven and decorated men's belts, which were regulation dress for Ottoman officials or military, have not been made since the collapse of the Ottoman Empire. They include the belts worn exclusively by the Circassian Guard, who stood guard outside the European embassies.

Worn with the fez (*tarbush*), which first became wide-spread in Syria because of the Ottoman dress regulations, is a cloth (*aghabani*) which is wrapped round the lower third or lower half of it. This cloth had a dual purpose: it was a decorative and prestige cloth like the turban, but also a means of stating the social position of the person wearing it. The Ottoman government laid down various colours for the different religious groups, and religious dignitaries still distinguish themselves in this way today. But nowadays the fez is seldom seen.

223

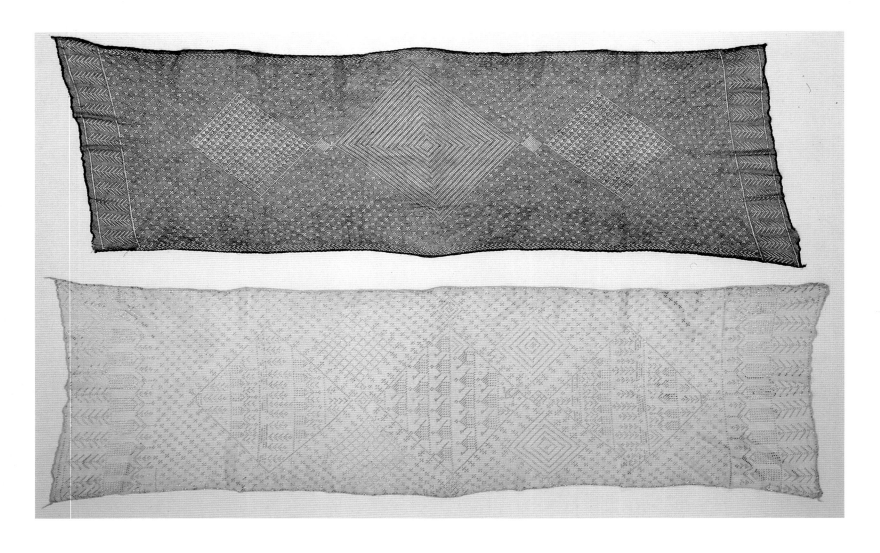

547—549 Tulle veils decorated with beaten silver tinsel yarn. Originally these cloths were produced at Baalbek.

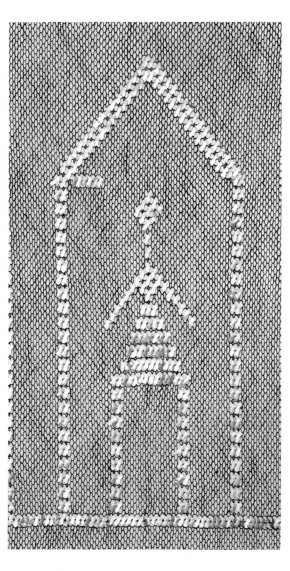

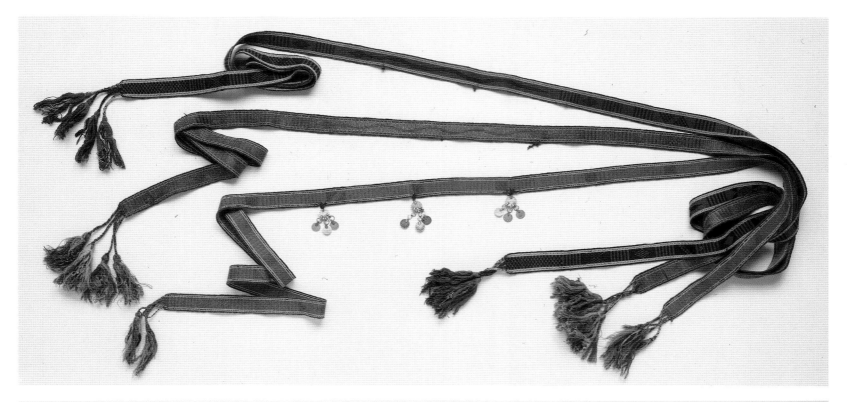

550 Tablet-woven women's belts with the snake motif, presumably made in Damascus.

551 & 552 Sashes for men: imported from Kashmir (bottom right), second half of the nineteenth century; and an imitation of Kashmiri work, made in Aleppo, early twentieth century. Such cloths are no longer produced.

553 Bottom left: belt in fine tablet weaving, which also serves as a purse for money. These too are no longer produced.

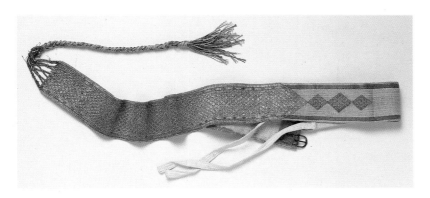

554—557 Lancé and brocaded silk bath cloths, Aleppo.
The head cloth is decorated with a fish
in damask weave and inscribed with the name Aziza.

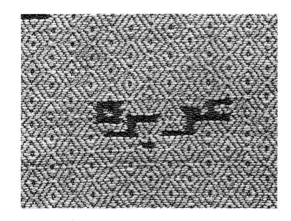

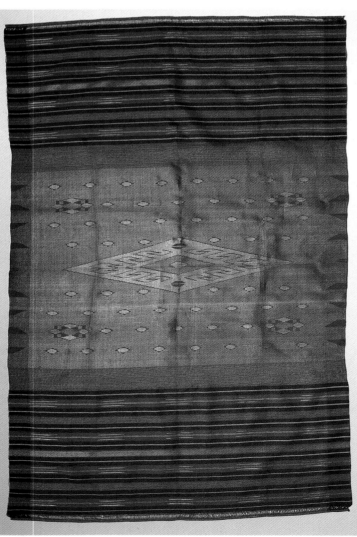

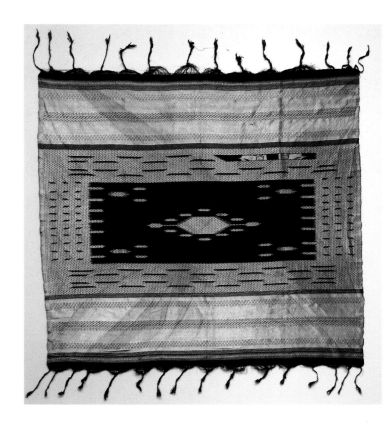

558—563 Heavy silk scarves (of the Kasrawaniye/Homsiyye type) lancé and brocaded with silver and gold threads. The cloths come from Aleppo and are signed with the mark of the master and his workshop (two lions and the name of the weaver).

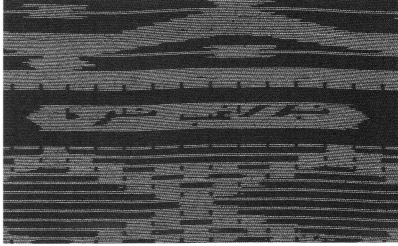

564–567 Silk scarves from Homs, lancé and brocaded with silver. The one above was woven by Mounir Raghib Mushalwat. The old master is no longer alive, but his sons still have a shop in the *suq*, where they sell scarves like these. They are produced by a number of weavers.

Textiles from Homs

Homs has a tradition of textile production that reaches back to antiquity. Today it is best known for its kerchiefs woven from heavy silk with lancé and brocaded decoration in gold and silver threads. These are called *kasrawaniyye* or (after the city) *homsiyye* and their background colour is usually black or more rarely red. The brocaded kerchiefs are also known as *musawwara* ("picture cloths"), an allusion to the optical impression created by their patterns. The silver and gold threads are also made in Homs, at a factory founded at the beginning of the century and equipped with French machines from Lyon, though it has long since ceased working to its full capacity. Many weaving workshops are in the residential areas, on the ground floor of houses and most of the weavers in Homs are Christians.

568 & 569 Factory in Homs making silver and gold thread. The portrait shows the present owner's grandfather, who founded the firm. According to the old card index of customers, before the Second World War it was supplying not only weavers in Homs, but also clients in Damascus, France, Italy and India.

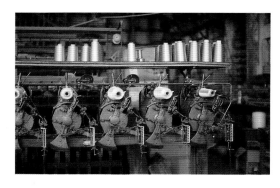

570 & 571 Weavers in Homs, weaving (above) and brocading (below) a scarf.

572 Scarf from Homs, woven by Habib Huri. He stopped working a long time ago. According the seller, cloths of this type are worn, for example, at Mhardah and in the villages east of Homs.

The kerchiefs are produced exclusively for the peasants from the surrounding villages and the nomads. Many of them still wear them as traditional head coverings, and Homs serves them as a busy little market town. The colouring and patterns are to suit the preferences of the various villages or the nomads who do their shopping in Homs. The kerchiefs are mainly used by women, but for family occasions or village festivals they are also worn by men. The livelihood of the weavers is ensured by this clientele keeping to its customary dress, and the people are apparently willing and able to pay for the superior quality of the goods. The fact that the weavers are able to meet the demand and that the traditional production of these textiles can continue in Homs, is also connected with the fact that the weavers are better supplied with silk. Homs is situated near the region where many peasants still breed silkworms (between Safita and Ain al-Wadi). In this region sericulture was introduced and promoted in the first years of the French Mandate in connection with the development of silk in the region which was then the Alawite state. In 1927 two million mulberry trees were planted around Tartus, Safita, Masyaf and Banyas. The quantity of silk produced in the region remained marginal, however, when measured against the demand of the French textile industry, and it was used mainly to supply the Syrian market. The region was therefore less badly affected by the decline of Lyon and the movements in the world market after 1930. For the Alawite peasants silkworm cultivation was a viable source of income and still is. Their customers are still the agents from Homs, who are based in the old silk *han*. The weaving of silk kerchiefs in Homs also binds the city to the countryside, to the peasants who provide the silk, and to the peasants and nomads, who have continued with tenacity to use these beautiful textiles and so ensure their continued production and the livelihood of the craftsmen.

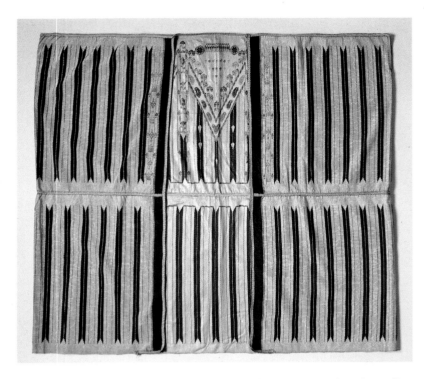

573 *Abaye*, gold brocade with silk, 1937 (Museum für Völkerkunde, Berlin).

Damascene brocade, Damascene damask

Silk damask and gold brocade were and are the most costly of the traditional textiles produced in Damascus. After the collapse of the textile market in the mid-nineteenth century, Damascus deliberately concentrated on the production of these luxury fabrics for a well-heeled local and European clientele. But despite many efforts and the introduction of Jacquard looms, the production of the beautiful fabrics with their delicate and complicated patterns has now almost vanished. Of the old looms only a handful are still in operation, most now lie unused as sad piles of timber. There was nostalgia in the eyes and voice of the merchants and the old weaver of Nassan & Co. in Damascus when they showed us their brocades and explained the patterns with their romantic names: one pattern that is still sought-after is called "Queen Elizabeth" or "Lovebirds". According to the stories, Queen Elizabeth of England was asked at the time of her coronation what she wanted as a present from Syria. Her reply was silk brocade. When she was asked about the pattern, she is supposed to have drawn the "Lovebirds", which were then woven by the weavers. Also impressive are patterns such as the "Rose of Damascus", "Narcissi", in the silk damasks fine paisley patterns, the "Fighting Crusaders" and "Paradise Lost" – the latter only exist as pattern samples kept with their punched cards in the hope that they may one day be ordered again by a customer. Nassan & Co. is a family business. During the Ottoman Empire and at the beginning of the century it was still a large factory and untaxed, with such a big turnover that the owners could afford the money necessary to spare their staff military service. Until around 1958 two workers operated each of the twenty or so looms, weaving the brocades in three, five or seven colours with the corresponding patterns. Today only two looms are left. In the past the making of brocade and damask was almost exclusively the preserve of Christians, but gradually an increasing number of Kurdish weavers have been moving into this field. The cards for the few Jacquard looms still in operation continue to be made by Armenians. Until the 1960s tourists were still frequent customers, but now production is mostly for the local market, since damasks and brocades have become very popular as upholstery materials, and are hardly used at all for clothing. The goods for sale are accordingly sorted, above all by colours and patterns, and new ones to suit the wishes of the customers are designed to order. The new patterns are not, however, woven on the old looms operated by hand, but on the electric looms. Nevertheless brocade is still a very costly textile and, like Syria's other traditional fabrics, it is coming under increasing pressure from the cheaper textiles made of artificial fibres. Among these other textiles no longer produced in Damascus is Damascene ikat. The introduction of artificial silk around 1930 caused the first setback for ikat cloth, then in 1947 the war in Palestine meant the loss of the traditional market for the material, since Damascene ikat had been bought mainly by Palestinians.

It is probably too late to increase the production of brocade and damask – and this is true also of other traditional crafts. The old weavers are no longer working and there is no new generation to follow them. So these precious fabrics seem destined for a marginal existence, appreciated by only a few and by foreigners. Some of the merchants are less sentimental. Some people die at the right time, said one of them, perhaps the weaver will die when nobody wants his textiles any more. Of course this is very sad, for the silk will die with him.

The old weaver, bent over his loom with tired eyes, concentrating hard, paused in his work to show us with a smile the damask he was weaving. Presumably he never possessed a piece of this cloth himself. The fine silk damask with its shimmering colours was exquisitely beautiful. We were allowed to take a pattern strip with us – we chose "Paradise Lost" in blue.

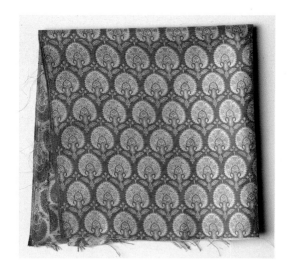

575 Punched pattern cards for Jacquard looms.

574 A weaver in Damascus.

576–579 Fragments of damasks from Damascus with paisley patterns and floral motifs – bottom right: "Paradise Lost".

A Mosaic of Syrian Ornament

Johannes Kalter and Antoine Touma

In the pre-Christian period Syria was for centuries exposed to strong Mesopotamian influence. The conquests of Alexander the Great linked it to the Hellenistic world. Syria was a Roman province, then came under Iranian influence in the middle of the third century AD, and was reconquered by Byzantium as part of the Eastern Roman Empire. From 661 to 750 it was the centre of a great Arab empire extending from the Atlantic Ocean to the Indus. All the conquerors and rulers of Syria have left buildings behind them, and the decoration of these has influenced the ornaments used in folk art. Syria was linked by the Silk Road with China, Central Asia, India and Iran. Goods, forms and ideas were carried along the road and became common property. The Turco-Mongolian conqueror Timur abducted the craftsmen of Aleppo and Damascus in the early fifteenth century and took them to Central Asia. In his wake Turcoman and Uzbek groups came to Syria and they still live there as ethnic minorities. They brought their own set of forms with them and retained it. In the later period of the Ottoman Empire the Ottoman provinces of Syria received an influx of people from the European parts of the Empire, such as Albania, Bulgaria and Greece, as well as from the mountainous region of the Caucasus.

It is therefore not surprising that the ornament of Syrian folk art contains echoes and remnants of all the cultures mentioned. The title of this chapter is not simply a play on words but is intended to encourage the reader to look through the whole book again and consider the ornaments illustrated from the point of view of the influences suggested here. With this background knowledge the reader will be able to categorize much of the material immediately, but in other instances the process of fusion and overlap make it extremely difficult to ascribe the ornament to particular cultural regions.

The strict geometric patterning of much woodwork, engraved metal decoration of trays, and the structure of kelim patterns is a legacy of late antiquity and latterly of Byzantium. Thus far Syrian ornament stands in the general Islamic tradition: it took classical models and developed them to create, for example, a star-interlace decoration of such perfection that this motif became next to the arabesque probably the most common and characteristic in Islamic art.

The vase with life-giving water and the tree of life are doubtless motifs which Syrian art inherited directly from Byzantium. In Islamic art we find it for the first time in

580–583 Examples of classical and Islamic ornaments. Top left: vine rinceau and stylized tree of life, Roman relief from southern Syria, second/third centuries; top right: detail of a Roman mosaic, Bosra; below: geometric interlace patterns from the Great Mosque in Aleppo, Mamluk period, thirteenth century.

584 View of a gateway arch with floral decoration strongly influenced by Iranian art, Palmyra, second century AD.

585 & 586 Details of the façades of the so-called treasury and the courtyard of the Umayyad mosque in Damascus. The heavily restored mosaics date back to the building of the mosque in the eighth century. They include vase motifs, palms and cypresses – motifs which have survived in Syrian folk art up to the present day.

587 Detail of a panel of tiles with strongly geometrical cruciform blossoms, Damascus, sixteenth/seventeenth centuries.

588 Detail of a group of tiles. Vase motifs with tulips, hyacinths and blossoming branches; the border at the top is in the form of battlements. Made in Damascus in the seventeenth century and strongly influenced by the Ottoman court tile works at Iznik.

591 Cosmetic flasks in the form of cypresses. The application stick of the flask on the left is surmounted by a bird (perhaps the sun-bird), chased silver. Damascus, nineteenth century.

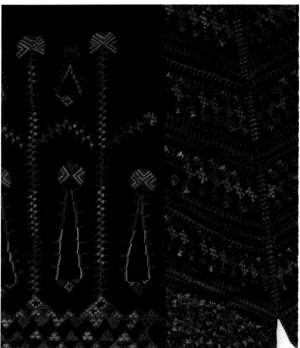

589 Above: opus sectile on a fountain in the Azem Palace, trees of life in the form of highly stylized cypresses. Damascus, seventeenth century.

590 Detail of embroidery from the oasis of es-Suchne with cypresses surmounted by a disc (perhaps the sun), early twentieth century.

592 The front of a peasant chest. The middle panel has cypresses under arcading, while the outer panels have interlace enclosing stars decorated with intarsia. Cedarwood with mother-of-pearl inlay. Damascus, nineteenth century.

Seljuk carpet fragments, as well as in Ghasnavid and Seljuk metalwork. In Syria it is found, influenced by Iznik tiles, in the tile patterns of Damascus, and in many embroideries of urban and peasant origin. The starting point for this development may have been the mosaic decoration of the Umayyad mosque in Damascus, where the abundance of representations of trees and vase motifs would have provided a wealth of visual material and stimuli.

The tree of life, a symbol plenty, wealth and fertility, has the same historical background as the vase motif. Representations of trees of life can be traced back as far as the ancient Near Eastern cultures. But the Turcoman and Uzbek intruders from Central Asia must have brought with them the northern Asian idea of the tree of life as the axis of the world linking the underworld, the world in which we live and the sky. These two ideas have apparently overlapped in Syrian folk art. The striking frequency of cypresses as a tree motif may originally have been of Syrian origin. Cypresses are among the most distinctive trees of the Mediterranean-influenced agricultural regions of Syria. The association of cypresses with representations of round discs above them, as for example in embroideries from es-Suchne, suggests a Zoroastrian influence from Iran. This would not be surprising since the city of Yazd, the most important centre of the Iranian Zoroastrians up to the modern period, was a major trading centre on the Silk Road. The combination of cypresses and birds (probably the sun bird), another motif that is often seen, also suggests Zoroastrian influence. In my view, the representations of mountains with trees are certainly of north Asian origin.

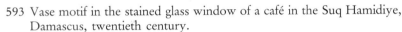

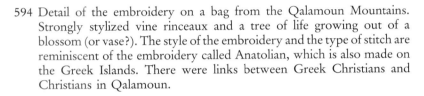

593 Vase motif in the stained glass window of a café in the Suq Hamidiye, Damascus, twentieth century.

594 Detail of the embroidery on a bag from the Qalamoun Mountains. Strongly stylized vine rinceaux and a tree of life growing out of a blossom (or vase?). The style of the embroidery and the type of stitch are reminiscent of the embroidery called Anatolian, which is also made on the Greek Islands. There were links between Greek Christians and Christians in Qalamoun.

595 Tree of life on the door of a house in Hama, modern wrought iron work.

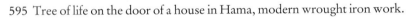

596 Detail of a raw silk dress with silver appliqué work made in Hama using *plangi* technique, for bedouin women. Birds on the tree of life, twentieth century.

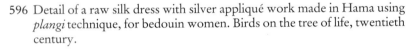

597 Lower hem of a woman's coat, embroidery with metal threads on velvet. Trees of life on mountains. Qalamoun mountains, twentieth century.

598 Strongly stylized tree of life in a style common in Central Asia (e.g. among the Turcomans), on the back of a woman's dress. Chan Shei-chun, twentieth century.

235

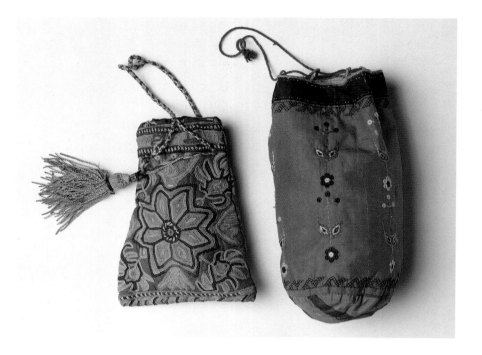

599 Top left: bag from northern Syria. The borders, the emphasis given to the centre and the trees of life growing out of the corners are reminiscent of the embroideries of the Yomut Turcomans, twentieth century.

600 The best bags were acquired in 1891 from a Syrian Christian. The style corresponds exactly to old Turcoman embroideries (Museum für Völkerkunde, Berlin).

601 & 602 Sleeve band and lower end of the sleeve of women's dresses from the Hauran. The motif could be read as ram's horns on a mountain and appears in comparable form on Uzbek embroideries. Southern Syria, twentieth century.

603 Appliqué work from the facing of a Druze coat. The technique and the motif of the ram's horns can be compared directly with Uzbek textiles from Central Asia.

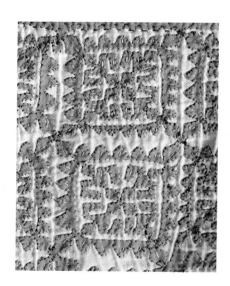

604 Coat with *boteh* motifs, printed cotton, Aleppo, twentieth century.

605 Peasant chest, cedarwood. The interlace band on the front is found in Ghasnavid and Seljuk metalwork of the twelfth century. Damascus (?), nineteenth century.

606 Detail of a coffee tray. The motif of the gazelle hunt is in the style of prehistoric rock paintings. Southern Syria, twentieth century.

607 Gold printing on a woman's coat from Aleppo. Peony branches in the Chinese style. Twentieth century.

608 Carved wooden architectural fragment, severe kufic with forked-leaf rinceaux; on the right, a vase with a tree of life. Damascus, twelfth century.

609 Detail from a woman's dress embroidered with the name of Allah, Hauran, twentieth century.

They probably represent a combination of the ideas of world tree and world mountain. In the textile art of northern Syria especially, a number of motifs, such as mountains surmounted by rams' horns or the "double *kochak*" motif, are undoubtedly of Turcoman origin. *Botehs* (almond leaf patterns) are found on printed fabrics. They may have come to Syria as an ornament with the highly prized Kashmiri shawls. Peony branches printed in gold, also on a coat, appears unmistakeably of Chinese provenance. Calligraphy, usually an important element in Islamic surface decoration, has almost no place in Syrian folk art.

An incised drawing on a coffee tray shows how the bedouin milieu retained ideas and motifs which go back far into prehistory. The motif of a hunter chasing an antelope recalls prehistoric rock paintings in its manner of representation.

To sum up, it can be stated that Syrian folk art does not really have Syrian ornamentation, but rather that the richness and variety of its ornaments are a mirror of Syria's changeful history.

610 Bonnet and headband of an Armenian woman, Aleppo *c.* 1890. Petit-point embroidery. Geometric motifs and stylized trees of life in the Central Asian style. Crosses are embroidered on the headband. (Museum für Völkerkunde, Berlin).

Bibliography

Baldensperger, P. 1895: The Immovable East, London

Bonn, Foreign Ministry 1988: Länderaufzeichnung über die Arabische Republik Syrien. Stand 15.03.1988, Bonn

Bouchemann, A. de 1934: "La sédentarisation des nomades du désert de Syrie", in L'Asie Française, No. 320, Paris

Bouchemann, A. de 1935: Matériel de la vie bédouine. Recueilli dans le désert de Syrie (tribus des Arabes Sba'a), Documents d'Études Orientales No. 3, Institut Français de Damas, Paris

Bouchemann, A. de 1937: Une petite cité caravanière: Suhné, Documents d'Études Orientales, No. 6, Institut Français de Damas, Paris

Bouron, N. 1930: Les Druzes. Histoire du Liban et de la Montagne Haouranaise, Paris

Browne, W.G. 1800: Reisen in Afrika, Aegypten und Syrien in den Jahren 1792 bis 1789 (German translation from the English), Leipzig/Gera

Burckhardt, J.L. 1822: Travels in Syria and the Holy Land, London

Bühler, A. 1943: "Materialen zur Kenntnis der Ikattechnik", Internationales Archiv für Ethnographie, supplement to vol. XLIII, Leiden

Chevallier, D. 1982: Villes et travail en Syrie du XIXe au XXe siècle, Paris

Clauss, L.F. 1933: Als Beduine unter Beduinen, Freiburg i. Br.

Collison et al. (eds.) and Seccombe, I.J. (compiler) 1987: Syria, World Bibliographical Series, Oxford/Santa Barbara/Denver

Cornand, J. 1986: "L'Artisanat du textile à Alep. Survie ou dynamisme?", in Bulletin d'Études Orientales de l'Institut Français de Damas 36, Paris

Dalman, G. 1937: Arbeit und Sitte in Palästina, vol. V, Gütersloh

Dyson-Hudson, R. and Dyson-Hudson, N. 1980: "Nomadic Pastoralism", in Annual Review of Anthropology 9, Cambridge

Euting, J. 1896-1914: Tagebuch einer Reise in Inner-Arabien, Leiden

Firro, K. 1990: "Silk and Agrarian Changes in Lebanon 1860-1914", in International Journal of Middle East Studies 22

Frank, H. 1989: Syrien, Schauplatz der Geschichte, Bonn

Gaube, H. and Wirth, E. 1984: Aleppo, Wiesbaden

Goodrich-Freer, A. 1924: Arabs in Tent and Town: An Intimate Account of the Family Life of the Arabs of Syria with a Description of the Animals and Plants of their Country, London

Graham-Brown, S. 1988: Images of Women, London

Grant, C.P. 1937: The Syrian Desert: Caravans, Travel and Exploration, London

Leach, E. 1976: Culture and Communication: the Logic by which Symbols are Connected, Cambridge

Hopwood, D. 1988: Syria 1945-1986. Politics and Society, London

Ismail, K. 1975: Die sozialökonomischen Verhältnisse der bäuerlichen Bevölkerung im Küstengebirge der Syrischen Arabischen Republik, Berlin

Issawi, C. (ed.) 1966: The Economic History of the Middle East 1800-1914, Chicago

Joumblat, F., Seeden, H. and Atallah, M. (eds.) 1989: Past and Present, (exhibition catalogue) Rashid Karameh Museum, Beiteddin

Korsching, F. 1980: Beduinen im Negev (exhibition of Sonia Gidal Collection), Mainz

Land des Baal. Syrien – Forum der Völker und Kulturen 1982 (exhibition catalogue), Mainz

Langenegger, F. 1911: Durch verlorne Lande: Von Bagdad nach Damaskus, Berlin

Lewis, N.L. 1987: Nomads and Settlers in Syria and Jordan 1800-1980, Cambridge/New York

Lombard, M. 1978: Les textiles dans le monde musulman du VIIe-XIIe siècle, Paris

Masters, B. 1990: "The 1850 Events in Aleppo: An Aftershock of Syria's Incorporation into the Capitalist World System", in International Journal of Middle East Studies 22, Cambridge

Mershen, B. 1982: Untersuchungen zum Schriftamulett und seinem Gebrauch in Jordanien, Mainz

Moser, R. 1974: "Die Ikattechnik in Aleppo", in Baseler Beiträge zur Ethnologie 15, Basle

Musil, A. 1927: Arabia Deserta, American Geographical Society. Oriental Explorations and Studies No. 2, New York

Musil, A. 1928: The Manners and Customs of the Rwala Bedouins, American Geographical Society. Oriental Explorations and Studies No. 6, New York

Onne, E. 1980: Photographic Heritage of the Holy Land 1839-1914, Manchester

Oppenheim, M. von 1939: Die Beduinen vol. I: Die Beduinenstämme in Mesopotamien und Syrien, Leipzig

Owen, R., The Middle East in the World Economy 1900-1914, London

Raswan, C.R. 1934: Im Land der schwarzen Zelte, Berlin

Schienerl, P.W. 1984: Teildarstellungen im Islam, Göttingen

Schneider, J. 1963: Vorbereitungsmaschinen für die Weberei: Ein Handbuch für Spinner, Weber und Wirker, Berlin

Schubert, G.H. von 1839: Reise in das Morgenland in den Jahren 1836 und 1837, vol. III, Erlangen

Seale, P. 1965: The Struggle for Syria. A Study of Post-War Arab Politics 1945-58, London

Naval Intelligence Service of H.M.G., April 1943: Syria, Geographical Handbook Series, (no place)

Van de Velde, C.M.W. 1854: Narrative of a Journey through Syria and Palestine in 1851 and 1852, 2 vols., London

Völger, G., Welck, K. von, and Hackstein, K. (eds.) 1987: Pracht und Geheimnis. Kleidung und Schmuck aus Palästina und Jordanien (catalogue of the Widad Kawar Collection for an exhibition at the Rautenstrauch-Joest Museum in Cologne, in collaboration with the Institute of Archaeology and Anthropology of Yarmuk University Irbid) (= Ethnologica NS, vol. 13), Cologne

Volney, C.F. 1787 (reprinted 1959): Voyage en Égypte et en Syrie pendant les années 1783 1784 et 1785, Paris

Weir, S. 1976: The Bedouin, Westerham

Weulersse, J. 1940: Le pays des Alaouites, vol. I, Tours

Weulersse, J. 1946: Paysans de Syrie et du Proche-Orient, Paris

Winkelhane, G. 1987: "Textilgewerbe und Karawanenhandel Syriens im 19. und 20. Jahrhundert", in Völger, v. Welck and Hackstein (eds.), Pracht und Geheimnis, Cologne

Winkelhane, G. 1987: "Traditionelle Kleidung und europäische Durchdringung - Damaskus in spätosmanischer Zeit", in Völger/v. Welck/Hackstein (eds.), Pracht und Geheimnis, Cologne

Winkelhane, G. 1988: "Artisanat du textile et commerce caravanier en Syrie", in Institut du Monde Arabe 1988

Wirth, E. 1969: "Der Nomadismus in der modernen Welt des Orients – Wege und Möglichkeiten einer wirtschaftlicen Integration", in Nomadismus als Entwicklungsproblem, Bielefeld

Wirth, E. 1971: Syrien: eine geographische Landeskunde, Wissenschaftliche Länderkunden 4/5, Darmstadt

Wöhrlin, T. 1990: Gestaltendes Bauhandwerk im Orient (photographic exhibition) November-December 1990, Freiburg i. Br.

Bibliography to the Essay by P. Pawelka

van Dam, N. 1981: The Struggle for Power in Syria (1961-1980), London

Hinnebusch, R.A. 1989: Peasant and Bureaucracy in Ba'athist Syria. The Political Economy of Rural Development, Boulder/San Francisco/London

Hourani, A.H. 1954: Syria and Lebanon, Oxford

Islamoglu-Inan, H. (ed.) 1987: The Ottoman Empire and the World-Economy, Cambridge/Paris

Keyder, C. 1987: State and Class in Turkey. A Study in Capitalist Development, London/New York

Longrigg, S.H. 1958: Syria and Lebanon Under French Mandate, London

Mahr, H. 1971: Die Baath-Partei. Porträt einer panarabischen Bewegung, Munich/Vienna

Ma'oz, M. 1968: Ottoman Reforms in Syria and Palestine, Oxford

Ma'oz, M. and Yaniv, A. (eds.) 1986: Syria under Assad, London/Syria

Marsot, A.L. al-S. 1984, Egypt in the Reign of Muhammad Ali, Cambridge/London

Owen, R. 1981: The Middle East in the World Economy 1800-1914, London/New York

Pawelka, P. 1985: Herrschaft und Entwicklung im Nahen Osten. Ägypten, Heidelberg

Pawelka, P. 1991: "Von der Metropole zur Peripherie: Der sozioökonomische Abstieg des Vorderen Orients", in Pawelka, P. and Pfaff, I. and Wehling, H.-G. (eds.) Die Golfregion in der Weltpolitik, Stuttgart

Rabinovich, I. 1972: Syria under the Ba'ath 1963-1966, Tel Aviv

Seale, P. 1986: The Struggle for Syria. A Study of Post-War Arab Politics 1945-1958, London

Tibawi, A.L. 1969: A Modern History of Syria, London

Wirth, E. 1971: Syrien. Eine geographische Landeskunde, Darmstadt

PHOTOCREDITS

2	Langenegger, F. 1911
3	Weulersse, J. 1940
5	Raswan, C. R. 1934
22	Grant, C.P. 1937
51	Grant, C.P. 1937
52	Grant, C.P. 1937
53	Seale, P. 1965
54	Seale, P. 1965
55	Seale, P. 1965
222	Weulersse, J. 1940
233	Grant. C.P. 1937
234	Weulersse, J. 1940
247	Weulersse, J. 1940
248	Weulersse, J. 1940
280	Langenegger, F. 1911
287	Raswan, C. R. 1934
321	Weir, Sh. 1976
325	Weir, Sh. 1976
337	Raswan, C.R. 1934
345	Raswan, C. R. 1934
350	Oppenheim, M. v. 1939
360	Oppenheim, M. v. 1939
361	Oppenheim, M. v. 1939
369	Oppenheim, M. v. 1939
370	Oppenheim, M. v. 1939
371	Graham-Brown, S. 1988
389	Graham-Brown, S. 1988
401	Graham-Brown, S. 1988
544	Graham-Brown, S. 1988
545	Onne, E. 1980
546	Onne, E. 1980